To the memory of master woodturner Steve Blenk,
a mountain of a man with extraordinary talent,
abundant kindness, great joy, and saintly patience
when teaching his craft and art to others

D1535931

Acknowledgments

I'd like to thank all the hospitable crafts-persons who allowed me to come into their shops and take the photographs that illustrate this book: Jim Tolpin; Doug Warren; Curtis Erpelding; Michael Dresdner; Steve Blenk; Roger Heitzman; Cliff Friedlander; Jim Casebolt; Carol Reed; Pat Curci; Del Cover; Pat Edwards; Michael Cooper; Jeff Traugot; Sam Maloof, his son Slimone, and his employees Larry White and Mike Johnson; Michael Burns and James Krenov at the College of the Redwood's School of Fine Woodworking; David Marks; Art Espenet Carpenter; Dan Stalzer; Owen Edwards; Jim Budlong; Jeff Dale; Richard Wedler; Joe O'Rendy; Stan Wolpert; Frank Klausz; Ian Kirby; Wendell Castle; Michael Dunbar; Garrett Hack; Alec McCurdy; John Manthei; David Ellsworth; Toshio Odate; and Jerry Bowden.

For their technical assistance and for providing information and products: Jean Brock; Mark Primack; Kevin Ireton, Chuck Bickford, and Charles Miller at *Fine Homebuilding* magazine; Michael Wolcott; Leonard Lee at Lee Valley Tools[SM]; Peter Spuller at Klingspor®; Andy Wolff at Dri-Dek®; Jeff Whittamore at Zip Wall®; and Paul Fitzmarice at Imre Communications.

And a big thanks to all my friends and colleagues who have helped: Michael Dresdner, for his kind assistance in helping me clarify my thoughts at a time when they were as cloudy as a dusty shop; Steve Robins, for his aid with photography; Drew Strizik, and the crew at Bay Photo Lab, for processing my film without fail; my parents, Lorant and Maria Nagyszalanczy, and my wife, Ann MacGregor Gibb, for their tireless support and boundless affection. Finally, I'd like to thank Bou Dou, my now-departed pal and the best shop cat ever, for his steadfast companionship.

Contents

Introduction

Given how so much has changed about the world in the half decade since the first version of this book was published, it's comforting to think that relatively little has changed in the actual practice of working wood. Sure, every year sees its share of new technologies, some quite relevant and others that are frivolous—paraded by tool manufacturers bent on convincing us that woodworking is barely possible without laser-guided saws, do-it-all benchtop machines, and nuclear-powered cordless power tools (okay, so there aren't any nuclear tools . . . yet).

Despite the proliferation of all the tools and gadgets, there still exists a magic place in the back of every woodworker's mind: a place where all the lumber is straight, the blades are sharp, the tools are precise, the benches are sturdy, the light is good, and the air and the floor are clean. While heaven might be the only place that most sawdust-slingers will ever experience all of these things at once, the place I'm talking about is the ideal woodworking shop.

It's clear that what constitutes an ideal workshop means different things to different people, but there are some basic qualities that any shop worthy of the name should possess. Without getting into an argument about the exact specifications of such a shop (its size and proportions, how it is laid out, where the best place is to put the workbench, and so on), here is a list of things I think most of us should expect from a first-class woodworking shop.

- Provide's a shelter that protects us (and our tools and supplies) from the effects of bad weather and harsh sun and keeps us warm in the winter and cool in the summer.

- Provide's a cozy place in which we can earn a living or escape from all the burdens and distractions of our daily lives.

- Provide's a secure place to keep our valuable tools and supplies.

- Control's humidity so that we can work comfortably, our tools won't rust, and our lumber won't swell or dry out excessively.

- Provide's fresh air to breathe and some means of controlling wood dust and fumes so we don't have to breathe them.

- Contain's and control's the noise generated by loud machines and power tools.

- Provide's abundant light, day or night.

- Provide's safe and adequate electricity to power our machines and portable power tools.

- Provide's a well-organized space to work in as well as easily accessible storage for building materials, small tools, accessories, and supplies.

- Provide's a space that's flexible enough for future changes in equipment or work style.

While it is well beyond the goal of this book to tell you exactly how to create a shop that would fulfill all these goals, I will systematically explore each of these elements, which are integral components of a complete woodworking shop. The intent is to give you the ideas and information you'll need to make the myriad decisions that face you, whether you are setting up a new shop for the first time or remodeling your present shop.

This new and completely updated edition of the book begins by looking at the nature of the physical structure itself: where it's located, how much space it provides, how easy the ingress and how secure it is, how to keep its climate comfortable and well ventilated, and how to provide adequate electricity and lighting. Subsequent chapters examine equipment: what kinds of hand tools, portable power tools, and machines are required for woodworking; how to decide what to buy (or what not to buy); how to get the most out of tools you already own; how to arrange machines and work areas to make your shop safe and efficient; and how to choose or build comfortable benches and workstations. The final chapters deal with several other important shop issues: storage of tools, lumber, and supplies; the control and collection of sawdust; the use of compressed air; and both personal and material safety issues.

All of the ideas and suggestions presented in this book are tempered with the knowledge that every woodshop is highly individual in character and substance: A strategy for storage or electrical wiring that is the Holy Grail for one woodworker may well be the Tower of Babel for another. That is to say, there is no single right way of doing something. This is especially true when it comes to things like shop layout, choosing equipment, and designing storage. What works for you and suits your tastes, budget, and style of work is best (and don't let any busybody know-it-all tell you any different!). That said, there are less-subjective elements of shop setup that are worth following more

closely, such as the design and installation of compressed-air and dust-collection systems.

Throughout the book, I invite you to learn and benefit from the experience of veteran craftspeople who have contributed to its pages so as to avoid their pitfalls and mires of frustration. While you can always remodel, reorganize, and rejuvenate your shop—which, incidentally, is part of the process of keeping pace with changes in the tools we own and the way we work—few of us have the time, resources, and patience to endure working in a shop that doesn't suit us like a comfortable pair of shoes.

Whatever a shop is to you, what it isn't is just some place with four walls and a door. Like the difference between a house and a home having to do with where the heart is, you have to follow your heart as well as use your mind when transforming a simple building that others might call a shed or a garage into what you proudly call your woodshop.

1

The Quest for Shop Space

> "Woodworkers all search for and establish a place to call their own workshop."

Having worked out of the same shop for nearly 20 years, it annoys me when a new visitor comes to my house and refers to the building at the back of my yard as my "garage." When I put my personal feelings aside and look more objectively at the rambling agglomeration of sheds and shacks that house all aspects of my woodworking pursuits—tools, benches, lumber, supplies—it looks less like a shop than it does a housing project for wayward trolls. What makes it a shop is that every aspect of that old building has been reworked, remodeled, and laid out to suit my own individual way of working with wood.

In many ways the only thing that distinguishes any old structure from a woodworking shop is that the latter provides a space to work in and is otherwise filled with tools and machines. Just about any building, shed, shack, or spare room can serve as a perfectly adequate woodworking studio.

Woodworkers all search for and establish a place to call their own workshop. But that space isn't always a matter of choice: If the basement or the garage is the only viable alternative to plopping a tablesaw in the living room, then that is where you're likely to end up making wood chips. Of course, it's a lot tougher when your first choice for shop space is a room that must serve double-duty as a part-time laundry room or a home for the family ping-pong® table.

Sometimes it's hard to imagine converting a shed or an available building into a viable shop space. I know one woodworker who does excellent work inside a structure that once served as a roosting space for a barnyard full of chickens! But if you have an old chicken coop or barn on your property that you're thinking of turning into a woodshop, it's best to weigh all the pluses and minuses before spending time and money on the conversion.

In this chapter, I'll examine a number of possible places in and around an average residential home, suburban lot, or country property in which you might locate a woodshop. I'll explore the advantages and disadvantages of each location and point out some things to consider. I'll also look at several ways to improve the space you already have by gaining floor space through shop reorganization or remodeling efforts.

His love of brick buildings led Garrett Hack to build his workshop from salvaged and recycled brick, slate, and granite. The building sits a short walk from Hack's rural Vermont home.

Advantages of a Home Woodshop

By far, the majority of woodworkers I know, both professional and amateur, have their woodworking shops at home. The convenience of strolling out the back door and into the shop to cut a few tenons or glue up a cabinet subassembly anytime you want to can be a real pleasure. You save a lot of time that you would have otherwise spent driving, riding, or walking if your shop were across town.

Whether you rent or own your home, chances are the cost of having a shop is included in the cost of paying for your home—a big savings over paying separate shop rent. And you don't pay a separate bill for basic utilities (gas, electric, water), so the overall cost of running the shop is also less.

A shady patio filled with exotic plants and cacti separates Del Cover's expanded garage workshop from his house a few yards away. Having your home and shop close to each other is not simply a convenience, it also helps deter the theft of valuable tools.

You'll be able to use your home's facilities (restroom, kitchen) and perhaps use the study or home office to take care of shop-related correspondence and to draft working drawings for shop projects. You'll also probably sleep more soundly at night with your expensive tools locked up within earshot rather than in some industrial space patrolled only by late-night alley cats.

But before you get swept up in the seductive convenience of having a work-shop at home, be sure to consider the downsides. Power tools make lots of noise that can quickly put you in the doghouse with your spouse or push your neighbors past their tolerance, especially if you run a router or tablesaw at night or during a Monday-night football game ("Hey Alice, that guy next door must be running his electric wood whacker again;

the Packers look all snowy, but they're playing in Arizona!").

Then there's the dust and debris that typically end up all over the floors, car-pets, and—if you come indoors for a quick siesta while that first coat of lacquer dries—all over the upholstery. If a home shop is where you earn your bread and butter or if you're a workaholic, you might find it hard to get away from woodwork-ing, such as when you end up in the shop at 4 A.M. sanding face frames because you can't sleep (it's happened to me).

But if you decide home is where you want your shop to be, the next step is fig-uring out where. The chart on the facing page sums up some of the problems of locating a shop in areas in or attached to the house. Now let's explore the types of home spaces in more detail.

PROBLEMS WITH HOME SHOP LOCATIONS

PROBLEM	ATTIC	BASEMENT	GARAGE	ROOM IN HOUSE
Noise	Floor vibration transmits noise to the rest of the house	Uninsulated floor transmits noise to rooms above	Uninsulated walls and doors transmit noise outdoors and to adjacent rooms of the house	Standard gypsum-board walls transmit sound to adjacent rooms
Dust	Fine dust wafts downstairs through doorways	Fine dust wafts upstairs; forced-air central heat may carry fine dust throughout the house	Dust gets tracked into the house; fine dust settles on cars and other items stored in the garage	Without sealing the doorway to the shop space and implementing an excellent dust-collection system, dust gets all over the house*
Heating, cooling, and moisture	Unvented attic spaces quickly become too hot for comfort, and uninsulated attics get too cold	Basements can be very damp and cold; walls that are not properly sealed seep moisture	An uninsulated garage must typically be heated separately from the rest of the house; moisture may invade through an inadequately sealed garage door	The temperature of the shop may be controlled by a thermostat in another room; air may be very dry in homes with forced-air central heat
Headroom	The size of the attic and the pitch of the roof limit headroom; a dormer can be added to increase headroom	Low floor joists, beams, or pipes may severely limit headroom and space needed to handle large stock	Low-hanging storage shelves around the perimeter of the garage may pose a headroom hazard	Standard ceiling height provides good headroom
Access	Narrow stairs and doorways limit the size of lumber and sheet goods going in and projects coming out	Narrow stairs and doorways limit the size of lumber and sheet goods going in and projects coming out	Large garage doors provide excellent access	Doors and hallways may be too narrow to provide access for machines and lumber
Structural limitations	Floor joists may be inadequate to handle the load of heavy machines	Basements with dirt floors or uneven concrete may be difficult to work in	A residential garage may lack adequate power to run machines	Rooms in a household residence are unlikely to have adequate power to run machines

*The room must not contain the air-return vent for the home's central heating/cooling system.

When Stan Wolpert built a new home, he added an ample woodshop above his three-car garage, making good use of the building's tall attic space. Benches and machines line the walls where the ceiling slopes down, and two dormer windows provide head space for additional machines and work areas.

Setting Up a Shop inside a House

Some might say that only an act of desperation would cause anyone to consider doing something as noisy, messy, and space consuming as woodworking inside a nice, clean house. As the chart on p. 7 shows, the problems involved with having a shop in your home can be daunting. But an in-house workshop might be your only recourse, short of renting workshop space nearby. Depending on the design of your home—and the scale of the projects you wish to build—basements, attics, porches, and even walk-in closets may be worthy of consideration.

ATTICS

Unless you're lucky enough to have a large attic space that's not above your living space, (see the photo above), the average home attic is usually a poor choice for a shop. Even attics with a fairly large floor space have limited headroom due to the slope of the roof. Access to an attic is typically up a narrow stairway, making transport of tools and materials difficult.

Attic floors are often inadequate to bear the weight of heavy woodworking machines, and the noise transmitted through floor vibration is likely to deluge the entire house. Because heat rises and attics typically lack adequate ventilation, an attic shop is often too warm even during periods of temperate weather.

All that said, if the attic is your only option, you'll need to exercise some creativity to turn it into a workable shop. Understand that your tool choices will probably be limited to hand tools or smaller models of machines. Fortunately, benchtop models of most woodworking machines are readily available and, depending on the kind of work you do, can be an acceptable solution.

BASEMENTS

If your house has a basement that isn't filled with clutter or doesn't fill up with water during the rainy season, it may be your best bet for an in-home shop space. Like an attic, a basement often presents access challenges. A basement shop needs wide stairs or a large door opening to the outside so that machinery and lumber can be brought into the shop and finished projects can be carted out.

Depending on the layout of the building, the floor may be supported by large posts or foundation members strategically placed in the basement. These structures can encumber free space and make handling long or large stock difficult.

If your home's central heating furnace is in the basement, you'll have to prevent sawdust from accumulating so as not to create a fire hazard. You'll also have to make sure that the system doesn't blow fine dust into every room of the house.

One advantage of a basement is built-in temperature control. It's typically cool even on the blistering days of summer; and since the house stands above, it's comfortably warm in winter.

A subterranean location can be an invitation to water seepage. Moisture coming through concrete or brick walls or, in some areas, outright flooding can endanger expensive tools and machines. In most cases, the water threat can be controlled by treating the walls with moisture proofing or by installing sump

pumps. Humidity problems can be cured with a dehumidifier.

Headroom Inadequate headroom is another bugaboo for basement shops. Wrestling large work in a low space can be absolutely maddening. Try assembling a tall bookcase or a hutch in a space with low ceilings.

If your basement lacks adequate headroom, you may be able to improve things in the course of a major house renovation. When woodworker/author Jim Tolpin remodeled his two-bedroom home, he raised it 2 ft., building a stub wall on top of its existing foundation.

Doing this increased the height of his basement shop to 10 ft., just enough to allow him to flip a long board or sheet of plywood end for end. The ground drops away toward the rear of his home so

Recessed Fixtures Improve Headroom

EVEN IF YOU CAN WORK IN A BASEMENT without whacking your head, you might find it difficult to add lighting fixtures that are above head level. Recessing fluorescent lights in between joists is one way to save space.

Although Ian Kirby's basement woodshop isn't particularly spacious, careful layout and organization make the space very workable.

Raising his home's foundation just 2 ft. gave woodworker and author Jim Tolpin enough headroom in his basement shop to maneuver long boards and large sheets of plywood.

that the rear wall of the shop is aboveground, providing easy access to the shop through a large, garage-type door.

Setting Up a Shop Attached to a House

For convenience, the next best thing to having a shop inside your house is having it just a few steps away. Getting the shop out of your immediate living quarters has real advantages. For starters, sawdust, finishing vapors, and some noise stay out of the main part of the house. And, generally, lumber and machinery are easier to get in and out of a garage or enclosed porch than your home.

GARAGES

If an alien race were to study the average home woodworker's lifestyle, I'm sure it'd conclude that garages were designed to house tools, machines, and workbenches and that the family automobile was meant to live in the driveway. Thank goodness modern cars have paint jobs that can withstand the rigors of outdoor life.

While many garages become places of woodworking out of default—there being nowhere else to set up a shop—the average two-car garage can provide a woodworker with all the comforts of a proper workshop. As far as amenities are concerned, the average garage has a level floor, typically a concrete slab; is weatherproof; and has at least rudimentary power and lighting. In many smaller homes, the garage doubles as a laundry room, so it's likely to have 220v electricity and even a sink with running water. In an early 1950s housing development I once visited, the home's garage came complete with a "handyman" bench and storage cabinets built against one wall.

Containing noise and dust Machine noise can be a problem inside your home. A shared wall between the garage and the house easily transmits vibration that can be nerve wracking—especially if you like to work late in the evening or when housemates are trying to concentrate or relax. This can seriously restrict the hours of power-tool operation in your shop.

Wood dust and chips can also become a problem for home garage shops. Fine dust wafts into the house through open windows and doors, and sawdust gets tracked in on the soles of unwiped shoes. If your home's water heater or central heating unit is inside your garage, watch for dust accumulation on or near the unit and its ductwork to avoid a possible fire hazard.

Converting the garage into a shop

The process of transforming a garage into a workable shop ranges from effortless to extensive, depending on the kind of work you want to do and how much equipment you have. Even if your shop has only one electrical outlet, a couple of good extension cords and power strips can power a few small stationary machines and portable electric tools. But a larger complement of machines, some with 220v motors, generally calls for additional circuits to be added or a full-blown electrical upgrade (see "Upgrading Your Electrical System," on p. 47).

The average garage's single bulb or 4-ft. fluorescent fixture hardly provides

Not big enough for his needs as it stood, Del Cover's single-car-garage addition nearly doubled the length of the existing structure, providing enough floor space for a basic complement of stationary machines, bench/assembly areas, and storage.

The Indoor/Outdoor Shop

ALMOST EVERY GARAGE has some kind of large door, which is perfect for a shop: You can drive a pickup right inside to unload a stationary machine or a stack of plywood or lumber. Leaving the door open can provide useful light and ventilation as well as give you room to pass boards that are too long to cut, plane, or joint inside. And a big door allows you to drag out a workbench or to wheel out mobile machines, so you can annex your driveway or patio to work outside on a sunny day.

Careful layout and planning accompanied by the use of portable work surfaces and mobile tool bases make it easier for a single garage to accommodate both woodworking and the family car.

adequate lighting for safe woodworking, so you'll want to add an extra circuit for new light fixtures as well. And if working with the garage door closed is paramount for good neighborhood relations, you might also want to add a couple of new windows or skylights to help illuminate the enclosed space (see "Getting the Most out of Natural Light," on p. 64).

Most home garages are uninsulated and lack any sort of heating, which may or may be an issue, depending on your local climate and time of year in which you want to work. Insulating your garage's attic space or roof can go a long way toward keeping it comfortable during winter's bitterest chill or summer's worst heat wave (see "Insulation," on p. 27). Insulation can also help reduce moisture problems that result in rust on steel and cast-iron tools.

Since 99 percent of garages have concrete floors that are murder on human leg joints, you'll also want to consider installing cushioning floor mats (see "Floor Mats and Cushioned Tile, on p. 37).

Sharing the garage with vehicles
If your garage will continue to serve double-duty as shop and nighttime refuge for the family car, the layout of machinery and workspace must be compact enough to provide room for both uses, or you must make your benches and machines mobile to allow the shop to be compressed into a smaller space when not in use (see "Creating Convertible Spaces," on p. 134). If you are tired of sharing space, most garages are good candidates for a floor-space-expanding remodel job.

ENCLOSED PORCHES

An attached porch can offer a good amount of floor space that's easy to enclose to form a woodshop. Because the porch is attached to the house, one wall already exists and the other walls can be fitted between the porch's roof support posts, with windows and doors added where they'll serve best (see the drawing below). After you run a few electrical circuits, hang some light fixtures, and add a little insulation (if you need it), you'll be ready to make sawdust.

Setting Up a Shop in an Outbuilding

If you live on a farm or ranch, you probably have no shortage of choices of where you can locate a shop: an old tractor shed, a bay of a big hay barn, a Quonset® hut, a corrugated metal building, or even a large chicken coop. Semirural properties and suburban tracts often include an outbuilding that can be successfully converted into a serviceable woodshop. New and clean or old and rustic, an outbuilding shop can give you the square footage you need to run a small cabinet or furniture business or just to pursue a woodworking hobby in style.

The issues of converting any outbuilding into a woodworking shop depend mostly on what the structure was previously used for. Older buildings that were used to house animals typically had dirt floors, which aren't very practical as shop floors because they don't provide a solid surface for heavy machines and they

Reinforcing Porch Floors

Make sure your porch's floor is strong enough to support the weight of heavy cast-iron machines before you roll in your planer and tablesaw. If the floor needs reinforcement, you can add additional piers and floor joists or block up to the floor directly underneath heavy machines.

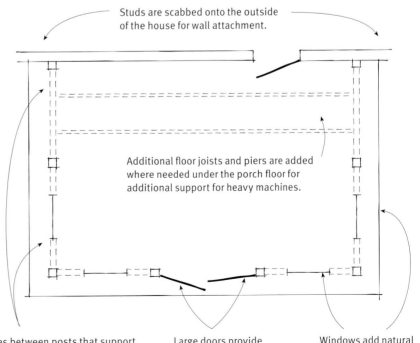

An Enclosed-Porch Woodshop

A porch with a shed-style roof is attached to the outside wall of the house.

Studs are scabbed onto the outside of the house for wall attachment.

Additional floor joists and piers are added where needed under the porch floor for additional support for heavy machines.

Spaces between posts that support the porch roof are filled in with stud walls to enclose the shop.

Large doors provide easy access for machines and supplies.

Windows add natural light and ventilation to enclosed walls.

readily transmit rust-promoting moisture. They also retain odors that are hard to get rid of and irritating to live with.

Unless a building was designed for housing equipment, such as milking machines, it doesn't have adequate power to run an average power-tool woodshop,

An iron angle brace, cut in the shape of a snake, adds a blacksmith's touch that reinforces the frame of the corrugated fiberglass–roofed front addition of Budlong's shop.

Once a traditional blacksmith's shop, the simple wood-and-block building (shown below) was converted by Mendocino, Calif., cabinetmaker and furniture maker Jim Budlong into a one-man shop with small living quarters above

and new wiring may have to be run from some distance away. Depending on the climate, an outbuilding's lack of insulation can also present problems. But despite these drawbacks, such a structure may have the makings of the shop of your dreams.

To gain the space he needed, Mendocino, Calif., woodworker Jim Budlong converted a former blacksmith shop into a very serviceable woodshop (see the photos at left). To increase the floor space, he added on to the basic structure several times; the upstairs was remodeled to create a small residence.

BARNS

A barn can offer a woodworker a particularly spacious and comfortable place to work. Barns typically have lots of unencumbered space—large doors for easy access, windows for ventilation—and may have a hay loft, which can be used for shop storage. The open space found between the loft bays in most barn structures have a high ceiling that's great for headroom when building big projects and/or working with large sheet goods. Adding skylights further increases the feeling of spaciousness and gives an otherwise dark barn building loads of light.

CORRUGATED-METAL BUILDINGS

Relatively inexpensive to build, a corrugated-metal shop requires only a slab and wall-stud structure, which is then covered with corrugated-metal walls and a roof.

Carol Reed transformed her small barn into a compact, functional woodshop. The structure's large windows and doors provide lots of light and ventilation and make it easy to move supplies, machines, and finished projects in and out.

You can take best advantage of a tall shop structure by adding a partial loft, whvich provides some storage for supplies while retaining the spaciousness of the high ceiling.

Metal buildings often have corrugated fiberglass panels around the roof, replacing occasional sheet-metal panels, to serve as skylights. Fiberglass can also replace sections of siding high on a building to let in sunlight similar to a clerestory window. Because thin sheet metal transfers heat readily, a metal structure may need substantial insulation in a cold climate.

MOBILE-HOME SHOPS

Older mobile homes are self-contained buildings—typically complete with doors, windows, insulated walls and ceilings, heat, electricity, and plumbing—that can often be bought for a paltry sum (especially if they are in aesthetic disrepair). And, true to their name, mobile homes can be moved from one place to another.

A mobile home can be converted into a very serviceable shop space if you have the patience to deal with a few shortcomings (see the photo on the facing page). First, the space is narrow. Unless you can get your hands on a double-wide unit (which is more expensive and much harder to move), most mobile homes are only 8 ft. wide at the most. This means you'll have to do all work with large sheet goods outdoors. You'll probably also have to step outside to flip long boards end for end.

A shortcoming that can be a serious problem for a power-tool woodworker is floor integrity. The floors in most mobile homes are not designed to handle the weight of a heavy stationary machine, such as a tablesaw, bandsaw, or planer.

In lieu of reinforcing the entire understructure of the mobile home, the

Although modest in size and design, a corrugated-metal building is easy to erect and can provide enough room for a basic complement of woodworking machines as well as storage space for lumber and materials.

Owen Edwards gave new life to this old mobile home tucked into the woods in Mendocino, Calif., when he converted it into a novel woodshop equipped with a full complement of woodworking machines.

Careful layout and organization allow woodworker Owen Edwards to handle long lumber and to build fairly large casework inside his narrow mobile-home shop. (He cuts full-size plywood sheets to size outdoors.)

strategy that Mendocino, Calif., furniture designer/craftsman Owen Edwards used to strengthen the floor beneath his heavy machines, such as his cast-iron-framed Davis and Wells 18-in. bandsaw, was to crib up short lengths of lumber underneath the area of the floor where the saw was mounted. (Concrete blocks are also a good choice.) Edwards purposely located the bandsaw near the door, so it wouldn't have to be carried to far.

Building a New Shop

Every now and again, some lucky woodworker gets to live a dream come true: to build his or her own woodshop from the ground up, exactly the way he or she wants to. The prospect can be intimidating, and keeping up with all the decisions

Before You Invest in a New Shop, Think Twice

Despite the appeal of building a new shop—especially the idea of having everything exactly as you'd like it—it's probably your most expensive option. When you consider the cost of the necessary permits, ground preparation, materials, and labor, building a new shop might not be as cost effective, square foot for square foot, as remodeling an existing structure. But if there's more wrong with your current shop than there is right, making a fresh start may be well worth it (as old-timers say, "no use in polishing dirt").

To give himself enough room for boat work and specialty architectural work such as stairway construction, Washington State woodworker Doug Warren built his new shop 40 ft. long by 20 ft. wide with big, double doors for ventilation and access.

that need to be made along the way can be daunting.

If you build from scratch, you have the opportunity to design exactly the kind of space you want and not have to make do with the shortcomings of an existing space. You can plan a space that has enough square footage for your needs with high ceilings, insulation, heating, electricity, and lighting.

Building a new shop can afford you the opportunity to create a space that accommodates more than just woodworking. Part of your new shop may include office space or studio space for another craft or discipline. Master chairmaker Michael Dunbar's spacious New Hampshire shop was designed with class-room space and facilities that serve as a woodworking school.

Even if lack of space restricts the size of your dream shop to that of an oversize garden shed, built in a corner of your yard, careful planning and ingenious storage can yield a shop large enough to accommodate small projects and weekend puttering. By locating the new shop building carefully, you can minimize the effect of noise (and dust) on your family and neighbors.

Before you do any building, make sure you check with the local authorities about any zoning and building restrictions. You should also get all the required permits before you start. Even if you think you know exactly what you need, it

Pastorally sited next to a pond, this architect-designed Connecticut shop is a model of comfort, with all the amenities a dream shop should have: ample lighting and electricity, good insulation and climate control, comfortable wood floors, and a full central dust-collection system.

After running a chairmaking school for several years in a rented building, "King of Windsor" chairmaker Michael Dunbar and his wife, Sue, built a spacious two-story building that serves as a woodshop and a classroom for their Windsor Institute.

Although only 10 ft. wide by 16 ft. long, this diminutive backyard workshop provides its owner with a cozy, well-organized space in which to work on small projects.

FLOOR PLAN
160 SQ. FT.   SCALE 1/4"=1'-0"

may save time, effort, and materials to hire an architect, especially if the structure will be attached to your house. In some municipalities, an architect's plan is required to get building permits.

But don't think your "ideal" shop will necessarily be your last shop. If you're like most woodworkers, you'll be second-guessing decisions you've made about the size, organization, and features of your new shop before you've even finished building it. Many craftsmen say that getting a shop to function well and suit the work habits and tastes of its user are more evolutionary processes than revolutionary ones.

Remodeling a Shop

The day comes in every woodworker's life when he or she realizes that the shop is woefully undersize and there is little hope of completely renovating it or relocating to a spacious shop anytime soon. The trick here is to come up with a way of gaining square footage without having to dip into your kids' college fund or take

A Truck Box Extension

PETALUMA, CALIF., WOODWORKER JEFF DALE came up with a clever and effective way of adding floor space to his small shop, and he did it without having to pour a foundation. Dale bought a used 8-ft. by 12-ft. truck box (the enclosed box on the back of a small commercial truck) for $650 and located it directly adjacent to his shop. Because the truck box is a self-contained structure that sits on concrete piers, it doesn't require a building permit. The only major modifications Dale did to the box were to insulate, roof, and add a skylight and a window. With extension cords carrying power from the main shop, Dale uses his truck-box expansion to house a thickness planer and an edge sander. A small bench at one end allows him to use his routers without filling up his main shop with chips and dust. A powerful ventilation fan under the bench blows the dusty air outside.

out a second mortgage on your house. Fortunately, there are inexpensive ways of adding on structurally without bottoming out financially.

Take for example, Jim Casebolt's shed-roofed addition to his single-car garage, shown at right. By using simple, inexpensive construction methods, including concrete piers and a stud frame, topped by a translucent corrugated-fiberglass roof (which lets in loads of sunlight), furniture maker and boatbuilder Casebolt created enough extra space to house several new machines. By wrapping the L-shaped addition around his shop, he also acquired space along the side of the garage, which he

An inexpensive addition to the rear and side of Jim Casebolt's single-car garage doubled the size of his shop. By using a translucent corrugated-fiberglass roof, he gained loads of natural light as well.

Built on the site of his original undersize shop, Cliff Friedlander constructed a larger (and more colorful) shop nestled behind his backyard deck and hot tub.

uses as a lumber room and for storage of tools and materials, all without getting into a major construction project.

As with homes that need a little special stretching after a new baby comes along (or an in-law comes to visit and won't leave), a capacity-challenged shop can often be remodeled to gain more floor space. Like adding a bedroom or family room to your home, putting an addition on your shop may allow you to double its size and get you all the space you need, as well as add to the value of your property.

It's almost always easier and cheaper to remodel a shop than it is to build a new shop. But before you start knocking down walls, consider all the costs involved in addition to materials and labor: construction permits; property reassessments, which may result in higher taxes; and shop down time during construction, if woodworking is a source of income.

Curtis Erpelding's Two-Car Garage Shop Remodel

A complete remodel of his two-car garage doubled the size of Northwest woodworker Curtis Erpelding's shop while adding a second-story office and storage space to the structure.

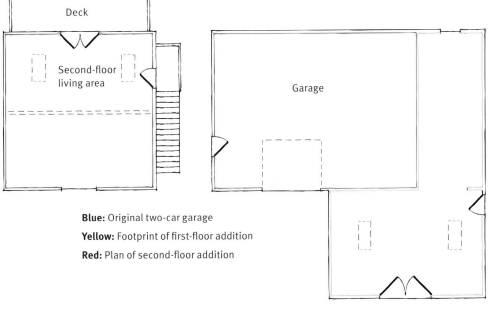

Deck

Second-floor living area

Garage

Blue: Original two-car garage
Yellow: Footprint of first-floor addition
Red: Plan of second-floor addition

Remodeling can be especially problematic if you live within city limits and must deal with local zoning and planning-department limitations, which can put the kibosh on new construction in your yard.

But sometimes a partial remodel just won't do. When Santa Cruz, Calif., woodworker Cliff Friedlander purchased his home, there was a small building in the backyard that he used as a shop for several years. Instead of just reworking the too-small building, he razed the structure and replaced it with a much larger, well-designed building. His new shop provided the space he needed to conduct his business building kitchen cabinets and furniture.

Walls, Ceilings, and Floors

"I want my shop to be cozy and comfortable, to provide protection against the elements, and to be a space that I (and my tools) can live and work in safely"

One of the first workshops I ever set up for myself had a dirt floor and paper-thin walls—it was a teepee-style structure with long redwood poles that supported a plastic tarp cover. The space was cold on foggy mornings, hot on sunny afternoons, and subject to every breeze and gust of wind that blew sawdust around. Its dirt floor was damp at best and quickly became wet and muddy whenever it rained. With no protection from the elements, my tools rusted quickly and, since there was no closeable door, occasionally disappeared entirely. I actually built some pretty nice pieces in that shop, but I was young and foolish and willing to put up with such shortcomings. Now I want my shop to be cozy and comfortable, to provide protection against the elements, and to be a space that I (and my tools) can live and work in safely.

Walls and Ceilings

The most basic elements of a workshop—the walls that protect us from wind and rain and keep hooligans from making off with our precious implements—are easy to take for granted unless they're not there. Noted furniture maker Sam Maloof told me that when he built his first proper workshop, almost two years elapsed between the time he put up the walls and roof and when he put on the sheathing and siding to enclose them. During the interim period, Maloof moved in and worked in the shop daily, simply covering up his machines at night to keep off the morning dew.

While I assume that the walls of your shop are at least sheathed on the outside, most small shop spaces that I have visited have exposed stud walls inside, including most home garages and sheds. Covering the inside walls not only makes the inside of the shop feel more finished but also can improve the quality of the workspace.

Light-colored interior walls bounce around both natural and artificial light, improving the effectiveness of the light

coming in through windows and skylights as well as the artificial light produced by light fixtures. And covering your shop's interior walls also provides an opportunity to add insulation, possibly the most important physical improvement that will make your shop more comfortable.

WALL MATERIALS

Ease of installation and availability make two materials ideal for shop walls. Gypsum wallboard, commonly called drywall or Sheetrock®, is the most commonly used interior surface material. But if you like the "wood look" you can install thin wood paneling, quickly and efficiently.

When renowned furniture maker Sam Maloof moved to Alta Loma, Calif., in 1952, he built a new shop out of lumber a local dealer gave him on credit, but it was nearly two years before he was able to complete the shop's redwood siding. Maloof built several additions to the shop, including the bench room shown here.

Drywall Drywall is inexpensive and readily available; it's relatively easy to install; and most important, it retards the spread of fire in a building, which is why many building codes require it for interior surfaces. While drywall's heavy weight makes it a chore to install on high walls and ceilings, its density helps reduce the amount of machine noise that escapes from the shop. And if you can live with an interior that Martha Stewart wouldn't be incarcerated in, you can skip the most difficult part of a drywall job: taping, texturing, and painting.

Insulating and paneling interior shop walls make a shop more comfortable. Light-colored drywall helps bounce light around the shop and, should a shop fire occur, retard the rate of it spreading.

If you cut and fit individual pieces together, mounting them with drywall screws on walls and ceilings, you can drywall a small shop in a day, ending up with an off-white interior surface that's clean looking, even if it's not entirely finished.

The only problem with drywall is the effect it can have on sound quality inside your shop. Smooth, hard drywall tends to reflect high-frequency noise very effectively, which can make running a router or tablesaw with a whiney blade unpleasant.

Fortunately, adding shelves, cabinets, and even machines to the shop helps dampen reflected sound. If your shop has one or more large, open drywall surfaces, you can attenuate interior noise by installing sound channel and covering the surfaces with sound board (see "Reducing Machinery Noise," on p. 42) or a heavy, pleated drape made of loosely woven fabric, such as burlap.

Wood paneling Thin wood paneling, which is typically made from cheap plywood or composite board covered with "photo-grained" vinyl to resemble real wood, is relatively light and inexpensive, especially if you buy one of the less-popular styles that your local lumberyard has on sale, such as "marshmallow ash" or "ultra-pecky pecan."

Choosing a light-color finish is important, as it will help bounce and diffuse lighting. Darker natural-wood finishes can make the shop feel warmer and more traditional, though it's probably best to install it on only one or two walls; dark

Choosing and installing insulation that's R-rated for your climatic zone in both ceilings and walls is a necessity if you live in an area with harsh winter weather.

paneling an entire shop can make a small space feel like a cave.

Wood paneling is easy to cut and trim, and large pieces can be nailed or stapled (using a pneumatic gun) to studs and joists in minutes. Unfortunately, paneling doesn't prevent the transmission of noise in the way drywall does. Because the thin material can resonate like the top of a guitar from the lower-frequency noise produced by machines, it's a good idea to run a bead of construction adhesive along framing members before nailing

panels in place to prevent the paneling from rattling and buzzing.

INSULATION

If you're heating an uninsulated shop, your heating bill might amount to the equivalent cost of a new cordless drill or a set of fine chisels every winter. And if your heating system can't keep up with your shop's heat loss, the shop will still feel cold and uncomfortable during the coldest months of the year.

Installing insulation in shop walls before paneling them is a breeze. Here insulation specialist Jean Brock fits bats of R-11 fiberglass insulation in a stud wall.

Insulation Priorities

Practically speaking, it's always better to install insulation and hang drywall or paneling before you move into your shop, before machines, shelves, and storage cabinets go in. If your budget is limited, insulating only the ceiling will gain you the lion's share of insulating benefits. You can always insulate the walls at a later time, if you wish.

Adding insulation to your shop's ceiling and walls isn't particularly difficult—you can do the work yourself—and is an expense that will add value to your shop while making it more comfortable to work in. If you work in a typical wood-stud garage or outbuilding with a ceiling (or at least existing ceiling rafters) located in one of the country's more temperate zones, the cost of insulating is likely to run under a dollar per square foot of floor area.

Walls are generally much easier to insulate than ceilings and roofs. You don't need to worry about ventilation, and the size of the wall studs determines which insulation to use: R-11 or R-13 for 2×4 walls and R-19 or R-21 for 2×6 walls. (R-value refers to how well a material insulates: The thicker and better an insulator, the higher the R-value number.) Shops with walls that have already been paneled or drywalled can have insulation blown in (call your local insulation contractor for more information).

Because heat rises, a shop will rarely benefit from having its floor insulated, except in some cases where the underside of the floor is exposed, such as a shop built high on piers or on a hillside that drops away.

Insulating conventional ceilings If your shop has a drywall ceiling with an attic space above it that's big enough to crawl around in, you've got it made. Insulation is simply a matter of laying bats of fiberglass insulation between the ceiling joists.

Just make sure the attic space is ventilated so you won't have moisture problems. The climate you live in and how temperate you want your shop to stay will determine the insulation you'll choose in terms of R-value. See "Regional Insulation Recommendations for Residences," on the facing page, for a general guideline on how much ceiling and wall insulation is recommended for various climate zones around the country.

REGIONAL INSULATION RECOMMENDATIONS FOR RESIDENCES

ZONE	CEILING INSULATION*	WALL INSULATION*	
1	R-19	R-11	
2	R-30	R-11	
3	R-38	R-13	
4	R-38	R-19	
5	R-49	R-25	

*R-values represent a major insulation-manufacturer's recommendation for meeting the latest energy standards for new and existing homes.

An Unvented Insulated Vaulted Ceiling

Night Cooling Creates Moisture
At night, the cooling of the hot, uninsulated rafter bays allows condensation to form, causing moisture damage and fungal growth.

Heat Builds during the Day
By day, the insulated rafter bays collect heat. The hot unvented air eventually transfers heat through the insulation into the shop.

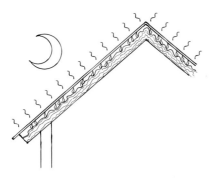

Ridge Venting a Vaulted Ceiling

A ridge vent atop the roof allows hot, moist air to escape.

An air space of at least 1 in. between the insulation and the sheathing allows for air movement.

Screened vent holes in the ends of the rafter bays allow cool air to displace escaping hot air.

Insulating a vaulted ceiling The job of insulating becomes a bit more difficult and costly if your shop has a vaulted ceiling (free space all the way to the building's rafters) or a flat roof with no attic above it. Technically, you should not install insulation in enclosed spaces that are not properly ventilated. The reason for this, as shown in "An Unvented Insulated Vaulted Ceiling," on p. 29, is that moisture-laden air, which is trapped in the enclosed space between the roof sheathing, rafters, and interior paneling, is heated by the sun during the day and then condenses during the coolness of the evening.

Depending on your climate, the type of roof and sheathing, and how much sun the roof gets, this condensed moisture may be minor, perhaps encouraging the

When insulating the roof of a shop with a vaulted ceiling, leave at least 1 in. of air space between the insulation and the underside of the roof sheathing for ventilation. A trio of holes bored in rafters just below the skylight shown here ventilate hot air from the insulated rafter bay below the skylight to the adjacent bays

A simple ridge vent installed at the peak of the roof allows hot air to escape from the rafter bays of a shop's vaulted ceiling.

growth of mold and mildew, or severe, creating a significant amount of water that will stain paneling and cause mysterious drips. Over time, unventilated insulated spaces can even cause wood rot and damage the structure.

The proper way to insulate between rafters to prevent moisture problems is shown in "Ridge Venting a Vaulted Ceiling," on the facing page.

Here are the factors to keep in mind:

- Leave an air space of at least 1 in. (2 in. is better) between the top of the insulation material and the underside of the roof sheathing (see the bottom left photo on the facing page).

- Install a ridge vent to allow hot air to escape at the highest point of the rafter bays, as shown in the bottom right photo on the facing page.

- Create ventilation at the bottom of each rafter bay, either by installing screened soffit vents or by boring holes through the freeze blocks. These allow fresh air to enter and displace the hot air escaping through the ridge vent.

- Ventilate any rafter bays that are below skylights. You can accomplish this by boring several 1-in. holes through the horizontal blocking in the rafter bays or by boring through rafters in the bay below the skylight.

The maximum amount of insulation you'll be able to fit into the rafter bays will depend on the width of the rafters in your shop. "Average Thickness of

Fiberglass Insulation," on p. 32, shows the thicknesses of typical fiberglass insulation bats of various R-values. For example, in a shop with 2×8 rafters (which are actually 7½ in. wide), R-19 is the thickest insulation you'll be able to use and still leave a 1-in. air space above the insulation.

Rigid foam insulation materials are generally too expensive for typical interior installations. But because they are thin relative to their insulation value and are easy to cut and install, rigid foam is a good choice in applications for which fiberglass would be impractical, such as when insulating flat roofs and large shop doors.

Although expensive, rigid foam insulation is easy to install and packs a lot of R-value into a thin layer, making it a great choice for insulating shop doors.

AVERAGE THICKNESS OF FIBERGLASS INSULATION

R-VALUE	THICKNESS (IN.)
R-13	3½
R-19	6½
High-density R-21	5½
Regular R-30	9½
Cathedral R-30	8½

MOISTURE BARRIERS

In some climates, a vapor barrier is required before drywall, wallboard, or wood paneling is installed over insulation. Some insulations come with a facing (foil or kraft paper) that functions as a vapor barrier. If using regular insulation, you can apply a 4-mil or 6-mil plastic sheeting such as Visqeen over it. The purpose of a vapor barrier is to keep moisture within the shop from getting into the insulation cavity. To be most effective, the barrier should be as continuous as possible. Selecting a clear barrier material will make it easier to see when stapling it to studs and rafters.

DOORS

If you work in a single- or double-car garage, you won't have any problems getting in and out of the shop because these doors open wider than a whale's mouth. If you are outfitting an outbuilding or shed to serve as a woodworking shop, fit at least a 36-in.-wide door as your entrance. It's even better to install double doors whenever possible, one of which can be used for everyday comings and goings. When you need to move a new wide-belt sander into the shop—or the sailboat you built out—both doors can be easily opened for access.

Big sliding doors—the kind commonly found on modern barns—also provide lots of access. They run on overhead tracks and can be sized as needed, right up to the length of an entire shop wall. However, such big doors can be tedious to deal with on a daily basis because they may require a lot of physical effort to

A pair of big double doors can make life in the shop a lot easier: One door provides daily access, whereas propping both doors open allows you to move large machines, materials, and projects in and out of the shop easily.

A sliding door, like the one shown here on furniture maker Roger Heitzman's Scotts Valley, Calif., shop, can be sized as big as necessary, right up to the length of an entire wall

slide open and closed. And when security is a factor, locking them properly is time-consuming. One solution is to add a smaller personal entrance through a big slider by cutting in and fitting a regular hinged door.

A big limitation of sliding doors is the length of the track, which is about twice as long as the door itself. This presents a problem when you want to put a big door on a small building.

One door style that's physically large yet is easy to fit on a small shop is the bifold door. Each bifold consists of a pair of doors, each with an outer frame made of 2×4 construction lumber that's covered with ½-in.-thick exterior-grade plywood. Two sets of hinges allow the door to be hinged out, then folded back. The two-piece doors take up a lot less room when fully open than a single-piece door would. One shortcoming with big

To spare the effort of moving a big sliding door every time he enters or exits, woodworker Dan Stalzer installed a standard hinged entry door directly into one end of the slider. He also added a long, translucent fiberglass-glazed window to let in natural light.

A set of large bifold doors provides Santa Rosa, Calif., woodworker David Marks ready access to his big lumber shed. Constructed from inexpensive plywood and 2×4s, bifold doors are easy to build and operate.

This simple mechanism—made of a weight, a pair of pulleys, and a length of thin cable—can be rigged to keep a door closed to prevent shop noise or dust from wafting outdoors or into clean spaces.

doors that have only a single skin is that they don't insulate well. You can improve the situation, though, by installing rigid insulation on the door's inside surfaces (see the photo on p. 31).

Separating workspaces If you have a multiple-room workshop, you'll want to keep dust from the machine room from wafting into "clean" spaces, such as offices, design studios, and bathrooms. This is a particularly big problem with home shops—dust goes everywhere. Keeping doors closed is one step toward preventing dust from getting out. You can fit spring-loaded hinges to replace standard door hinges, or you can build a simple automatic door-closing mechanism with an old sash weight, a couple of pulleys, and a length of cable or cord.

SHOP SECURITY

Unless you encounter a burglar with a serious attitude (and a wall-cutting chainsaw), windows and doors are the common routes of illegal entry. To protect your valuable investment in tools and machinery, it behooves you to do all you can to thwart would-be thieves from getting in through these vulnerable portals.

Thieves often enter a home or shop by kicking in the door. Most entry doors open in and are locked by dead bolts that secure into a wooden door frame, providing little resistance to a strong kick or battering ram. (Have you noticed how quickly officers knock down a suspect's door on those reality-TV cop shows?)

Reinforcing doors and frames You can make your shop doors more resistant by making them open outward and by reinforcing the door jam. Anyone trying to kick in a door is kicking against the entire door stop. The door should be fitted with nonremovable pin hinges and a steel security plate mounted over the lock area. The additions of a steel lock strike/reinforcing plate in the jam and another around the lock assembly make the door extremely resistant to any attempts at knocking in or prying open.

Protect any extra doors your shop has by barring them, especially if they open onto alleys and passages where thieves can hide. Steel bar brackets, which take a regular 2×4 bar, should be through-bolted with carriage bolts or heavy lag bolts to the studs on either side of the door.

Electric openers You can add security as well as convenience to garage doors or to sliding sectional doors by installing an electric opener, which prevents the door from being lifted without activation via remote or key switch. For even more security, shut off the opener or flip its "security" switch on when you leave the shop for extended periods, lest some electronics-whiz crook cracks your remote-control code. Very wide doors that could be twisted to gain entry can benefit from the addition of latches or hasps and padlocks on both sides.

A shop entrance door that opens outward is more resistant to forced entry than one that opens inward. A strong deadbolt and strike-protection plate further help thwart break-ins by late-night intruders.

A set of steel bar brackets and a brace cut from a standard 2×4 will effectively seal little-used shop doors and prevent unauthorized entry.

Locking shop entrances with a strong hasp and high-quality padlock is a tremendous hedge against shop burglaries. The lock shown here has a design that protects the hardened shank from sawing, prying, or hammering.

Avoid Temptation with Window Covering

Don't forget the value of window shades or blinds for keeping beady eyes from peering into your shop in search of valuables. This is especially important if your shop faces a public thoroughfare.

Padlocks If you padlock shop doors, don't scrimp on the size and strength of the lock: Cheap combination locks can be knocked off with a sledgehammer faster than you can say "illegal entry." The best hasps and locks are designed to protect the padlock's shank from tampering, as shown in the photo above. (Although hardened lock shanks are resistant to shearing with bolt cutters, they can still be shattered by quick freezing with canned freon, then being struck with a hammer.)

Often, a thief won't even bother trying to remove a padlock—he'll simply pry off the entire hasp assembly. Make certain the hasp is securely mounted to the door and jamb. Through-bolt hasps to both the door and the jamb with carriage bolts, using large washers inside keep "prying" thieves from success.

Screws and bolts Short of installing electronic security, the best protection for windows is making sure they can't be opened from the outside if the glass is broken. Many window styles can be fitted with keyed locks, but it's cheaper to drill holes and add screws or bolts through window members to secure them. Bolts or screws should be relatively easy to remove from the inside, so you can open the window when you need to.

You can also bolt or screw a window partially open to allow a little ventilation without compromising your shop security entirely. Aluminum sliding windows are especially vulnerable to thieves. Adding locks or bars that keep them from sliding generally isn't enough because an entire window can be pried out of its frame. Screw such frames shut or add bars for the best security.

Steel bars If you wish to have more complete protection, even when windows are left open, steel bars are a good choice. These are typically through-bolted on from the outside to prevent removal. Bars may also be fitted inside window openings behind the glass, which can keep your shop looking less fortress-like.

Floor Treatments

Feeling the earth beneath your feet is a good thing, at least when you run around at the beach for a few hours on a warm summer day. But doing woodworking in a shop that has a hard, damp floor is uncomfortable at best and can cause your feet, ankles, knees, and hips to ache after an average work session.

Having a shop floor that's comfortable to stand on is just as important as wearing sturdy shoes that fit correctly. Therefore, choose your flooring carefully

Covering your shop's cold, hard concrete floors with rubber floor mats in work areas and in front of machines can make standing for long periods of time a lot more comfortable and easier on your knees and feet.

when building a new shop or, if your existing flooring is poor, make the effort to improve it to make it more healthy and comfortable.

CONCRETE FLOORS

Until God gives us more resilient knees (or medical science enables us to replace every baby's knees with shock absorbers at birth), concrete is by far the harshest flooring material. In addition to being hard on the body, concrete provides the least-flexible flooring system: You can't run electrical wiring or pipes under the slab unless it's done when the concrete is poured.

Also, a concrete floor is cold—a plus if you live in a very hot climate but more often a negative. Concrete can transmit dampness, raising shop humidity and making a somewhat slick surface all the more slippery. And slabs often crack,

especially in earthquake country like California (there's a fissure in the concrete pad in my shop where small ivy vines regularly appear).

On the up side, concrete floors are less expensive to build than most other flooring systems and are very easy to keep clean. If your pad was poured thick and level to start, a concrete floor has no problem supporting the heaviest of woodshop machines.

Floor mats and cushioned tile

If you're tired of living with a concrete shop floor's shortcomings, you can quickly improve things by simply adding floor mats. The cheapest way to go is to buy just enough mats to go in front of your benches and power tools. Rubber floor mats come in a staggering array of sizes; I find 24-in. by 36-in. mats to be right for most small-shop tasks.

Smooth Sailing on Hard Floors

IF YOU DON'T WANT TO BUY work-area floor mats, you can make ships' galley-style wooden-slatted mats for your bench and work areas instead. They're easy to build and a great way to use cutoffs from ripping stock.

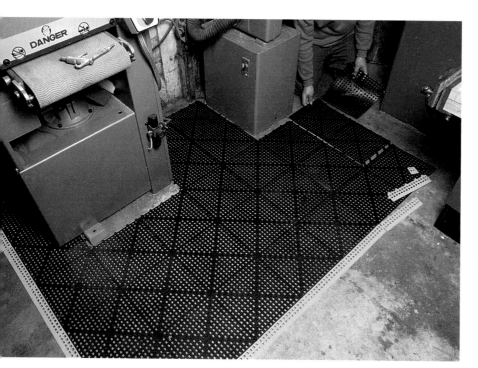

An interlocking floor-tile system, such Dri-Dek, uses 1-ft. squares that provide comfort, are easy to install, and allow flexibility. Floor tiles can be reconfigured at any time to suit new shop layouts.

The most basic design differences are open weave, or mesh-style, vs. continuous surface, or solid-surface, mats. The tradeoff is that solid-surface mats are easier to clean with a broom or vacuum but often don't provide the same amount of cushioning as thicker, mesh-style mats do. But while mesh-style mats tend to trap sawdust and small scraps (making it harder to find screws and small parts you accidentally drop), they also keep you from having to walk directly on top of flotsam and jetsam. And cleanup is not too bad: Lift up the mats and shake them out, making sure you don't forget to wear a dust mask, then vacuum the floor.

If you want to add the cushioning of floor mats to your entire floor or at least most of it, there are several good interlocking floor-tile systems that offer layout flexibility as well as knee protection. Dri-Dek® and other manufacturers offer easily installed 1-ft. by 1-ft. tiles in a variety of colors. While the initial cost is somewhat high, the advantage of these systems is their flexibility. If you move equipment around—or if you move to a new shop—you simply reconfigure the tiles to suit your new layout.

Painting concrete Moisture easily travels through regular concrete floors and can make a shop unpleasantly damp. Two coats of floor paint will prevent moisture migration to such an extent that the humidity in the shop will drop noticeably.

Besides hiding ugly stains, painting a dark, dingy floor with a light-colored paint, such as light gray, will help reflect light around your shop, resulting in better overall illumination.

Before painting, vacuum the floor and scrub it clean with a strong cleanser, such as tri-sodium phosphate (TSP), and let it dry. The floor must be completely dry and at least 50°F before painting, so it's best to paint during warm weather. If your floor is subject to water seepage and stays continually wet, you'll have to treat it with a masonry waterproofer first. Super-smooth concrete should be treated with a muriatic acid wash before painting to rough it up and help the paint stick.

To prevent slipping accidents on glassy-smooth concrete floors, mix clean sand or special nonslip grit into the paint. Alternatively, you can apply strips of high-friction tape, such as 3M's® Safety Walk®, to traffic areas. These tapes are sold by the inch at most hardware stores and home centers.

WOOD FLOORS

If you're building a new shop, a wood floor is a great investment toward making the space cozier, warmer, and feel better to walk and stand on. If you're currently stuck with concrete, adding a plywood

floor on top takes more effort than simply putting down mats, but it allows you to add a vapor barrier to reduce moisture and humidity in the shop. It even provides you with the opportunity of running electrical wiring and plumbing underneath the plywood.

A couple of coats of light-colored floor paint not only will hide stains and brighten up a dingy concrete shop floor but also will help reduce shop humidity by preventing ground moisture from seeping up through the concrete.

If you are tired of living with a cold concrete shop floor, installing a plywood floor over it will make working in the shop more pleasant and will allow you to run power directly to mid-floor machines.

Laying a floor over concrete Start by laying down a good continuous moisture barrier between the floor and the concrete. You have two choices: laying down plastic sheeting, typically 6-mil polyethylene, or coating the concrete with a penetrating sealant, such as Sinak. If you choose to lay down plastic, start in the center and work toward the walls, leaving enough around the baseboards to trim off later. Overlap any seams in the plastic by about 6 in., and seal them with duct tape after cleaning the seam area with denatured alcohol. If you seal the floor, you must first clean it thoroughly, then apply two light coats, following the manufacturer's directions.

There's just one possible snag: The warm air inside the shop and the cool air next to the concrete can create moisture problems beneath the floor. If you live in a wet area and anticipate moisture problems, it's prudent both to seal the floor and to lay down a moisture barrier.

This kind of floor is definitely not a good idea if the ground around your shop is wet and your slab has major seepage problems.

Next, lay down wooden members (known as screeds or "sleepers"), and fasten them over the moisture barrier or sealed concrete. Depending on how much under-floor space you desire, you can use 1×3s or 1×4s flat or 2×4s either flat or on edge. Although pressure-treated lumber is more expensive than standard construction-grade lumber, it is much more resistant to decay and is the best choice for sleepers.

Space the sleepers 12 in. to 16 in. on center and fasten them down to the concrete with powder-actuated fasteners, concrete anchors, or concrete screws, such as blue Tapcon® screws. The latter are the easiest to use, requiring only a $\frac{5}{32}$-in. starter hole drilled with a masonry bit.

Apart from driving the fasteners, take care not to penetrate or damage the plastic moisture barrier as you work; if you do, tape up any accidental tears completely. To best support heavy machines (such as tablesaws and planers), add sleepers directly underneath where the bases of the machines will be located. You can lag-bolt down machines to these sleepers after the floor is laid down.

Subfloor systems One of the big advantages of a raised wood floor is that you can run electrical circuits, compressed-air piping, and even dust-collection ductwork (if there's adequate clearance) below the floor where it's out of the way.

The clearance under a raised floor can allow not only electrical circuits but also compressed air piping and dust collection ductwork to run across the shop without getting in the way. The ductwork shown here removes sawdust from a tablesaw set in the center of the shop.

Run electrical circuits in conduit or use weatherproof Romex™, attaching it to the sides of the sleepers it runs along. Wherever wiring must cross sleepers, rout a narrow channel. If using Romex, cover the channel with a protective metal nail plate (see the bottom photo on p. 39). Avoid installing flush-mount electrical boxes in the floor because these can accumulate sawdust and create a fire hazard (see "Adding Electrical Outlets," on p. 51).

After you've run any wiring or plumbing between the sleepers, you're ready to apply a ¾-in. or 1-in. tongue-and-groove underlayment-grade plywood flooring. Plan any cuts you need to make so that butted ends will have mating tongues and grooves. Screwing down the floor with galvanized deck screws will prevent floor squeaks while allowing you to pull up a section of floor should it become damaged or if there are moisture problems underneath.

Sound Abatement

If your shop is in a residential area (and you want to stay on good terms with your family and neighbors), it's important to keep the copious amount of noise generated by machine woodworking at

How Sound Travels

SOUND IS TRANSMITTED from the shop space to the outside world through vibration. Sound waves generated by machines and portable power tools travel through the air until they hit wall surfaces, doors, windows, and skylights, where they are transformed into vibrational energy. Machines mounted to wooden floors or tools used on thin work surfaces attached to outside walls, such as a router run on a plywood workbench, can send noise outside by directly vibrating the walls or floor. Joisted wood floors are the worst culprits, acting like soundboards that amplify the sound of a tablesaw or compressor just like the body of an acoustic guitar or ukulele amplifies the vibration of the strings.

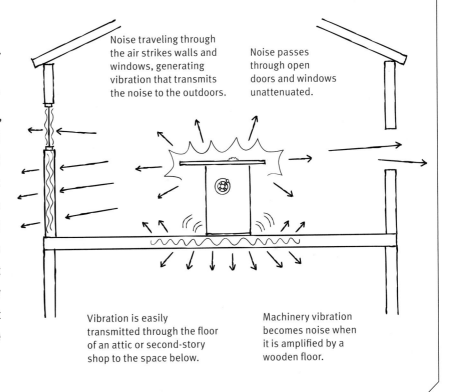

Noise traveling through the air strikes walls and windows, generating vibration that transmits the noise to the outdoors.

Noise passes through open doors and windows unattenuated.

Vibration is easily transmitted through the floor of an attic or second-story shop to the space below.

Machinery vibration becomes noise when it is amplified by a wooden floor.

bay. "Average Sound Levels of Various Machines," below, compares the decibel levels of selected power woodworking activities.

The walls, door, and windows of your shop provide the primary means of containing machine noise. But if thin walls, close proximity to cranky neighbors, and the fact that you like to run your router in the middle of the night require that you reduce your shop's noise output, then alterations to your shop are probably called for.

AVERAGE SOUND LEVEL OF VARIOUS MACHINES

SOUND SOURCE	SOUND LEVEL* (DB)
12-in. radial-arm saw	113
3½-hp router	104
10-in. tablesaw	100
14-in. bandsaw	93
8-in. jointer	90
1-hp dust collector	82
Drill press	75
Normal human speech	60
Whisper	40
Threshold of human hearing	0

*If two machines are running at the same time, do not add decibels (dB) together. Because the decibel scale is logarithmic, any sound that doubles is raised by only 3 dB. Therefore, the sound level of two tablesaws running simultaneously would equal 103 dB, not 200 dB.

REDUCING MACHINERY NOISE

To reduce the noise that machines transmit through a wood floor, first try to isolate the base of the machine from the floor. Placing the machine legs or base atop rubber or dense foam pads can cut down the noise. For devices such as compressors and central dust collectors that must be bolted down, purchase anti-vibration pads.

You can reduce noise transmission both inside and outside your shop by reducing the transfer of sound energy through either the air or by direct vibration. Undoubtedly, you've noticed what a difference it makes just shutting the shop's doors and windows before running a tablesaw. You can further reduce noise by blocking off any unnecessary openings between your shop and the outdoors.

To reduce higher-frequency noises, such as screaming portable power tools, apply sound-deadening material to the inside walls of the shop. Probably the least-expensive material for this purpose is soundboard (sometimes called beaverboard), a compressed fiberboard that comes in ½-in.-thick, 4×8 sheets. The material can be nailed or screwed to the studs of unfinished walls, but it'll be more effective if attached on top of drywall. Not only does soundboard help cut some noise to the outdoors but it also reduces noise inside a shop by absorbing higher-frequency sounds and curtailing their reflection off of hard wall surfaces.

Unfortunately, the deep-throated roar produced by machines such as jointers, shapers, and planers is harder to control.

Smart Ways to Reduce Machinery Noise

YOU MAY WANT TO TRY REDUCING THE NOISE LEVEL that you create in the shop. The fewer decibels your machines produce, the fewer get transmitted outside. You can often make significant gains just by changing blades, bits, and cutters. For example, tablesaw blades vary considerably in regard to the amount of noise they produce. Fitting a planer or jointer with a helical cutterhead reduces noise dramatically.

Machines can also sometimes be quieted by adding a little judicious sound-deadening insulation. Enclosed metal stands can add significantly to the noise output of a machine. To reduce noise, try gluing foam insulation or soundboard inside the stand or stuff it with Styrofoam® scraps.

Noisy compressors, vacuum pumps, shop vacuums, and other cacophonous pieces of equipment can be quieted by setting them inside a sound-deadening "doghouse" cover, which you can build, as shown.

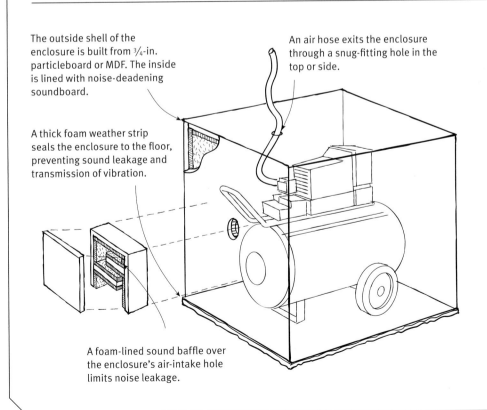

The outside shell of the enclosure is built from ¾-in. particleboard or MDF. The inside is lined with noise-deadening soundboard.

An air hose exits the enclosure through a snug-fitting hole in the top or side.

A thick foam weather strip seals the enclosure to the floor, preventing sound leakage and transmission of vibration.

A foam-lined sound baffle over the enclosure's air-intake hole limits noise leakage.

Using lightweight, compressed-fiber ½-in. soundboard to cover a layer of drywall provides inexpensive sound absorption that helps reduce machine noise both inside and outside the shop.

One of the easiest and most effective methods for damping these middle- and low-frequency sounds is to isolate the drywall/paneling from the walls and ceiling.

Here's how to proceed:

1. Starting with bare stud walls and ceiling joists, attach strips of resilient channel (also known as "sound channel") to the studs or joists at regular intervals.

2. Screw the drywall to these furring strips, which prevents vibration from being transferred from the drywall to the wall studs and outer sheathing.

3. Add a layer of fiberglass insulation between the studs before applying any wall covering. This will help keep your shop more temperate as well as quieter.

Windows and doors Windows and doorways are other conduits for sounds to escape your shop. Existing windows can be quieted by fitting double-glazed replacements, which work much the same way that double walls do to keep vibration from transmitting.

Don't overlook noise problems caused by cheap, hollow-core exterior doors. Replacing them with solid-core doors helps reduce noise.

If you're building a new shop, remember that you can control noise emission to a degree just by where you locate doors

Pressed-metal sound-channel strips mount directly to wall studs, providing a vibration-isolated mounting surface for drywall paneling and significantly reducing noise passing through shop walls.

Fitting a shop with double-glazed windows prevents the roar of tablesaws and routers from transmitting outdoors and helps keep the shop cooler in summer and warmer in winter.

and windows. Simply avoid locating windows on sides of the building that face areas you'd prefer not to shower with noise. For example, the shop shown on p. 23 has no windows or doors on the sides closest to the neighbors.

Special cases If your shop is already paneled or drywalled, you can dampen noise by adding mass to the wall. Fastening a second layer of ⅝-in. drywall over an existing ½-in. or ⅝-in. layer—or a layer of ¾-in. drywall over thin wood paneling—will prevent more noise from escaping your shop.

If you need to really put a cork in your shop's noise level (perhaps there's a new baby trying to sleep in a bedroom right next to your attached-garage woodshop), you'll get the greatest noise insulation by building a second interior wall to the shop. Wall coverings on separate stud walls, inside and outside, keep the transmission of vibrations through the wall to a minimum. While effective, this solution is complex and costly enough to warrant hiring an acoustical consultant before tackling this kind of job (ask a local contractor for a recommendation).

3

Electricity and Lighting

"What you do with the conduit that carries all that wondrous power, once it enters your shop, has everything to do with how conveniently and safely your machines plug in and your lights switch on."

Electricity provides the energy that brings a modern woodworking shop to life. Unless you're one of the rare individuals who works wood with only hand tools or who has a shop powered by steam or waterwheel, electricity is as necessary for productive work as having wood, glue, and finishing materials. In addition to energizing our machines, electricity provides essential light so that we no longer need to schedule our work by the rising and setting of the sun.

What you do with the conduit that carries all that wondrous power, once it enters your shop, has everything to do with how conveniently and safely your machines plug in and your lights switch on. Those of us who have struggled with a shop where the only power and light source dangled from a single wire suspended from the center of the ceiling know the value of good electrical distribution.

Properly designed and installed shop wiring will power the machines in the largest of shops without you having to constantly swap cords or reset tripped breakers or replace blown fuses. A further benefit of good wiring is efficient shop lighting, which illuminates the shop in a way that's easy on the eyes and promotes safe work by allowing you to see what you're doing at all times.

Upgrading Your Electrical System

If you've been calling your garage or basement "home" for your woodworking pastime, chances are you've gotten really good at getting by with extension cords. Utility spaces designed mostly for storage or for a limited amount of work rarely have enough outlets to satisfy a typical woodshop.

Upgrading the power by adding wall outlets is often a pivotal step that

Working Safely with Electricity

- Never do any electrical work unless you follow safe practices and know exactly what you're doing.

- Never work on live electrical wiring. Always turn off the electricity at its source. Put a sign on the box while you work telling others not to turn on the power.

- Connect all ground wires on all circuits properly. Never cut these wires off or fail to hook them up.

- If you're unsure of any aspect of a wiring job, hire a qualified electrician to do the job.

WHEN WORKING WITH POWER TOOLS

- Never cut the ground pin off a tool's power cord; use a three-prong adapter that's been properly grounded.

- If working outdoors or in damp conditions, plug the tool into a ground-fault circuit interrupter (GFCI) protected circuit or power strip, or switch to cordless power tools.

changes a space from being just a garage to being what you can call a true shop. Or maybe your shop is in an old building that has "knob and tube" wiring that needs modernizing for the sake of safety as much as efficiency. For such a case, here is an outline of what you'll want to do to upgrade your shop's electrical system.

How to Upgrade Your Shop's Electrical System

Follow these steps to safely upgrade the electrical system in your shop. Call an electrician if you're uncomfortable doing any of the following.

1. Check your service panel to make sure it has adequate amperage capacity and room to add new circuit breakers.

2. Make an electrical layout drawing of your shop, showing existing circuits and their outlets, fixtures, and switches.

3. Sketch in the new circuits that you plan to add, noting the voltage of each. Carefully plan the location of outlets and fixtures and the of route the wiring back to the breaker box.

4. Calculate the number of amps each new circuit must handle, and choose the appropriate cable type, wire gauge, breaker amperage, and receptacle type for each circuit.

5. Install the electrical boxes, and drill holes for wiring to pass through framing. In paneled or masonry-walled shops, prepare surface-mount cables or install raceways.

6. Run the cable for each circuit around the shop from the breaker box to each electrical box it services (or pull wires into BX cable or install wires in raceways). Leave loops of extra wire at each end.

7. Wire outlets, switches, and fixtures, making sure all connections and ground wires are proper and secure.

8. With the main power switched off, install new circuit breakers in the box and connect wiring from each new circuit.

9. Flip the breakers off, restore power, then turn the circuits on one at a time to test.

DOING IT YOURSELF VERSUS HIRING A PRO

Shop wiring is generally not very complicated. If you've done home wiring tasks before, you'll be up to the task of adding new circuits and outlets around the shop. But if you haven't done much wiring or if your home doesn't have an electrical service panel with enough extra capacity to handle the needs of power-tool-intensive woodworking, upgrading your shop's wiring can be intimidating. This section won't tell you all you need to know to wire the entire shop yourself; you can get more information about that from any good book on basic electrical wiring.

If you have any reservations about doing the work, don't hesitate to hire a certified electrician. Even if you don't do the work yourself, at least you can provide the electrician with a carefully thought-out plan for how you want your shop wired.

SAFETY FIRST

When upgrading your electrical system, safety should be foremost in your mind, and that is why you *never* work on live electrical wiring! The truth is that it doesn't take an enormous surge of power—one that fries internal organs and leaves skin burned to a crisp— for electricity to kill.

Most people who are electrocuted die from cardiac arrest when their bodies serve as a pathway for electric current, typically when a live wire has been contacted while standing on a concrete floor or damp ground. Insidiously, even a relatively small electrical current (less than 100 milliamps—that's less current than it takes to power a night light) can upset the delicate electrical balance that keeps your heart beating. "Working Safely with Electricity," on p. 47 contains a list of electrical do's and don'ts that you should pay attention to when working with electrical wiring.

START WITH THE SERVICE PANEL

Before you begin any effort to upgrade power in your shop by adding new outlets or circuits for new machines, you must determine whether your existing electrical service and wiring can handle your shop's needs. Start by examining your service panel (the metal box just downstream from your electric meter that's fed directly from the power lines coming into your home/building).

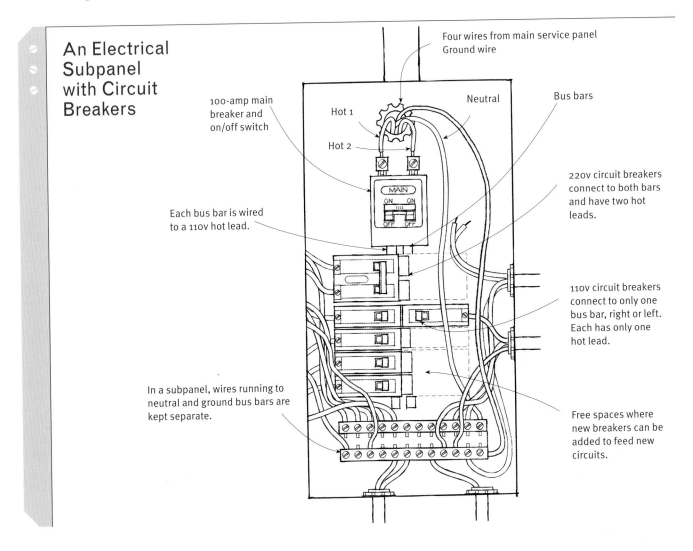

An Electrical Subpanel with Circuit Breakers

Four wires from main service panel
Ground wire

100-amp main breaker and on/off switch

Hot 1

Hot 2

Neutral

Bus bars

MAIN
ON   ON
OFF   OFF

Each bus bar is wired to a 110v hot lead.

220v circuit breakers connect to both bars and have two hot leads.

110v circuit breakers connect to only one bus bar, right or left. Each has only one hot lead.

In a subpanel, wires running to neutral and ground bus bars are kept separate.

Free spaces where new breakers can be added to feed new circuits.

If your home/shop building was constructed before the 1950s, chances are you have only a 30-amp service (with two 15-amp fuses) or a 60-amp service (with four 15-amp fuses). The circuits running off these 15-amp fuses aren't beefy enough to handle many standard shop machines, such as tablesaws, shapers, and thickness planers. Moreover, many older systems offer only 110v power, which means you can't run machines with 220v motors—a serious limitation for a modern woodshop.

Getting rid of the fuse box

Older fuse boxes can't be easily upgraded. The only solution is to contact your local power company and ask them to upgrade your service to a modern, 100-amp, 150-amp, or 200-amp service, and then hire an electrician to install the new service panel.

A modern service panel has three wires coming into it: two 110v hot wires and one neutral wire. In a breaker box, which uses circuit breakers instead of fuses to protect wiring from shorts or overloads, the hot leads are wired to two bus bars.

Depending on the type of circuit breaker and how it is installed, the hot lead for a 110v circuit can be run off of a 110v bus bar (see "An Electrical Subpanel with Circuit Breakers", on p. 49). A 220v circuit has a breaker that connects to both bus bars and has two hot leads and a neutral wire.

Even if you're fortunate enough to have a modern breaker box, make sure there is room for adding another breaker before you plan additional shop circuits. If there are no unbroken knockouts on the panel's cover plate, you'll have to add an electrical subpanel for the new circuits.

Adding a subpanel
If your existing service panel has no room for expansion or if you find yourself running to the other end of your property each time you trip a breaker or need to shut a circuit

Installing an electrical subpanel in your shop provides room to add separate circuits for shop lighting and outlets and for powering large, amp-hungry machines. It also makes it easier to locate and turn breakers off when working on shop circuits or to reset them after an overload.

Use the Right Capacity Breaker or Fuse

You might be tempted to "upgrade" the capacity of some of your existing shop circuits by replacing a fuse or breaker with a higher capacity one, for instance fit a 20-amp fuse in place of a 15-amp fuse. I have just three words: *Never do this!* The wiring for any circuit is designed to safely handle only so many amps. If you change the circuit's fuse/breaker protection, you are creating a severe fire hazard.

down at the main panel, it's probably time to install a separate subpanel in or near your shop.

In a home with a standard 200-amp service, you can have a 100-amp or 70-amp circuit run to your shop. If you can't safely turn the power off at your main panel, you'll need to have the subpanel installed by a qualified electrician.

Before you choose a particular brand of subpanel box, it's wise to check the cost of circuit breakers that fit it because some brands cost much more than others.

ADDING ELECTRICAL OUTLETS

Can any shop ever have too many electrical outlets? Probably not, and the number of extra outlets you install should be

Electrical Wiring in a Typical Woodshop

- 1: 110v/15 amp; bandsaw and drill press
- 2: 110v/15 amp; outlets for bench area
- 3. 110v/20 amp; outlets on back wall and router table
- 4: 220v/20 amp; planer and jointer
- 5: 110v/15 amp; overhead fluorescent lights
- 6: 220v/20 amp; tablesaw
- 7: 110v/20 amp; outlets on front, side walls, and combo sander
- 8: 220v/15 amp; radial-arm saw

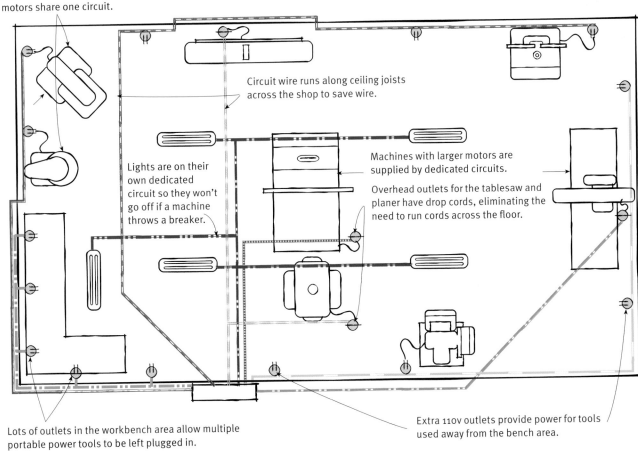

Machines with relatively small motors share one circuit.

Circuit wire runs along ceiling joists across the shop to save wire.

Machines with larger motors are supplied by dedicated circuits.

Lights are on their own dedicated circuit so they won't go off if a machine throws a breaker.

Overhead outlets for the tablesaw and planer have drop cords, eliminating the need to run cords across the floor.

Lots of outlets in the workbench area allow multiple portable power tools to be left plugged in.

Extra 110v outlets provide power for tools used away from the bench area.

Easy-to-Reach Bench Outlets

IF YOUR SHOP HAS BUILT-IN BENCHES along one or more walls, a convenient strategy is to install 110v outlets at regular intervals both along the backsplash and just below the front edge of the benchtop. The backsplash outlets provide power for benchtop machines, such as drill presses and disc sanders. The lower outlets are great for running portable power tools without having to drape their cords across the bench, where they're likely to get in the way

limited only by your shop-wiring budget. Try locating more outlets in areas where you will be likely to use portable power tools, lights, a compressor, or dust collector. A circuit diagram showing various outlet locations in a two-car garage-size shop is shown in "Electrical Wiring in a Typical Woodshop" on p. 51.

Normal outlets in open shop areas should be at least 12 in. from the floor. However, in areas where shop machines and/or workbenches will be placed close to walls, mount outlets about 42 in. up from the floor. If you have wood floors, avoid recessing outlets directly into the floor, where they can quickly collect sawdust and become a fire hazard.

Unless you're sure you'll never again remodel your shop, it's better to spread outlets around the shop as uniformly as possible, rather than locating each one closest to the machine that it feeds. Extra 110v outlets located away from machines and workbenches are likely to come in handy when new small machines are added or for running portable power tools, such as when you must assemble a big cabinet or build a canoe in the middle of the shop floor.

NEW CIRCUITS FOR MACHINE TOOLS

If you have a one-person shop where only one machine is run at a time, it is normal to have individual circuits that may service three, four, or more machines, even if their combined motor amperage requirements exceed that circuit's capacity. However, it is best to run separate, dedicated circuits for larger machines so that you can run, say, a tablesaw and a jointer concurrently, which can save time when you're dressing and ripping wide boards. Dedicated circuits are also necessary for powerful air compressors and dust collectors, which run in tandem with machines.

In a shop shared by several woodworkers, all machines should be powered by dedicated circuits to prevent an overloaded motor. When one person using a machine throws a breaker that cuts off power to a machine someone else is using, it is a situation that's at best annoying and at worst dangerous.

When planning new circuits, be sure to size the wiring and circuit breaker to handle the recommended maximum motor amperage that's safe to run. "Maximum Capacity of Typical Shop Wiring Gauges," below,

shows recommended wire gauges and circuit-breaker sizes to handle various motors. A motor's amp rating is typically printed on its name plate or in the machine's manual, but if you don't know it, "Approximate Amperage for Different Motor Horsepowers," on p. 57, shows typical requirements for common motors.

If you have a machine motor that can be run on either 110v or 220v power, it's better to run the motor on 220v whenever possible. Doubling the voltage cuts the amperage in half so that, for example, a 3-hp tablesaw motor that draws 15 amps at 110v requires a 20-amp circuit run with 12-gauge wire. That same motor operated at 220v draws only 7½ amps, so it may be run on a 15-amp

MAXIMUM CAPACITY OF TYPICAL SHOP WIRING GAUGES

APPLICATION	COPPER WIRE GAUGE (AWG)			
	14 GAUGE	12 GAUGE	10 GAUGE	8 GAUGE
Maximum sustained amperage a circuit may handle (110v or 220v)	15 amps	20 amps	30 amps	40 amps
Recommended maximum motor size (amperage) that's safe to run on a circuit*	12 amps 110v or 220v	16 amps 110v or 220v	24 amps 110v or 220v	32 amps 110v or 220v
Typical circuit application for wire size	Lighting circuits	Outlets for 110v tools and machines	Circuits for large 110v or 220v machines	

*Electrical motors draw extra power when starting up, resulting in a surge that pulls more amperage through the wiring.

Blind Loops for Future Outlets

IF YOU REARRANGE THE MACHINES IN YOUR SHOP as often as you change your socks, here's an economical trick that will keep your electrical layout more flexible. While you're wiring new circuits, add more receptacle boxes than you plan on using.

Run a loop of the circuit wire through all of the unused boxes, and fit them with blank cover plates (as shown here). Wiring the shop this way is an especially good idea if you drywall or panel the walls, which makes it difficult to make wiring changes later.

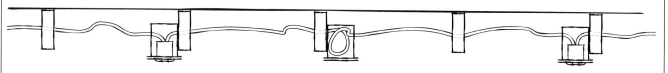

Leaving a wire loop in a box with a blank cover plate allows the unused box to be easily converted into a working outlet when it's needed.

A cord hanger provides strain relief for an electrical power cord that is dropped from an overhead outlet, serving to protect the cord from damage and prevent it from being pulled out accidentally.

circuit wired with 14-gauge cable. Not only do you save money by being able to use less expensive wire (lower-amperage breakers are often cheaper too) but also the motor will run more efficiently on the higher voltage.

Powering machines away from walls One of the biggest shop wiring dilemmas is how to power tools located in the middle of the shop. If you don't have a raised floor under which to feed electrical wiring (see "Subfloor Systems," p. 40), you'll have to devise a way to get the power cord to the tool without it being in the way. Using special cord-relief hardware, you can drop a power cord from the ceiling or overhead beam to a machine, as shown in the photo at left.

The trouble is that drop cords have an almost magical ability to snag long boards and pipe clamps as you carry them around the shop. If you wire a drop cord for your tablesaw, locate it near the extension table's far right corner. But if you regularly work with large sheet-goods, any tablesaw drop cord is likely to present a continuing nuisance.

Routing power cords across the floor isn't a much better solution because cords can create a tripping

A molded rubber-like cord duct covers an electrical power cord that runs across a doorway or floor to feed machines used in the center of the shop. It prevents cord damage and tripping accidents.

hazard. About the best you can do is to run the cord to the machine in a spot with the least foot traffic and cover it with a cord duct, which will protect the cable and minimize the tripping potential.

One strategy is to install an overhead outlet in a spot where you can easily reach it. Then, wire up a longer power cord to the tool, routing it where it is least in the way, such as down a support post. This is the safe way to go because it allows you to disconnect the power to that tool before changing blades or bits or adjusting the tool.

ADDING LIGHTING CIRCUITS

It's very important to run separate circuits for power tools and lights. This is to avoid leaving you in the dark if a breaker trips while you're working with power tools at night.

Routing a power cord from a stationary machine to an overhead electrical outlet located within easy reach provides a convenient way to disconnect power to safely change blades or make major adjustments.

220v Plugs and Outlets

TAKE SPECIAL CARE WHEN BUYING plugs and outlets for connecting 220v machines. There are many different styles and types (single and three phase, for example), each rated to handle a given maximum amperage.

Not only are electrical plugs specified to handle either 110v or 220v but they're also specified for amperage and number of wires. Shown here (left to right) are 15-, 20-, and 30-amp 220v plugs, with three or four prongs.

Although they're much more expensive than standard duplex 110v electrical outlets (right), spec grade outlets (left and center) are made from sturdy plastic with metal reinforcements, making them a more durable and long-lasting choice for woodshop installations.

WIRING WITH SHEATHED CABLE

Because it is inexpensive and easy to work with, nonmetallic sheathed cable (NM cable), such as Romex™, is the cable of choice for small-shop wiring. Most local codes allow you to wire circuits with NM cable, as long as it's installed in places where it won't get wet or damaged. A special kind of nonmetallic cable, called UF cable, can be used for outdoor and underground wiring, if, for instance, you're running cable from your main service panel to a subpanel in the shop.

When estimating the amount of cable you'll need for your new circuits, figure an extra foot at each outlet box and breaker box connection. Also, add a couple of extra feet for each long cable run to allow for unexpected twists and turns and cable sagging.

Although they're more expensive, plan on buying and installing "spec grade"

When running circuits for new lighting, calculate the number of watts each circuit must handle, following the appropriate formula given in "Light Circuit-Capacity Calculations," on p. 58. Note that different formulas are used for incandescent and fluorescent lighting. On circuits with mixed light types, use the fluorescent formula.

APPROXIMATE AMPERAGE FOR DIFFERENT MOTOR HORSEPOWERS

MOTOR HORSEPOWER	110V MOTOR	220V MOTOR	220V, 3-PHASE MOTOR
1/4	6 1/2	3 1/4	n/a
1/3	7 1/4	3 1/2	n/a
1/2	10	5	2 1/2
3/4	14	7	3 1/2
1	17	8 1/2	4 1/2
1 1/2	20	10	6
2	23 1/2	12	7 1/2
2 1/2	26 1/2	14 1/2	8 1/2
3	33	17	9 1/2
5	n/a	27 1/2	16

110v outlets on all 110v circuits. These are much more durable and less prone to breakage and failure during the heavy use they'll get in the shop. If you're adding 220v circuits, make sure you buy the right type to fit the plugs on your machine power cords (there are many styles; see "220v Plugs and Outlets," on the facing page). Plugs, as well as the wiring and circuit breakers that feed them, should be sized to handle 25 percent more amperage than the machines they serve (for example, a 15-amp machine requires a 20-amp plug and circuit). Most 220v machines have three wires—two hot and a ground—and require a plug with three prongs. If your machine's cord has four wires, use a four-prong plug—*do not* connect the neutral and ground wires to each other! If you are installing overhead outlets, consider twist-style plugs and outlets, which will keep power cords from accidentally coming unplugged. Also, make sure to buy receptacle boxes that are big enough for large 220v outlets (as well as for ground-fault circuit interrupter [GFCI] outlets; see "GFCI Outlets and Breakers," on p. 232) since they typically don't fit into smaller-style electrical boxes.

The Shortest Distance between Two Points

You can typically save cable by routing it across the ceiling or through the attic, which is often the shortest route for circuits on the opposite side of the shop.

It's best to have a systematic approach to installing wiring, which follows:

1. Mount electrical boxes as per your circuit layout drawing, nailing or screwing them to studs and joists or popping them into cutouts in the drywall or paneling.

2. Drill holes through studs to pass cables through: ½-in. holes for 14-gauge or 12-gauge NM cable; ⅝-in. holes for 10-gauge cable. Center the holes in the studs, drilling at least 1½ in. below the top edge of each joist. On studs with

electrical boxes, drill holes 4 in. to 6 in. above or below the box. In corners, it's often easier to saw and notch the studs, rather than trying to drill through.

3. Using U-shaped insulated staples, attach the cable about every 4 ft. where it runs along a stud or joist, 8 in. to 12 in. from each box, and wherever the cable changes direction.

4. Pull the cable into boxes, leaving at least 6-in. to 8-in. hanging out of each box and an extra 6-in. to 8-in. loop of cable just above or below each box to

Light Circuit-Capacity Calculations

NONFLUORESCENT LAMPS

To figure the maximum amperage recommended for sustained use of regular incandescent and tungsten/halogen lamps, use the following formula.

$$\frac{\text{Total wattage of lamps on circuit}}{\text{Voltage (typically 110v)}} = {}^{8}/_{10} \text{ of circuit amperage}$$

EXAMPLE

If you have seven 75w light bulbs and three 250w halogen bulbs on the circuit, your total wattage equals 1,275w. Use the formula to determine the amperage:

1,275w ÷ 110v = 11.5 amps

In this case, a 15-amp circuit will handle the total light wattage:

0.8 × 15 amp = 12 amps

FLUORESCENT LAMPS

Because fluorescent lamps require additional power for their ballasts, you must add another 20 percent of wattage to the calculation.

$$\frac{\text{Total wattage of fluorescent lamps + 20\%}}{\text{Voltage (typically 110v)}} = {}^{8}/_{10} \text{ of circuit amperage}$$

EXAMPLE

If you have 15 twin-bulb fluorescent fixtures with 40w bulbs in your circuit, the total wattage is 1,200w; 20 percent of 1,200 is 240. Use the formula to determine the amperage:

1,200w + 240w = 1,440 amps

1,440w ÷ 110v = 13 amps

In this case, a 15-amp circuit isn't quite enough to handle the wattage, so upgrade to a 20-amp circuit:

0.8 × 20 amp = 16 amps

provide a margin of error and to make future wiring changes easier. Leave at least 12 in. to 15 in. of extra cable for each circuit at the service panel end for connection to breakers. If you plan to panel the shop after wiring, install metal nail plates where the cable runs through studs and joists to prevent metal fasteners from accidentally being driven into live wires—a shocking situation.

5. Once all the cables have been installed, wire up each outlet, switch, and light fixture, taking great care to wire each one correctly (the package the item comes in typically has wiring instructions, or you can consult a basic wiring book). Be sure to attach all ground wires properly, as they can save your life in an accident. When mounting an outlet or a switch in a box, fold the excess length of wire into a zigzag and press it carefully back into the box.

6. After all circuits have been wired at the boxes and cover plates have been installed, you're ready to connect the wires to their circuit breakers. After making absolutely sure the power is completely off at the service panel, remove the cover plate and install the new breakers, which snap into place on the bus bars. Feed the cables from the new circuits into the box, then strip and wire each circuit, running hot wires directly to the breakers. In a regular service panel, neutral and ground wires are connected to the same bus bar. However, for additional grounding safety, it's important that subpanels have these wires connected to separate bus bars that are electrically isolated and connected

When You Run Short of Cable

If you run out of cable in the course of a run or if you need to relocate an existing box, make the splice between cables inside a junction box (an electrical box with a cover plate). Never connect two ends of a wire or cable without housing it inside a box.

separately to the neutral and ground wires that feed the subpanel from the service panel (see drawing on p. 49).

When all wires have been secured, replace the cover plate, remembering to remove the knockouts for the new breakers, and turn off all the new circuit breakers before restoring power to the box. By flipping each circuit on individually, you'll know right away if there are any shorts or other problems (an instantly tripped breaker or a burning smell are pretty good indications).

Once all your circuits have checked out, take a few moments to label them (for example, Circuit 1: 110v outlets, west wall; Circuit 2: tablesaw, jointer; Circuit 3: overhead lights). Better yet, sketch a circuit map of the entire shop, noting which circuit each outlet and lighting fixture is on. Keeping the sketch handy, such as taping it inside the service panel, will prevent you from having to play "flip breakers until the lamp goes off that's plugged into the circuit in question." Labeling outlet cover plates is another way of keeping track of what each circuit is powering.

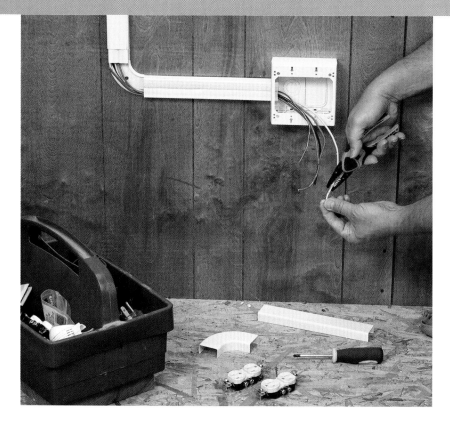

Electrical raceway is an enclosed metal or plastic channel that attaches to any kind of shop wall. Connected to surface-mounted electrical boxes, the raceway's removable lid provides fast access to wires, allowing you to easily add new shop circuits or modify existing wiring.

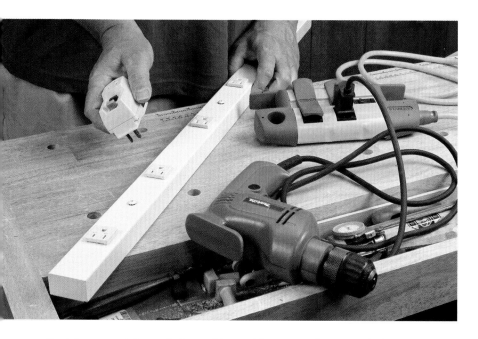

Electric power strips and plug molds provide a convenient way of adding more outlets in the shop without running new electrical circuits. A separate GFCI plug-in accessory provides protection for any power strip.

INSTALLING SURFACE-MOUNTED WIRING

Rewiring the inside of a house is a tough job because wiring has to be snaked around framing members hidden inside walls finished with plaster or drywall. If your shop has finished stud walls, you'll save considerable time and hassle by running new circuits using surface-mounted cables or electrical raceways. These also can be used to run circuits across concrete or brick walls.

An electrical raceway system provides a very flexible means of installing surface-mounted wiring because it has an enclosed channel with a removable cover that allows wiring changes. Raceway can be mounted at baseboard level, connecting to surface-mounted boxes for new light fixtures, switches, and outlets. When purchasing raceway, check the particular product's current rating because some systems are designed to handle only low-amperage wiring for home appliances.

Flexible armored cable (BX cable) is often used to wire shop circuits since it's easily surface mounted and new wires can be added or removed from inside the metal cable as needed. If you choose BX cable, select one with a large enough diameter to accommodate the gauge and number of wires you want to pull through it (using a fish tape).

POWER STRIPS AND EXTENSION CORDS

An easy way to gain more outlets in an existing shop without having to chop holes in walls and run wire for additional circuits is by employing electric power strips and plug mold (see the bottom photo on the facing page). These strips have become ubiquitous now that electronic devices and gadgets have overrun our homes and we need about 10 times the number of outlets that most older homes offer.

You can fashion your own multioutlet power box by wiring outlets into a metal electrical box at the end of a heavy-duty sheathed extension cord. But it's easier to buy a commercial power strip or plug mold that features four, six, or even more three-prong (grounded) 110v sockets. Most power strips feature a small circuit breaker so that you won't accidentally overload the capacity of the strip's wiring. Some strips even include GFCI protection, essential when working with power tools outdoors.

Unless you are running sensitive electronic equipment in your shop, such as stereos, computers, and CNC machines, pass on fancier, more expensive power strips that include surge protection and RFI filtering. The performance of standard woodworking power tools won't benefit from these features.

When using extension cords, it's critical that you not connect tools or machines that draw more amperage than a given cord is rated to handle. "Maximum Extension Cord Lengths" at right shows what size wire the cord should have to handle various power loads. Exceeding a cord's rating will diminish the performance of the tool;and serious overloading creates heat, which could pose a fire hazard.

Using a thicker extension cord with heavier-gauge wires (a 12-gauge cord shown here) for large portable power tools not only prevents overheating and fire danger but ensures better tool performance.

MAXIMUM EXTENSION CORD LENGTHS

MOTOR SIZE (AMP)	WIRE SIZE (GAUGE)	MAXIMUM LENGTH OF CORD (FT.)
3 ½	16	100
5	16	75
5	14	100
7	16	50
7	14	75
10	12	100
12	14	50
12	12	75
15	12	50

A self-retracting cord reel mounted near the shop door provides a handy means of feeding a long extension cord to power tools used outside the shop. For safest operation while using portables outdoors, such as this circular saw being used to cut plywood, the reel's 50-ft. cord should be plugged into a GFCI outlet.

tool in your hand can leave your local emergency room staff with lots to talk about ("So that's what happens when you catch your untucked shirttail in a spinning router bit!").

There are several strategies you can use to keep the electrical snakes from multiplying.

• Keep portable power tools plugged into a multioutlet electrical power strip. By mounting the power strip underneath or near your workbench or table and having a shelf or cubbies on which to store your tools, you can keep all your daily-use tools powered and ready to go.

• Install one or more self-retracting cord reels around the shop. Typically loaded with 50 ft. of power cord with a multi-plug outlet on the end, cord reels allow you to quickly pull out the exact length of cord you need. This way cords on portable power tools can be kept short and easy to manage. Just a slight tug and the device reels the cord back in. These are terrific when working away from outlets in the shop and—when plugged into a GFCI outlet (for protection from electrical shocks)—outdoors as well.

Managing cords One of the single biggest challenges in most shops is figuring out how to manage the twisted piles of black-rubber-covered spaghetti that seem to fill up benchtops and choke open-floor areas like unruly snakes. Tangled power cords from portable electric tools can make woodworking a hassle at best; running out of cord in the middle of a cut can ruin expensive workpieces. Loose cords on the floor love to trip you when you least expect it; and, worse, getting tangled in a cord with a whirring power

• Install short "pigtails" on your power tools and use them with extension cords. Twist-lock-style plugs are favored for this because standard two-prong plugs pull out easily. This is the most expensive solution, but it might be right for you if you work in a one-person shop and typically use only one or two tools at a time. Pigtails are especially good for tools that are commonly transported and used at job sites. Constant wrapping and unwrapping of cords often causes shorts and failures, and eliminating long cords also eliminates tangles and makes tools easier to store. On the down side, connecting and disconnecting tools from necessary extension cords can be time-consuming.

• Switch to cordless tools. Battery-powered tools get more powerful and versatile every year. Once only drills came without cords, but now you can buy cordless screwdrivers, sabersaws, circular saws, reciprocating saws, and more (see "Battery-Powered Portables, on p. 109). At this rate, the woodshop of the future could be nearly cord free.

Three strategies for preventing long cords on portable power tools from ending up snarled and tangled are (left to right): Buy tools with detachable power cords, such as this Sawzall®; fit each tool a short pigtail and plug it into an extension cord (using locking plugs) before using it; and refit existing power cords with tangle-resistant, self-retracting coil cords.

Keep Portables Ready to Run

KEEPING YOUR FREQUENTLY USED portable power tools connected to a multioutlet electrical power strip mounted below your workbench will save the time and trouble of plugging and unplugging tools every time you need them. Consider creating workstations where the tools are most often used.

Lighting Your Shop

I'll never forget the time I first visited a blind woodworker. His wife let me in the front door and pointed toward the basement stairs. "He's down there," she said. I could hear a mute roar as I opened the door and to my astonishment, the basement was pitch black! It took me a few seconds to realize that the only lighting necessary in that shop was for a sighted visitor like me.

Unfortunately for sighted woodworkers, even the most mundane tasks are dangerous or impossible without fairly copious amounts of light. Without light pouring in through windows or illumination provided by artificial means, most of us are as helpless as deaf bats.

Ideally, light for your shop should come from a combination of sources. Natural sunlight coming in through windows, open doors, and skylights is free and creates a healthy, natural light during the day. This is supplemented on cloudy days and at night by some network of artificial lights to provide general illumination for the whole shop. Finally, both natural and general lighting are further augmented by task lighting, which adds a little extra light at specific locations where it is needed for visually demanding tasks, such as layout and joinery work or carving.

GETTING THE MOST OUT OF NATURAL LIGHT

If you want to keep your electric bill to a minimum, design your shop so that natural lighting provides all the unregulated illumination you need during the day. Then depend on artificial light only at night.

But before you punch a bunch of holes in your shop walls and roof, remember that you can have too much of a good thing. Direct shafts of sunlight streaming into the shop can be too bright to work in, especially when adjacent areas of the shop are dark (which can cause eyestrain). And sunlight brings some added baggage: heat. A southern wall riddled with windows can generate stratospheric levels of heat and turn your space into an inferno. Also, direct sunlight has the annoying propensity to fade or change

The good lighting in this wood-shop comes from multiple sources. Natural sunlight comes through windows, doors, and skylights during the day and is supplemented with artificial light from overhead fluorescent bulbs, for general illumination, and with incandescent task lamps, for use at specific machines or wherever more light is needed for visually demanding tasks.

A half-dozen small skylights provide all the light Fort Bragg, Calif., woodworker Jim Budlong needs for seeing fine details as he works on a handsome walnut and ebony tabletop.

brightly colored materials. Gorgeous, colorful lumber and veneer exposed to direct light can dull dramatically.

Capturing the best natural light

If your shop doesn't already have enough natural light, then you should consider letting more in via windows or skylights. Not only will this upgrade improve the comfort of working in your shop during the day but it can also add to its future value, even if the next occupant/owner uses it for a different activity. Assuming your shop offers flexibility as to where windows and skylights can be placed, you'll get the most out of them by carefully planning their location relative to the layout of tools and machines within the shop.

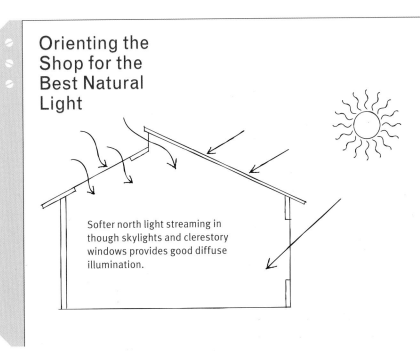

Orienting the Shop for the Best Natural Light

Softer north light streaming in though skylights and clerestory windows provides good diffuse illumination.

To fill a shop with natural light-ing that's pleasant and dif-fuse—rather than hot, direct sunlight with harsh shadows and glare—install skylights on north- or east-facing roofs.

This large skylight, which keeps the author's window-challenged woodshop bright, was shop-built using a 2×6 lumber frame covered with translucent corru-gated fiberglass glazing.

The sky at the horizon is only about one third as bright as the sky that is directly overhead. Hence windows and skylights located high on walls gather more light than windows placed close to the ground. If your shop currently has only a few windows near ground level, adding windows high on the end walls of a gable-roofed structure, for instance, or at the top of a wall above an adjacent roof (known as a clerestory) will substan-tially increase the amount of daylight that finds its way into the shop.

Locating light entry points When-ever possible, try to locate high windows, skylights, and clerestories on north-, northeast-, or east-facing walls and roofs. This reduces the amount of strong light that will stream directly into the shop, creating a nice, diffuse light, rather than glaring sunlight and harsh shadows. Light from north-facing openings also helps keep the shop cooler during brutal summer afternoons. A possible exception is if your shop is in a cool climate where conditions are frequently cloudy, such as in the Pacific Northwest. There, south-facing skylights and windows maximize the amount of cloud-diffused light that enters the shop.

Windows and skylights Windows are available ready-made in a wide variety of types and sizes, including both standard casement and sash. The simplest metal-framed windows are sturdy, durable, and affordable. And windows are relatively easy to install into most types of shop walls. Skylights also come ready-made in dozens of designs and types that are easy to install on just about any type of roof. You can also build your own simple sky-light by constructing a lumber frame and using safety glass or corrugated fiberglass as a glazing.

Unless you live in a very mild climate, install double-glazed windows and sky-lights that feature "low-E" glass. Low-E glass not only reduces heat loss in the winter but also reduces heat transmission in the summer. Double-glazed windows and skylights do a good job of cutting down on noise leakage from the shop to help keep the area around it quieter. Double-glazing also helps prevent condensation drips from skylights, an annoying and potentially destructive problem. If shop overheating is an issue, choose a skylight that may be opened for ventilation.

Spotlight Your Work Areas

YOU CAN MAKE THE MOST of whatever natural light enters your shop by locating machines and workbenches to take advantage of it. However, avoid placing a machine or bench so it faces a window or skylight that receives direct sunlight when you work. Having strong light just where your eyes are focusing creates a lot of eyestrain, and such an arrangement is also likely to cause glare. Instead, orient the machine/bench so that the light comes from behind where you stand while working. If that's not possible, the window can be treated to attenuate its light.

Remember to Ventilate Rafters below Skylights

If the skylight is installed through an insulated roof, don't forget to ventilate the rafter bay below the skylight (see "Insulating a Vaulted Ceiling," on p. 330). Not doing so can create condensation drips that make the skylight look as though it were leaking.

Diffusing and controlling natural light As anyone who has gotten a nasty sunburn knows, too much sunlight can be a decisively bad thing. Fortunately, we can tame the harsh rays of the sun by blocking or filtering them, thereby lowering their intensity. Opaque curtains, shutters, and reflective Mylar® coverings can be used to block light coming into your shop, which might be necessary on some south-facing windows during the most solar-intensive months of the year.

To reflect the most heat, the outward-facing surface on window treatments should be white or silver. Collapsible auto window shades can make good temporary coverings, as can aluminum foil. Thicker window coverings, such as thermal window shades, will help keep a heated shop warmer in winter, especially if the windows are only single glazed. Skylights receiving too much direct sunlight can be fitted with a roll-up-style vinyl shade on the underside, which will allow you to block the light when necessary. Just remember to keep all shades vacuumed to reduce fire danger.

If you don't want to block the light coming in through windows but just want to filter it to make it more pleasant, translucent treatments, such as white canvas awnings, light fabric curtains, and paper shades, will diffuse sunlight and cut down on glare and harsh shadows. To diffuse direct light that comes in through skylights, choose a skylight that has a frosted, not clear, outer glazing. If your shop already has clear skylights, you can diffuse light by mounting a prismatic lighting panel on the inside of the glazing. These thin, inexpensive plastic panels, available in large sheets from plastics stores and home centers, are the kind that you often see covering commercial fluorescent light fixtures.

INSTALLING ARTIFICIAL LIGHTING

The biggest shortcoming of using sunlight to illuminate the shop is that it is inconsistent, changing with every hour of the day and every cloud that passes overhead. Also, it's nonexistent between sunset and sunrise. Unless you're willing to restrict your woodworking to the hours of daylight, you need to have some kind of artificial light in your workshop.

Unlike our forefathers who had to illuminate their shops with candles or oil lamps, modern woodworkers have the convenience of clean-burning, electric lighting at their disposal. But even with this advantage, many woodworkers settle for shop lighting that even colonial chairmakers might have considered too subdued.

You can't work comfortably and safely without adequate lighting—a few bare bulbs dangling around the shop or a single double-bulb fluorescent "shop light" aren't enough. Even if you have a large enough volume of light, poor or uneven placement can create eyestrain and glare. And the choice of lighting type—tungsten, halogen, or fluorescent—affects the way colors look.

In this section, I examine the factors involved in choosing and installing artificial lights in your shop. The goal is to enable you to make informed decisions

Overhead Light Placement for Work Areas

Fair: The lights illuminate the area without glare but can create some shadows.

Best: The lights illuminate the entire work area without blinding the woodworker.

Poor: Lights that are too far in front of the work area or too low throw light directly into the eyes of the woodworker.

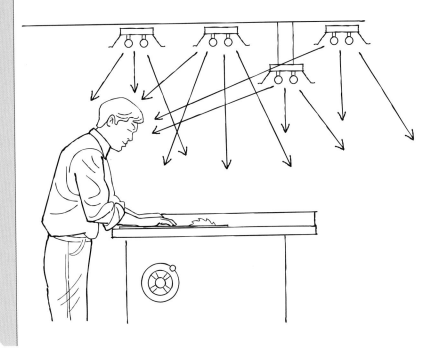

if you choose to install, upgrade, or replace lights in your shop, so that you will end up with lighting that's adequate for safe and comfortable work with minimal eyestrain.

Start with good general illumination To see best, you need to illuminate your workshop with the right intensity of light. If the light is too low, you strain to discern detail and color. If the light is too high, your eyes are dazzled by the brightness and glare and you must squint,

which leads quickly to eye fatigue. This means you'll need to install enough fixtures to get the amount of light you need and locate the fixtures properly for ideal lighting.

There are two ways of putting light to work in the shop: General lighting, from both natural and artificial sources, provides the bulk of the light around the shop so you can see well enough to know what you're doing in any given area of the shop. Task lighting acts as a supplement to general lighting, using portable lamps

Background Lighting Counts

Why not just use light only where you are working in the shop? You see best when the object you're concentrating on is the brightest thing in your immediate field of vision with the background less bright but still in the same general range of brightness. This formula for good lighting is the reason it is best to use both general lighting and area-specific task lighting in concert.

Light Surfaces Reflect Light

YOU CAN IMPROVE THE EFFECT of whatever general illumination you now have in your shop—natural or artificial—by simply painting the walls a light color. White or light gray surfaces bounce light back, instead of absorbing it, providing more usable illumination from the same amount of lighting energy. You can get a reasonable amount of light bounce by installing reflectors above light fixtures, both fluorescent and incandescent. (This is especially important if fixtures are hung down a good distance from the ceiling, such as incandescent drop lights on cords.)

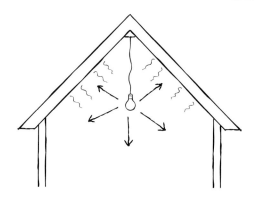

The combination of no reflector above the bulb and dark walls means that light is not reflected down into the work area.

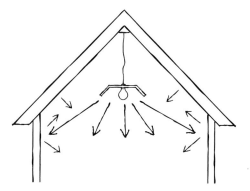

Adding a reflector above a bulb directs more light down into the work area. Painting walls and ceiling white bounces light around, making the whole shop lighter.

or fixtures in areas where you need just that extra bit of light to do fine work.

While there are highly scientific formulas for determining the size, number, and location of lighting fixtures for an indoor space, lighting is really a subjective endeavor. One person's perfectly lit shop may be considered to be a bit dim by a person who prefers brighter working conditions. And as you age, your eyes often need more light to see clearly than they did when you were younger. Variables such as the amount of natural light that's available, the reflectivity of the shop's interior, and even how much light is absorbed by dark machines, cabinets, and workbenches further confound the use of any easy shop-lighting formula.

Planning lighting Rather than leaving you in the dark (pun intended), let me offer what I think is a good starting point for planning the lighting for a small shop. If you're building a new shop or doing a total renovation, make a plan-view drawing of your shop and note the areas where you work most of the time. You'll want the best general light at machines, workbenches, and assembly areas. You won't need as much light in corridors, storage areas, or where compressors and dust collectors are located.

For both good light and best economy, I recommend using multiple 4-ft. two-, three-, or four-tube fluorescent lights for general lighting, then adding incandescent portable lamps or installed fixtures as task lights. On your plan, locate at least one fluorescent fixture above each machine/work area. Try to locate the fixtures so that they are either directly above the machine/work area or above where you stand when working, as shown in "Overhead Light Placement for Work Areas," on p. 69.

Avoid locating lights in front of machines and work areas where they will cast light in your direct field of vision. Generally, this means mounting fixtures high on walls or up on the ceiling. Plan for adequate light in work areas that receive sunlight during the day so you are able to work at night or on heavily overcast days. If you have doubts about your fixture-location decisions, wire up one fluorescent with a cord and plug and hang it up temporarily.

When installing new general lighting in a shop, it's a good idea to arrange the light circuits in two banks (or more in a large shop), as shown in "Wiring Twin Lighting Circuits" at right. This arrangement allows you to turn on only half your lights on a cloudy day and still have even illumination all over the shop. At night, both banks can be turned on for full artificial light.

Adding task lighting Now that you have the general lighting in your shop up to snuff, it's time to turn your attention to adding an extra bit of lighting where it's needed via task lights. Whether a task light is a plain old adjustable drafting lamp, halogen work light, or a sophisticated lamp that features daylight-like lighting, task lights give you the ability to add just the amount of light you want, when you want it, and where.

Adjustable, drafting lamps are ideal task lighting fixtures for the workshop. Most lamps come with a base that clamps onto a thin tabletop, or you can fit the lamp's base stem into a ½-in. hole drilled into a benchtop or wooden mounting block.

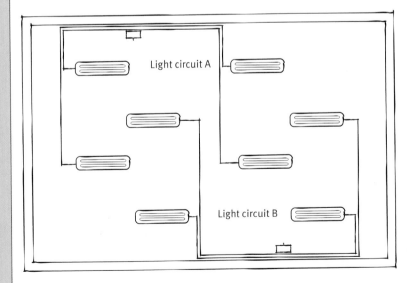

Wiring Twin Lighting Circuits

Light circuit A

Light circuit B

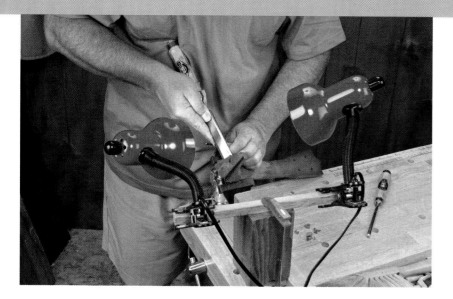

Portable lamps provide ample, adjustable lighting for doing intricate work, such as carving, inlaying, or trimming a dovetail, as shown here.

A gooseneck lamp with a magnetic base makes a handy task light that can be quickly mounted to the metal body or table of a machine, such as this bandsaw set up for resawing, to shed light exactly where it's needed.

By aiming the light carefully, a task light can make it easier to read the fine scale on a caliper or rule or to see fine checks or sanding scratches in a turning blank. For really fine, closeup work, consider setting up two task lights, such as the clip-on lamps shown in the photo above. By fitting the lamps with two different-strength bulbs (say 40w and 60w) and aiming them at your workpiece from two different locations, your eyes will better see and resolve very fine details.

Alternatively, you can employ a single task light to create shadow and glare and put it to good use. For example, it can be particularly difficult to see how a clear finish is going on wood when you're brushing or spraying it. By placing a task light at the same angle and exactly opposite the vantage point at which you are viewing the surface being finished, you can use the reflection of the light to see a polished or finished surface very clearly (see "Locating a Light Source for Wood Finishing" below). Positioning a task light this way also works when you need to see imperfections or fine details, such as when checking for sanding scratches before staining and finishing a panel.

While most lamps used as shop task lights use tungsten or halogen bulbs that put out a strong, harsh light, most lamps can also be fitted with small fluorescent

Locating a Light Source for Wood Finishing

Position a task lamp opposite the worktable so that light will reflect off the surface of the workpiece. This allows you to best see how the finish actually looks as you are applying it.

bulbs. These not only deliver a much softer, diffuse light, but also run cooler and with great energy savings over regular incandescents.

There's no shortage of possibilities in how to mount task lights. Gooseneck lights with magnetic bases are a good choice for adding lights to your machines since they will stay put on any metal surface you set them on. Because the life of conventional tungsten bulbs is considerably shortened by vibration, fit such lamps with mechanic's drop-light bulbs, which feature thicker filaments that are shock resistant.

COMPARISON OF COMMON ARTIFICIAL LIGHTING SOURCES

CHARACTERISTIC	TYPE OF ILLUMINATION		
	TUNGSTEN	HALOGEN	FLUORESCENT
Efficiency (watts per lumen)	Low: 9–29	Low: 20	Medium to high: 20–80
Bulb life (hours)	Short: 750–2,000	Short: 400–4,000	Long: 7,500–20,000
Initial cost	Low	Medium	Low to medium
Operating cost	Medium to high	High	Low
Quality of light	Harsh to medium soft; low to medium glare	Harsh; high glare	Soft; low glare
Color rendition	Fair	Fair	Poor to good
Heat generated by bulbs	Medium to high	High	Low
Other factors and special considerations	There are no replacement parts to maintain in fixtures (except bulbs). High-efficiency fluorescent bulbs are available to retrofit standard incandescent sockets.	There are no replacement parts to maintain in fixtures (except bulbs). Compact fixtures put out a lot of light for their size. Don't locate fixtures where they may accumulate sawdust and create a fire hazard.	Starters and ballasts in fixtures require occasional replacement. Ballasts give off a low hum that some find nervewracking. Lights don't operate well at low temperatures and flicker below 50°F, although there are special ballasts available that operate under cold conditions. Tubes are insensitive to vibration; they're good for rough work.

Cost of Bulb Upgrades May Be Worth It

AFTER COMPARING COSTS OF FLUORESCENT BULBS with various color ratings, I decided to change all the 8-ft. twin-tube fixtures in my shop to daylight-type bulbs with a high color rendition index (CRI). Such bulbs are available at lighting stores. The results were dramatic. Colors that were previously odd and muted seemed to come alive. The upgrade bulbs cost only modestly more than the cool whites they replaced, so they were a bargain, considering how much they improved the light and comfort of working in the shop.

If you've ever doubted that the sickly green light produced by inexpensive fluorescent shop lights could affect colors, look at these two photos, both taken with daylight-balanced film: The one on the top was lit by a typical cool white bulb, whereas the photo on the bottom used a C-50 bulb that produces light much closer to natural sunlight.

Choosing the type of light The three most common types of electric lighting for shops are tungsten (regular household light bulbs), halogen, and fluorescent (see "Comparison of Common Artificial Lighting Sources" on p. 73). There are significant differences among these lighting types, such as the cost of buying new fixtures, their efficiency or cost of operation, and their maintenance expenses (including the cost of replacement bulbs). Naturally, these issues are of greater concern the larger your shop is and the more lights you have to install and operate.

When comparing various bulbs, note that their wattage ratings only describe the amount of energy going in, not the amount of light coming out. The figure you want to compare is the "lumens," which is a measure of a bulb's light output. Lumen ratings reveal why modern fluorescent bulbs are such a good choice for shops. For example, a typical 100w tungsten light bulb produces about 1,600 lumens, whereas a single energy-saving 32w T8 fluorescent tube generates as much as 2,800 lumens—more than five times as much light for the same input power. A by-product of their efficiency is that fluorescent bulbs burn much cooler than incandescents.

The color and quality of light

Incandescent and fluorescent bulbs create different qualities of light, which affect the softness or harshness of the light they produce and how well they reveal the true colors of the objects they're illuminating. Because our eyes have evolved to see in natural sunlight, we perceive the colors of the world as being most "natural" when we view them in the sunlight. Researchers studying seasonal affective disorder (SAD) say that it's very important for human beings to live and work in areas close to natural sunlight.

All light has a color temperature that is measured in degrees Kelvin. On a clear day at noon, the sun has a color temperature of around 5,000 K, which is the reference by which all other light sources are measured. Unfortunately, most artificial light sources are far from the color temperature of natural sunlight and are deficient in one or multiple parts of the light spectrum. Your eyes and brain do an amazing job of compensating for color discrepancies, but you can still get into trouble when evaluating colors under lights with a poor color rendition index (CRI), such as when choosing a stain color for a project or matching colors when blending in furniture touchups with the surrounding finish. The two photos on the facing page show the same objects under different types of fluorescent lights.

"Colors of Shop-Light Sources" at right compares the color temperatures of tungsten, halogen, and fluorescent lights. Incandescent sources (fire, candles, tungsten or halogen light bulbs) make things look more reddish than they appear in sunlight. Fluorescent light fixtures often

COLORS OF SHOP-LIGHT SOURCES (DEGREES KELVIN)

Daylight at sunrise	1800 K
Daylight at noon	5000 K
Incandescent lamp (tungsten)	2600 K
Halogen lamp	3200 K
Warm white fluorescent lamp	3000 K
Cool white fluorescent lamp	4100–4200 K
Full-spectrum fluorescent lamp	5000 K

COLOR RENDITION INDEX OF FLUORESCENT BULBS

TYPE	CRI*
Warm white	53
Cool white	62
C-50	85
CWX	89
Daylight	100

*The higher the CRI, the closer the bulb is to natural sunlight.

Much of the information you need to know about the wattage and type of fluorescent tube is printed near the end of the tube. The three shown here are (front to back): 40w daylight, 32w cool white energy saver, and 32w warm white energy saver.

come with cool white or warm white bulbs that cast a greenish blue light. However, there are many types of bulbs, both fluorescent and incandescent, that create light with a color quality much closer to daylight. This is measured as the CRI. Bulbs with a higher CRI number are closer to natural daylight. On fluorescent bulbs, the CRI is printed directly on the bulb along with the wattage and other features (such as energy-saving status). Notice in "Color Rendition Index of Fluorescent Bulbs," on p. 75, the low CRI for cool white fluorescent tubes; no wonder working in a shop lit only with fluorescents can make you feel as if you were working under water. In contrast, other types of tubes, such as daylight and full-spectrum types have much higher CRI ratings. For incandescent fixtures, you can buy special (but expensive) natural daylight (ND) bulbs that have a very natural color temperature of 5,000 K.

Electronic Ballast Fluorescent Fixtures

IF YOUR SHOP IS IN A COOL CLIMATE (and isn't heated or insulated as well as it could be), chances are your fluorescent light fixtures function badly on cold days. Fixtures with standard ballasts will often flicker when first switched on and hum excessively. The best remedy is to install newer fluorescent fixtures that feature electronic ballasts that run bulbs flicker free, even in the coldest shops.

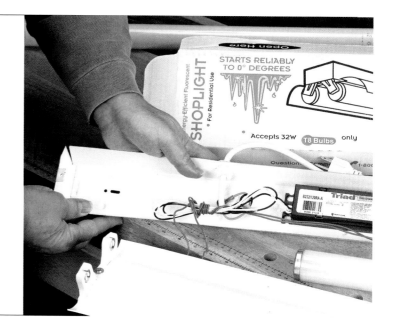

Heating and Ventilation

4

"A shop with good temperature control provides a comfortable environment that doesn't require you to dress as if you were on an expedition to Antarctica."

Despite the complex and ingenious physiology of the human body, it is difficult to feel warm enough or cool enough without the aid of clothing to wear and buildings to live in. Your shop is an enclosure that not only provides a comfortable environment for you to work in but also keeps your tools and supplies dry and prevents them from overheating or freezing during an average year. In all but the mildest climates, a shop must be actively heated during the cold seasons and insulated against outdoor heat (and possibly cooled) when the mercury soars. We must control not only the temperature of our shops but also the humidity, because too much can rust metal tools and too little can warp or crack precious lumber.

Another element of any comfortable living space—including a shop—is that its occupants should always enjoy a supply of fresh air. Having adequate ventilation isn't much of an issue when you're marking out a mortise or handplaning a frame member, but kick up a cloud of fine dust or fill the shop with adhesive or finish fumes and ventilation becomes necessary for comfort and safety. Ventilation may also provide most or all of the cooling your shop needs during hot weather.

In this chapter, I examine the ways of heating a woodshop effectively and economically as well as dealing with harmful humidity. I also look at several methods of providing ventilation for your shop, both for cooling and comfort and for exhausting dusty air and fumes produced during finishing operations.

Heating Your Shop

The simplest solution to working inside a cold shop is to keep yourself warm by wearing thermal underwear, socks, and insulated boots. (Avoid wearing bulky or loose clothes because these can catch in spinning power tools and keep you warm all the way to the emergency room.) But a shop with good temperature control provides a comfortable environment that doesn't require you to dress as if you were on an expedition to Antarctica.

Even if you're a naturally warm person, a cold shop can present other problems. When the temperature plummets, icy metal tools can be downright painful to pick up (they can even stick to your skin!), and wood and glues can be too cold to bond properly. Cold temperatures can cause wood and veneers to check and even crack if warmed too quickly. Many finishes won't dry and/or cure properly

---

Bigger Isn't Always Better

Surprisingly, experts say that it's better to err on the side of a shop heater that's slightly undersize rather than one that's too big. Unless you're planning for a future shop expansion, a heating system that pumps out more BTUs than necessary in daily operation costs more to purchase and operate and wastes more valuable space than a smaller heater that's adequate most of the time but may leave you rubbing your hands together on winter's chilliest days.

HEAT REQUIREMENTS BY REGION

SHOP LOCATION (LATITUDE; SAMPLE CITY)	BTUS PER SQUARE FOOT PER HOUR	
	INSULATED SHOP	UNINSULATED SHOP
N 32°; Jackson, MS	7	15
N 36°; Las Vegas, NV	14	30
N 38°; St. Louis, MO	28	60
N 40°; New York, NY	35	75
N 47°; Fargo, ND	49	405

below 55°F, and freezing temperatures will ruin water-based glues and finishes.

A correctly heated shop will help avoid these problems. This section will help you decide what kind of heat source will best serve your shop as well as give you an idea of how much it will cost to install and operate.

CHOOSING A HEAT SOURCE

Before rushing out and buying a new stove or installing a heating system, you'll want to consider just how much heat you need. Depending on your local climate, your needs might be best served by anything from a small portable unit that's used only during the coldest weeks of winter to a large wall heater or central unit that will run steadily for months. "Heat Requirements by Region," on the facing page, will help you get a rough idea of how much heat you'll need, specified in British Thermal Units (BTUs), the rating used to indicate the output of all heaters.

When choosing a type of heat source, consider all the costs. For example, the initial cost of one or two electric space heaters is quite low, yet the operating costs of a gas wall heater, which has a high installation cost, is much lower in the long run. Also consider the cost of fuel in your area (see "Average Output of Heating Systems Versus Unit and Installation Costs" at right, and "Comparison of Fuel Costs," on p. 80).

If you decide your shop needs more than a portable heater, your local stove shop or heating contractor should be able to steer you in the right direction in regard to choosing and installing a full shop heating system.

Insulate your shop first Whichever heating choice you decide on will require less wallet-robbing BTUs if your shop is well insulated (see "Insulation," on p. 27.) By using just average wall and ceiling insulation along with weatherstripping around doors and operable windows, you can cut down your heating bill by as much as 50 percent. Reducing heat loss

AVERAGE OUTPUT OF HEATING SYSTEMS VERSUS UNIT AND INSTALLATION COSTS

HEATING SYSTEM	RANGE OF BTUS PER HOUR	COST OF UNIT AND INSTALLATION (WHERE APPLICABLE)
Gas furnace	80 K–100 K	High
Radiant gas (wall heater)	25 K–40 K	Medium
Heat pump	80 K–100 K	Very high
Oil furnace	80 K–100 K	High
Boiler	80 K–100 K	Very high
Multifuel stove	80 K–100 K	Very high
Kerosene (unvented)	22 K–40 K	Low
Woodstove	8 K–50 K	Medium to high
Propane (portable)	8 K–40 K	Low
Electric (portable)	1 K–5 K	Very low

COMPARISON OF FUEL COSTS

FUEL TYPE	RELATIVE COST
Coal*	Very low to low
Wood*	Low to moderately low
Natural gas	Low
Wood pellets	Moderate
Kerosene	Moderate
Petroleum	Moderate
LPG (liquid propane gas)	Moderately high
Electricity	Very high

*Cost is highly subject to local availability.

by fitting double-glazed skylights and large windows can also make a big difference. And using insulated blinds or removable panels made of foam or other insulating material can significantly reduce heat loss.

Heat your shop safely Heaters that are powerful enough to offer usable indoor heat are also hot enough to set combustibles on fire, which is important to remember when you're heating a shop full of kindling-quality lumber. It's one thing to get away with not wearing hearing protectors or a dust mask, where negative effects occur little by little over a long period of time. But put a portable electric stove just a little too close to a small pile of shavings, and you'll witness the biggest and most costly science demonstration you're likely ever to see.

My recommendation is to save your risk-taking behavior for the stock market or your next card game. Why take a chance on losing your precious shop and all the tools in it when, with a little care and forethought, you can stave away the cold and still never have to make a hasty acquaintance with your local fire department?

Also remember that the use of any flammable finishing material automatically precludes the use of open-flame-type heaters, such as kerosene or propane portables. Electric heaters with

A good, efficient woodstove not only can take the winter chill off the shop but also can provide a way to get rid of cutoffs, wood scraps, and shavings.

exposed filaments should also be avoided, because these can also ignite flammables. The safest portable heat sources for finishing areas are sealed-beam heat lamps or radiant-style electric heaters.

WOOD-BURNING STOVES

A wood-burning stove in a woodshop illustrates a classic case of killing two birds with one stone—you get the heat necessary to keep your tootsies warm while ridding yourself of scraps and wood waste that you'd probably have to dispose of anyway.

Wood heat is pleasant, economical, and when generated by a well-designed, sealed stove, also very efficient. A single load of scraps is typically all that's needed to thwart the morning chill and get a properly insulated small shop up to a decent working temperature. Stoves also like a diet of large shavings generated by woodturning and planing, although finer sawdust must still be disposed of by other means because it smolders rather than burns.

Of course, if you live in Nome or Fargo (or if you've been miserly with your shop's insulation), it'll take more than a few armloads of cutoffs to keep your shop toasty all winter, so the cost of operating your stove may require the purchase of firewood as well. This is important to consider, since the installation cost of a good-quality wood-burning stove can run high. If your shop has a tall gable or attic space, the long lengths of triple-wall-construction stovepipe that you'll need can quickly equal or exceed the purchase price of the stove.

Installing a Woodstove in the Shop

Expensive triple-wall stovepipe is required wherever pipe passes through the ceiling, attic space, and roof.

Long lengths of pipe needed to vent the stove can easily equal the cost of the stove itself.

Locating a woodstove closer to the center of the shop helps it radiate heat more evenly throughout the space.

The minimum setback of the stove from an untreated wall is typically 12 in. to 24 in.

Some stoves may be vented directly through the wall.

Also, modern stoves that meet the U.S. Environmental Protection Agency's (EPA's) "Phase II" emission standards are expensive, a cost partially offset in the long run by the fact that they burn much cleaner and more efficiently than stoves made a decade ago.

If you live in an area where coal is readily available, you may want to consider buying a multifuel stove that can burn either wood or coal. Coal is by far a less expensive and more compact fuel

Get the Necessary Permits

Before buying and installing a wood- or coal-burning stove, you should check with your local building department and fire marshal's office. A permit, which will probably be needed, shouldn't be circumvented: An accidental fire in a shop with an illegal woodstove will almost certainly void your insurance, even if the cause of the fire had nothing to do with the stove. Your insurance company will also need to be notified.

source than wood, and coal fires burn longer and require less attention than wood fires.

Pellet stoves are another possibility, as they require less tending than regular woodstoves and are easier to install because they may be vented directly through a shop wall. However, as their name implies, they burn pellets made of specially compressed wood debris that you must purchase. Unfortunately, you can't use regular firewood or cutoffs from your scrap pile.

Obviously, safe placement of a stove in regard to combustibles—especially stored lumber and flammable liquids—is essential. Installing a stove in the center of a shop space is best from a heating standpoint, but practical issues of machine operation and work space often dictate compromise on its placement.

There are typically minimum setback requirements that must be observed when mounting a stove near a wall, as well as requirements for the size of a noncombustible hearth (a metal or masonry floor covering around the stove). Adding a sheet-metal hood and floor plate may be one way to reduce the amount of stove-to-wall clearance needed, and it also helps radiate heat into the shop. One plus of locating a stove near a wall is the possibility that stovepipe may be run horizontally out of the wall, although typically the vertical stack outside must still clear the roof line by at least 3 ft.

GAS HEATERS

Although gas heaters command a high initial purchase price and installation cost, they are very economical to operate. The most affordable units operate on natural gas, which must be piped into your shop. If natural gas is not available in your area, you must install a special heater that runs off a propane tank (or adapt a natural gas heater to run on propane), which adds to the cost of installation.

If you have a home shop and central heating, you might be able to heat your shop by adding a new register to the ductwork already running through your garage or basement shop space.

YOUR HOME'S CENTRAL HEAT

If you've set up a small shop inside your home in an unheated basement or in an adjoining garage, you might be able to use your home's central-heating system to warm your shop. If heating ductwork already runs through your shop space, it may be possible to cut into a duct and add a new heat register that will blow hot air into your shop.

Of course, your system's furnace must have enough capacity to handle the added heating burden. And the amount of heating that your shop receives will still be controlled by the thermostat inside the house, so you'll have less control than you might want. Also on the down side, forced-air heat can reduce the shop's humidity significantly, engendering dry skin and even checks and cracks in lumber.

One big problem often occurs in shops located inside the home: If the central-heating system is drawing air from inside the shop, fine dust can quickly clog your heater's filters and even create a fire hazard. An HVAC expert can guide you in the installation of filtration to prevent this problem.

UNIT HEATERS

One of the most popular means of heating shops, both small and large, is a gas-fired unit heater. Basically, a unit heater is a metal box with gas burners and a fan that distributes heat and circulates the air around the shop. Normally suspended from the ceiling, a unit heater works best in large, open spaces with ceilings that are at least 10 ft.

A gas-fired unit heater suspended from the ceiling can provide one of the quickest ways of heating a shop with high ceilings and a fairly large, open floor space.

Consult an Expert

Don't even consider using your house system for shop heat if your shop is big and uninsulated, unless you want your family to freeze all winter long. The best thing is to consult your local HVAC expert, who will be able to tell you if using your central system for shop heating is a good idea or not.

An alternative to a gas-fired shop heater, an electric unit heater runs on 220v power and has a heat output much greater than typical 110v portable electric heaters do.

high. Although it's a hefty investment for a small shop, even a small unit heater can crank out enough BTUs to warm a drafty space more quickly than most other types of heaters can.

Like wall or central heaters, a gas-unit heater requires proper, safe installation, including proper venting and an installation location that's a safe distance from combustible walls and objects. If you are considering a unit heater or any gas heater that requires permanent

installation, consult your local heating contractor for assistance, and be sure to get all necessary permits before installing it.

An electric alternative

If you want a more substantial heat source than portables can provide but your shop lacks gas piping, you might opt for an electric-powered unit heater. This type of unit uses 220v to output a much higher number of BTUs than portable electrics can. Just like its gas-fired cousin, an electric's powerful, built-in fan distributes the heat and circulates air throughout the shop. And the hanging design moves the heater farther from potential sources of combustion. As with a gas-fired unit heater, you do need to clean the heater often, especially if you produce a lot of fine dust in your shop.

Because an electric unit's cost of operation is much higher than that of a gas heater, it is not recommended for shops that aren't well insulated, otherwise your electric bill will go through the roof just as fast as your heat does.

HOT-WATER HEAT

Many old shop buildings in the East and northern Midwest have big metal radiators that pour out loads of heat without creating the same drying and dust-blowing problems of a forced-air system. A central boiler heats the water and pumps it through pipes to the radiators. In newer shops, radiators have been replaced by baseboard radiators, which are compact and distribute heat more evenly around the room. Installing this kind of

Keep Combustibles Clear

Be careful not to place space heaters too close to combustibles (which can be just about anything in a woodshop) or to accidentally drape a rag—or your pant leg—on top of them. Such fires can start in an instant. This is why every electric model has a built-in kill switch that turns the juice off if the heater is knocked over.

Portable electric space heaters are probably the most popular and easy way of heating a small woodshop. The unit on the left has two quartz elements and a fan and warms up very quickly. The radiator-like unit on the right encloses its elements in fluid-filled chambers for greater safety around wood dust.

central-heating system is a major project, typically only worth the effort if you're heating a sizable shop.

If you're building a new shop that will have a concrete floor, you might consider turning that slab into a giant radiator by installing a radiant-floor heating system. This system heats your shop with a central gas- or oil-fired furnace or heat pump that drives hot water through a long length of plastic tubing that is laid into your slab at the time it is poured. The piping is unobtrusive and maintenance-free, and the system is efficient and makes an otherwise cold concrete floor more comfortable to work on. Unfortunately, you can't retrofit this system into an existing floor.

PORTABLE HEATERS

Because of their low purchase cost and ease and flexibility of use, portable heaters are the most attractive solution for small woodshops. Because of their popularity for heating homes and patios as well as workshops, portables come in as many styles as cowboy hats at a rodeo. The amount of heat these units put out varies considerably, from a few hundred BTUs to thousands. They also run on different types of fuel: electricity, kerosene, or propane. But every type is not right for every kind of woodshop. You should consider the cost, safety, and practicality of operation before selecting a portable that's best for you.

Electric portables Probably the most versatile heaters on the market are of the portable electric variety. There are basically two types: units that have exposed heating elements and fans and those that use enclosed elements in fluid-filled chambers.

• **Exposed-element heaters** This type of unit provides shop heat through a combination of convection (heat transferred through the medium of the air) and radiation (heat transferred directly, the way we feel the warmth of the sun streaming through a window). These small electric space heaters come in a tall variety with reflectors behind the elements, which help direct heat radiation outward, and in a small box or cube type that relies on metal wires or ceramic elements. Both provide a good means of heating a small workspace rapidly.

• **Enclosed-element units** The enclosed style of electric heater contains

A bottled propane space heater is relatively inexpensive to run, but it should be used only in an open-air or a very well ventilated shop: The unvented heater expels noxious gases along with heat that can be both unpleasant and fatal to breathe.

the elements within a chamber or pipe filled with either water or oil. This pretty much eliminates the fire danger, but it also limits the type of heat output to convection only. Some portables look like small radiators on wheels, and the other popular style is a long, low baseboard-type heater. Higher-output 220v versions of these heaters are often used to heat all-electric houses. Because of the volume of heat necessary to get the fluid hot, it takes a while for these units to heat up. But after the initial warm-up period, they give off an impressive amount of heat and stay warm long after you've switched them off.

The downfall of these units is in providing the volume of heat necessary to heat the air in even a modest-size shop. They can be used as a primary source of heating only if your shop is quite small, say, two-car-garage size or less, and well insulated.

Propane and kerosene portables

Portable stoves powered by liquid kerosene or bottled propane are relatively inexpensive to buy, easy to start up, and cheap to run. And they're also light enough to easily move around the shop to supply heat closest to where it's needed. Unfortunately, because these are unvented stoves, the noxious products of combustion are produced along with copious amounts of heat.

Some woodworkers use portable stoves inside their shops, although manufacturers clearly state with these units that they are *not* to be used inside unventilated spaces. Even if you make a practice of thumbing your nose at official recommendations, this is one to heed. The gases put out by these stoves can at best leave you with a headache and at worst knock you out and kill you via asphyxiation.

Another more subtle problem with kerosene stoves in particular is that they add moisture to the air along with heat. This isn't necessarily a bad thing because heated winter air is typically bone dry. But if the wood projects you build are sensitive to moisture—if you're a luthier, for example—remember that kerosene heat is likely to increase the humidity of your shop.

Task heating Like light, heat can be applied to certain special situations. This saves energy and directs the heat to where it's needed most. Finishes and most wood glues are temperature sensitive and don't dry and cure well below a certain temperature—typically 55°F. If you leave an assembly to dry, say, overnight in an unheated shop, you might get an unhappy surprise the next day when you take the clamps off to find that the glue bonds are still tacky and weak. Worse yet, improperly cured glue bonds can fail sometime in the future.

An interesting and useful addition to any shop that's unheated or inadequately warm during the coolest months of the year is to build a separate, heated glue-up room. A glue-up room, as small or large as the biggest assembly you plan to put inside it, allows you to turn your

shop heat off at the end of the day and heat only the space in which your assembly is sitting. You can use an electric wallboard heater or any space heater that has a thermostat to heat the small space. By making your glue-up room only as large as it need be and by thoroughly insulating its walls, you'll save on energy because the heater will run only a small amount of the time.

If you live in a cold climate, using a separate heated glue-up room allows you to properly dry glued-up assemblies and cure clear-finished projects without having to heat the entire shop.

Similarly, you can enclose your finishing area and heat it at a different temperature than the rest of your shop, so finishes will dry and cure faster. Warm the area with heat lamps in portable light fixtures or with an enclosed-element heater that is safe for use around combustible vapors.

Ventilating Your Shop

The main reason to ventilate your shop is simple: to remove stale, musty air and replace it with cool, fresh air. Just like in your home or office, you'll feel better and breathe easier if your shop has a good amount of refreshing air circulating through it. This often doesn't require more than just opening a window or doorway. Circulating air also whisks away fumes from finishes and adhesives as well as very fine dust and smoke generated by wood scorched during sawing or shaping operations.

GETTING HEAT OUT OF THE ATTIC

Displacing hot air that accumulates in an attic or in the upper portions of a vaulted ceiling during bright, sunny days not only improves ventilation but keeps the shop cooler. The most effective way to remove that hot air is to vent it up through your shop's roof. If the roof doesn't have a ridge vent (see "Insulating a Vaulted Ceiling," on p. 30), installing an attic ventilator is the best solution. Ventilators that have a thermostatically controlled electric fan are a good choice for large attic spaces, especially in hot climates. But for smaller shops, a simple passive turbine ventilator is likely to be adequate.

Made from sheet metal and driven by even the slightest breeze, an inexpensive turbine ventilator is easy to install on most types of roofs, doesn't require power or maintenance, and is nearly silent. While the design thwarts rain from coming in, some water can get in during violent weather, so situate the turbine where drips won't rust machines or ruin valuable supplies.

A roof-mounted turbine ventilator can use the slightest passing breeze to draw hot air from a stuffy attic or directly from your shop space.

USING FANS

Compact and affordable, fans not only are a good way to cool the shop and keep it from getting stuffy but also can be remarkably effective at removing fine wood dust generated during sanding or machining operations. You can use a regular household box or circulation fan mounted in a shop window or buy special ventilation fans designed specifically for installation into a wall.

Just remember that if you're heating, cooling, or dehumidifying your shop, ventilation blows that conditioned air outside. If you're using ventilation to remove airborne dust, you'll be better off installing an air-filtration device (see "Air-Filtration Devices," on p. 210).

Exhausting Finishing Fumes from the Shop

A box fan exhausts fumes from the shop.

Air flow moves finish fumes away from the finisher.

Fresh air coming from an open window or door comes from behind.

A furnace filter over the opening keeps dust, pollen, and bugs out.

Give Fresh Air a Pathway

THE IMPORTANT THING WITH ANY FAN is to locate it on the opposite side of the shop from an open door or window to encourage flow-through ventilation. A simple and inexpensive box fan set into an open shop window might be all you need to exhaust fumes and fine dust generated nearby. Remember to keep a steady supply of fresh air flowing in through another window or door on the opposite side of the shop.

Ventilating Your Finishing Area

Whether you have a separate finishing room or you apply finishes on a clean benchtop, good ventilation will help you keep the air in your shop clean and healthy. Regardless of the kind of finish you apply, fumes should not be allowed to accumulate inside the shop. Fumes from solvent-based finishes, such as lacquers, varnishes, and polyurethanes, are unhealthy to breathe and—in the unlikely event that they are concentrated in a confined area and ignited by a spark—are explosive. (You'd probably pass out or run out of the room before the fumes in your shop became that concentrated.)

Although not explosive, many water-based finishes have strong, unpleasant ammonia fumes that should be removed from the finishing area. If your shop is in a garage or basement with a furnace, these fumes can have a more insidious effect than just offending your nose. Spraying a water-based finish can create strong alkali fumes that pit and corrode aluminum parts, such as your furnace's gas burners and heat exchangers.

CREATING GOOD AIR CIRCULATION

The most effective way to deal with finishing fumes is to create air movement that brings fresh air past you and blows fumes outdoors. You can ensure this by placing the piece being finished between you and the fan that's exhausting air to the outside and having an open door or window behind you to let in fresh air (see "Exhausting Finishing Fumes from the Shop" on p. 89). In most cases, wiping, brushing, or even dipping finishes generates a small volume of fumes that you can keep at bay with a simple box fan.

An even more effective ventilation technique for finishing or whisking away fine sanding dust is to use two fans: One that blows fresh air toward you while blowing sanding dust (or finish fumes) toward the second fan, set in a window or doorway that exhausts to the outdoors. Whether you employ one fan or two, switch the fan(s) on before you begin working, choosing a high or medium fan speed. And, of course, always wear a mask that's right for the job (see "Respiratory Protection," on p. 228).

When it comes to using a low-tech solution to removing fine dust and fumes from the shop, two fans are, indeed, better than one. As shown here, a powerful circulation fan blows dusty air away from the person sanding or finishing and toward the box fan mounted in the open doorway, which exhausts to the outdoors

MINIMIZING DUST

Keeping dust out of a fresh finish can be a major accomplishment in a typical small, single-room woodshop. Unfortunately, sucking air through the shop to remove finish fumes tends to stir up wood dust, as well as potentially pulling in pollen, insects, and dust from the outdoors.

An easy way to deal with this is to use inexpensive furnace filters over the doorway or window where fresh air is coming into the shop. These filters can be taped in place temporarily or you can make a frame to hold them and slide them in when needed. If you're lucky enough to have a dedicated finishing room, furnace filters will keep wood dust from the shop from being sucked into your nice, clean finishing space.

One way to allow fresh air into a finishing room that's adjacent to a shop filled with dust-spewing machines is to add vents to the finishing room's door. Regular-spun fiberglass furnace filters (or more expensive corrugated filters that are better at catching fine dust particles) fitted into the vent openings will keep fine dust out while allowing fresh air in.

It's best to locate the vents on the surface that's opposite the wall that contains the finishing room's exhaust fan. If the vents are near woodworking machines, you can keep flying chips and dust off the filters by fitting simple doors over the vents, as Santa Rosa, Calif., woodworker Dave Marks did (see the photo at right).

Woodworker David Marks uses inexpensive furnace filters fitted into cutouts in the door to his finishing room to allow proper ventilation yet prevent dust generated in his adjoining woodshop from ending up in a freshly finished turning or furniture piece.

When the Job's Done

Leave the fan on while you clean your brush and other finishing paraphernalia, especially if you use solvents to clean brushes and applicators. When you're done, turn the fan to a low setting, and leave it on until the finish is nearly dry to keep fumes from accumulating. For a fast-drying finish, this will be just a few minutes; for a slow-drying one, a couple of hours or more.

The temporary booth that wood-finishing expert Michael Dresdner uses for spraying water-based finishes is made from panels cut from a corrugated-cardboard appliance carton. Air is drawn through the knockdown booth by a powerful exhaust fan mounted to a wheeled dolly.

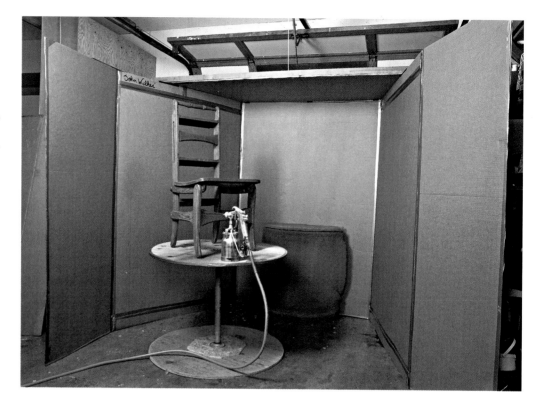

SPRAY BOOTHS

While you might get away with squirting a little finish from a spray can on a small part inside the shop, doing any serious amount of spraying puts out too much finish in the air for basic shop ventilation to handle. A spray booth should be used to keep the large volume of fumes generated during spraying from accumulating. Using a booth keeps the air cleaner to breathe and reduces the possibility of a fire when spraying flammable finishes. Just as important, a booth keeps overspray (finish particles that don't end up on the workpiece) out of the shop.

While spray finishing outdoors is an alternative, a good spray booth lets you spray finishes inside the shop more cleanly and predictably. A basic booth is simply a partially enclosed air funnel:

You stand at one end of the funnel and spray toward a fan at the other end that draws clean air past you and sucks fume- and overspray-laden air out of the shop. A filter over the fan keeps overspray from building up on it.

Folding spray booths When most people think of a woodshop spray booth, they think of a commercial type of metal booth that's large, expensive, and permanently installed. While this kind of booth is right for pros (see the photo on p. 94), you can make your own booth that's great for a small shop, one that's inexpensive to build and folds up and stores out of the way when not in use. You can build a full-size folding booth, which is big enough for spraying all but the largest furniture pieces and cabinets, or a pint-size version, which you can set up in a window or doorway for spraying small parts.

• **Full-size version** Designed for use with nonflammable water-based finishes, the large folding booth shown in the photo on the facing page is constructed from heavy, corrugated cardboard, the kind that refrigerator boxes are made of (ask for a discard at your local appliance store). The booth is made from six pieces that are roughly 3 ft. by 6 ft. each. Five pieces are hinged together with duct tape so that they'll fold in zigzag fashion, ending up as a flat bundle that's easy to store. The lower edge of the middle side is cut out to fit the exhaust fan, which should be a box fan or ventilation fan capable of moving 500 cfm of air or more. The inside surface of the fan enclosure is covered with spun-fiberglass filter material, which is available by the foot at home-supply stores.

The sixth piece of cardboard acts as a partial top for the booth, with a 1-in. by 3-in. wood reinforcement strip mounted on its forward edge. Velcro® strips on the lower edges of the top lock into mating Velcro glued to the top edges of the sides. These keep the top in place and allow the angle of the sides to be adjusted—more obtuse for large workpieces; more acute for small stuff.

Before use, the booth is set up in front of an open garage door or large doorway, and windows or doors are opened on the opposite side of the shop to create flow-through ventilation. Both the booth area and any loose dust in the shop must be

A box fan, a furnace filter, three pieces of cardboard, and a little duct tape are all it takes to build a simple spray booth that sets up in minutes in front of a window or doorway, allowing you to spray-paint or clear-finish parts and small projects.

vacuumed before use. Because ventilation is most effective when the spray gun is pointed toward the fan, it's best to put the work on a turntable of some kind, so it can be rotated during spraying.

• **A mini-booth** If you spray only small parts occasionally, you can build a petite version of the cardboard spray booth, shown in the photo above. Three pieces of cardboard are hinged together with

Get the Right Permits

In most cities and counties, your booth must be approved and certified by the local fire marshal, who can get you up to speed on the specific regulations required in your area for a spray booth. Such certification is an absolute must, lest you void your shop's insurance policy. Before building a booth, also check with your local building department because some air-quality jurisdictions require a special permit for a spray booth. Some areas severely limit the number of permits that are available.

duct tape, allowing the booth to fold flat. Tape holds the small, funnel-shaped booth to a regular box fan with a furnace filter taped on the intake side.

This mini-booth can be set up in minutes on a bench in front of an open window or on a stand in front of a doorway. Again, a turntable (this time made from a couple of plywood squares screwed to a lazy Susan bearing) allows the workpiece to be spun around during spraying.

Every component of a proper spray booth, such as this metal booth used by master guitar builder Jeff Traugott, is designed to allow the application of toxic and explosive solvent-based finishes safely and in a way that is environmentally friendly.

Permanent spray booths Although it is a major investment, a proper spray booth designed and built to approved safety standards is the safest and most environmentally friendly way of spraying toxic or flammable finishes. This kind of spray booth is required to have fire-rated walls, which are commonly fabricated from sheet metal (fire-resistant drywall is sometimes also permissible), explosion-proof fans, light switches and fixtures to prevent errant electrical sparks, and a sprinkler system in case of fire. A "radius rule" typically applies, stating that you must have explosion-proof fixtures up to a certain distance from the booth walls and doorway. There are even rules about the quantity of flammable finishes you're allowed to store inside the booth, on the floor, on shelves, and in special vented finish storage cabinets (see "Special Storage," on p. 188).

Controlling Shop Moisture and Humidity

Any shop that is allowed to cool past the dew point (the temperature at which moisture from the air forms dew) will allow condensation to form on exterior glazing (windows and skylights) and, most unfortunate, on many metal surfaces, such as machine tables and motors. Therefore, keeping a shop at a stable temperature through insulation (see "Insulation," on p. 27) and heating is the first step toward reducing excess moisture and the resulting humidity that can cause the formation of rust on tools

and machines as well as reduce warping and swelling problems in lumber. If your shop is built on a concrete slab, painting the concrete floor will prevent moisture from being wicked from the ground through the concrete (see "Painting Concrete," on p. 39).

REMOVING MOISTURE FROM THE AIR

If condensation and moisture are not a problem but your shop is in a hot, damp climate, you might consider installing air-conditioning, which removes

A portable dehumidifier can help you control excess humidity in your shop, which can rust tools and wreak havoc on the moisture content of lumber, wood parts, and projects.

A Perfect Humidity Level Is Hard to Achieve

What's the ideal humidity for a woodworking shop? That varies somewhat, depending on where you live and what kind of work you do. Guitar builders like to keep the tool rooms where they build and assemble guitars and store their parts and stock between 42 percent and 45 percent relative humidity (RH). Maintaining such a tight RH is not practical for most woodworkers, so the best that you might do is keep humidity from running too high and becoming a problem.

moisture from the air while making the temperature in the shop more bearable. If excess humidity is a nuisance even during cooler weather, a portable dehumidifier is probably the best way to take care of the problem. Relatively inexpensive to buy, dehumidifiers are sized according to how many pints of water they can remove from the air in a 24-hour period. The "Dehumidification Guide" at right will give you an idea of what size unit you need for your climatic needs.

A good-quality hygrometer that is accurate within 3 percent to 5 percent is an important tool for monitoring the relative humidity in your shop. It is essential if you build delicate wood projects, such as guitars and violins.

Dehumidifying the air in the shop also helps minimize problems with mildew and fungal growth, which are especially troublesome in tropical climates.

KEEPING TRACK OF HUMIDITY

Whether you're a woodturner who cuts his or her own stock and keeps a small supply drying in the shop or a luthier who needs to maintain constant humidity for proper construction procedures, it's a very good idea to monitor and control the humidity in your shop. Too much or too little moisture in the air can wreak havoc with your lumber and wood projects, causing warping and swelling or checking and shrinkage problems.

Hygrometers

The first step to controlling humidity is to keep tabs on how damp or dry the air is in your shop over the course of an average year. To monitor your shop's relative humidity (RH), it's important that you buy a good-quality hygrometer. Inexpensive units (models priced less than $15) simply aren't precise enough to judge shop humidity accurately.

Dial-type precision hygrometers that are accurate within 3 percent are sold through lutherie supply catalogs. And thanks to the microchip revolution, digital hygrometers that are accurate to within 5 percent to 6 percent are also an affordable choice.

DEHUMIDIFICATION GUIDE

SHOP CONDITION BEFORE DEHUMIDIFICATION	AREA OF SHOP (SQ. FT.)					
	500	1,000	1,500	2,000	2,500	3,000
Moderately damp (space feels damp and has musty odor only in humid weather)	10	14	18	22	26	30
Very damp (space always feels damp and has musty odor; damp spots show on walls and floor)	PINTS OF WATER REMOVED PER 24 HOURS					
	12	17	22	27	32	37
Wet (space feels and smells wet; walls and floor sweat or seepage is present)	14	20	26	32	38	44

Source: Association of Home Appliance Manufacturers (AHAM).

By monitoring shop humidity you'll know when the air is too damp and needs to be dehumidified or, if you live in a very dry climate like the Southwest, when it is too dry and needs more moisture, which can be accomplished by running a humidifier in the shop.

PREVENTING RUST

One of the things that happens when shop humidity runs too high is that steel and iron rust, which is a real problem

considering that most of your precious tools and machines are built from this moisture-sensitive material. But there is a lot you can do to eliminate or at least cut down on rust problems in the shop. Here are some strategies that will help:

- Prevent water and moist air from entering your shop. Keep your roof in good repair so it won't leak; mount a vapor barrier on walls, rafters/ceiling before installing insulation; paint concrete floors; and install weather stripping on doors and windows, including on the bottom of garage or barn-style sliding doors.

- Prevent moisture from condensing by fitting double-glazed skylights and windows, especially in harsh climates. Also, insulate vaulted ceilings to allow ventilation (see "Insulating a Vaulted Ceiling," on p. 30).

- Remove moisture from the shop air with a dehumidifier.

- Protect tools from humidity by using protective sprays and coatings. These sprays are especially good for large bare-metal surfaces, such as machine tables.

- Line drawers and cabinets with rust-inhibiting drawer-lining materials. This will keep moisture from turning your finest handplanes and Vernier® calipers into rusty paperweights. Don't use regular cloth or felt, which attract moisture and foster rust.

There is no shortage of products available that help protect your steel and iron tools and machines from the ravages of rust or to remove rust to restore metal surfaces, such as cast-iron tool beds and tables.

Prevent rust from ruining expensive tools and measuring instruments inside toolboxes and storage containers by placing one or more desiccant containers inside. These small, reusable aluminum packs are filled with silica gel, which absorbs moisture from the air inside the drawer or chest.

- If your shop isn't too damp to begin with, place desiccants in drawers and cabinets. A desiccant is a perforated metal container filled with chemically inert silica gel that will absorb moisture from the air within the enclosed space. Available in several sizes through catalogs and at stores that sell home safes, desiccants such as Hydrosorb™ often last for months before they need to be reactivated, which can be done by simply placing the containers in a 300°F oven for a few hours.

5 Equipping Your Shop

"Ultimately, the tools you choose should suit your style of woodworking."

So many tool catalogs, so few winning lottery tickets! For most of us, woodworking is a very equipment intensive pursuit. Perusing the Internet or flipping through the pages of the latest tool catalog is bound to give any woodworker a bad case of tool envy. And that applies not only to tools and machines but also to the devices, jigs, accessories, and supplies that go along with them.

Fortunately, a little ingenuity can go a long way toward helping you get the most out of the equipment you can afford—or already own. If you're just starting out, this chapter will provide some guidance and insight into what kinds of equipment might best serve your needs and how to stretch your budget to get the most bang for the buck. If you've had your own shop up and running for many years, you might want to check out this chapter for tips on even more neat stuff to add to your collection. Or perhaps curiosity will lead you to see if my suggestions for tool purchases agree with what you already own.

What Tools and Machines Do I Need?

Making a list of all the machines and tools needed for a complete workshop can be incredibly intimidating. You might feel that it's too expensive to even break into woodworking in the first place. And seeing those TV woodworkers who have more power tools than Jay Leno has expensive cars makes you feel as though your shop couldn't be "serious" unless you have all that stuff.

BUY TOOLS AS YOU NEED THEM

A useful strategy is to buy woodworking tools and machines as you need them. This not only prevents the rapid draining of your bank account but also gives you time to learn to use the tools as you acquire them. That doesn't mean you need to master all of your tools before you buy new ones, but it's important to develop a certain level of competency with what you already own. If not, you may become overwhelmed and discouraged.

Knowledge and experience will also help you make better-informed future purchases and will help you decide whether you need to upgrade your current crop of tools or make do with the gear you currently have.

But when you're just starting out, you might not know exactly what kind of woodworking you want to do. For example, woodturning calls for a very

What Kind of Woodworking Do You Do?

THE TOOLS YOU BUY should be based on the kind of woodworking you want to do. For example, a lathe is a key purchase if you wish to do woodturning, a scrollsaw is needed if you're doing Victorian fretwork, and a plate biscuit joiner is a must if plywood carcase cabinetry is your passion.

Basic Woodshop Tool and Machine Purchases

THE FOLLOWING TOOLS are listed in order of suggested purchase priority. If you don't have a particular machine or tool, alternative means by which you could perform its functions are given in parentheses.

STATIONARY MACHINES

1. Tablesaw (portable circular saw and fence, radial-arm saw*)
2. Jointer (handplane, router and fence)
3. Drill press (portable drill and jig)
4. Cutoff saw, sliding compound miter, radial-arm saw (tablesaw with miter gauge or crosscut jig, circular saw and fence)
5. Bandsaw (jigsaw, scrollsaw; tablesaw for resawing)
6. Thickness planer (handplane, router and jig)
7. Stationary sander: belt, disc, or combo (sanding disc in tablesaw, portable belt sander in accessory stand)
8. Shaper (router table, molding planes)

PORTABLE POWER TOOLS

1. Router (molding planes, handplane, scratch stock; saw and chisels for joinery)
2. Drill, corded or cordless (bit brace, geared hand drill)
3. Jigsaw (coping saw, frame saw)
4. Circular saw (panel handsaw)
5. Belt sander (handplane, scraper)
6. Orbital sander (sanding block)
7. Random-orbit sander (sanding block)
8. Plate joiner or biscuit joiner (router with kerf-cutter bit, or drill press with special attachment)

HAND TOOLS

1. Layout tools: tape measure, large and small try squares, marking gauge, marking knife, scratch awl, pencil compass, 6-in. and 12-in. rulers, 3-ft. straightedge, bevel gauge
2. Set of bench chisels, $\frac{1}{4}$ in. to 1 in.
3. Handplanes: jack, low-angle block, rabbet
4. Handsaws: dovetail, panel, or Japanese Ryoba and Dozuki
5. Hammer: standard nail or Warrington pattern
6. Mallet: wood or dead-blow-style plastic
7. Scraper blade or cabinet scraper
8. Spokeshave, flat or curved bottom
9. Rasps: coarse and fine cabinetmaker's style
10. Machine tools: set of wrenches, screwdrivers, Allen wrenches, pliers, Crescent wrench, pair of locking pliers

*Ripping on a radial-arm saw can be hazardous.

different set of tools from those needed for traditional cabinet making. And if you're like I was when I started, you're afraid of making the wrong purchases.

In the next few sections you'll find recommendations for a basic complement of stationary machines, power tools, and hand tools for a modern woodshop that is capable of making cabinets, furniture, and assorted DIY projects. See "Basic Woodshop Tool and Machine Purchases" on the facing page for an idea of the tools that are important for any woodshop.

Because most beginning woodworkers can't afford to buy all their tools and machines at once, I've listed the tools in each category in the order in which I think it's best to buy them. For the stationary machines and portable power tools, I've also included an alternative means by which you could perform their functions. For example, if you haven't yet bought a jointer, you could use a router or handplane for jointing a straight edge on a board. Or you could cut out a curved tabletop or furniture legs with a portable jigsaw instead of using a bandsaw.

STATIONARY POWER TOOLS

Ah, the big guns—the stuff that serious woodshops are made of (or at least the stuff that significant bucks are spent on). Unless you're a purist or are religiously prevented from using them, tablesaws, jointers, shapers, drill presses, and their companions are here to stay.

Modern woodshop machines let you work wood plain or fancy with more speed, accuracy, and convenience than any hand-tool-wielding craftsman could have ever dreamed of a hundred years ago. You can saw sensational scrollwork, plane a panel with precision, create consummate cope-and-stick work, make matchless mortises, and drill a hole dead-on all with the flick of a switch and with less skill and practice than it takes to do any of these operations by hand. But such a world of wonder comes at a

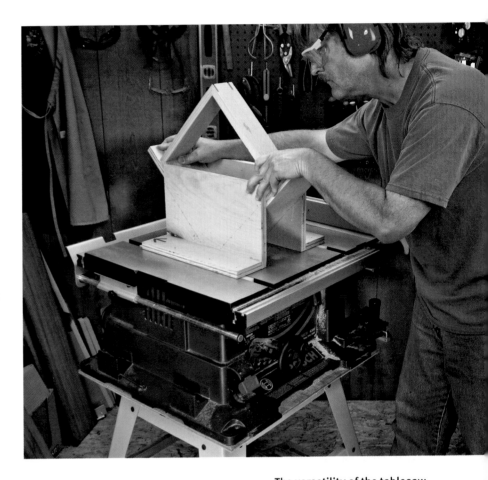

price. And it's a big price, literally. With the money it costs to buy a bargain-quality tablesaw you could fill a tool chest with the greatest hand tools.

Speaking of which, the first machine you'll undoubtedly want to buy for a woodshop is a tablesaw. Whether you purchase an expensive cabinet saw or a more affordable contractor's-style model, a good, basic tablesaw is an essential tool for many kinds of work: cabinetmaking and furniture making, home repair and remodeling, instrument making, boatbuilding, model making, and architectural millwork. Used with the right accessories and a little imagination, a tablesaw can perform basic ripping,

The versatility of the tablesaw makes it the centerpiece of most woodworking shops. A basic tablesaw easily rips, crosscuts, grooves and dadoes wood; and when fitted with the right accessory or jig, it can cut miters, coves, tenons, tapers, and an extensive array of joinery.

Rapidly replacing the radial-arm saw as the crosscut saw of choice in the woodshop and on the job site, the versatile, portable sliding compound miter easily tackles mitering and beveling tasks as well as crosscutting and trimming stock up to 12 in. wide.

crosscutting, and dadoing as well as a staggering variety of different cuts and types of joinery and machining work.

Because accurate work depends on having a straight edge to butt up to a fence, a jointer is an important early purchase for shops that do a lot of "straight line" work, such as cabinets and stick furniture. A good jointer not only helps straighten out crooked boards but also is needed to flatten stock that is cupped, bowed, or twisted ahead of thickness planing.

Although you can bore holes with any old hand drill, a drill press provides an accurate way to bore them square to an edge or surface or at precise angles. Further, you can chuck a wide variety of accessories into a drill press to do jobs

such as hollow-chisel mortising, surface planing, and even biscuit joining.

While parts can be cut to length on a tablesaw, having a dedicated crosscut saw makes part cutout a lot easier. The radial-arm saw, once a shop standard, has been virtually replaced in recent years by versatile, compact, and easier-to-set compound-miter and sliding compound-miter saws, which handle a slew of crosscutting duties from mitering and beveling to trimming stock to length.

Other basic machines for a core woodshop include the following: A bandsaw cuts out curved and circular parts, saws branches and burls into lumber or turning blanks, and resaws thick planks into thinner, matched-grain boards or veneers. A thickness planer surfaces rough planks into smooth lumber and changes the thickness of parts. Stationary sanders abrasively shape parts, smooth surfaces, and trim edges. A shaper profiles edges, creates moldings, and raises panels.

Because the basic size and capacity of all woodworking machines vary considerably, it can be confusing to know which to choose. "Stationary Machine Recommendations" on the facing page offers some suggestions for the appropriate sizes and capacities of machines for hobby, do-it-yourself, and professional woodworking shops.

Space-saving machines Because most woodworkers are pack rats as well as tool junkies, the practical limit to tool acquisitions is often the sheer capacity of one's shop (and, for the most seriously

STATIONARY MACHINE RECOMMENDATIONS

MACHINE	HOBBY SHOP; COMPACT WOODSHOP	DO-IT-YOURSELF; SMALL TO MEDIUM WOODSHOP	PROFESSIONAL FURNITURE OR CABINET SHOP
Tablesaw	Benchtop; 8-in. to 10-in. blade; universal motor	Contractor's saw; 10 in.; $1\frac{1}{2}$-hp to 3-hp motor*	Enclosed-base cabinet saw; 10 in. to 12 in.; 3-hp to 5-hp motor
Jointer	Benchtop; 4 in. to 6 in.; universal motor	On metal stand; 6 in.; $\frac{1}{2}$-hp to $\frac{3}{4}$-hp motor	Enclosed base; 8 in. to 12 in.; $\frac{3}{4}$-hp to $1\frac{1}{2}$-hp motor
Drill press	Benchtop; 8 in.; $\frac{1}{4}$-hp to $\frac{1}{2}$-hp motor	Benchtop or floor model; 14 in. to 16 in.; $\frac{1}{2}$-hp to $\frac{3}{4}$-hp motor	Floor model; 16 in. to 21 in.; $\frac{3}{4}$-hp to 1-hp motor
Cutoff saw	Powered miter saw; 10-in. blade	Sliding compound miter saw; 10-in. to 12-in. blade	Radial-arm saw; 12-in. to 16-in. blade (or 12-in. sliding compound miter saw)
Bandsaw	Tabletop or stand mounted; 9-in. to 12-in. wheels;* $\frac{1}{3}$-hp to $\frac{1}{2}$-hp motor	Stand mounted; 14-in. to 16-in. wheels; $\frac{1}{2}$-hp to $\frac{3}{4}$-hp motor	Heavy framed; 18-in. to 36-in. wheels; 1-hp to 3-hp motor
Thickness planer	Portable; 10 in. to 12 in. universal motor	Portable or stationary; 12 in. to 15 in.; $1\frac{1}{2}$-hp to 2-hp motor	Stationary; 15 in. to 24 in.; 2-hp to 5-hp motor
Stationary combination sander	Benchtop combo; 4-in. × 24-in. or 4-in. × 36-in. belt with 6-in. disc*	Bench/stand-mounted combo; 6-in. × 48-in. belt with 8-in. to 10-in. disc	Floor stand–mounted combo; 6-in. × 48-in. belt with 12-in. disc (or edge sander with 6-in. × 80-in. belt*)
Shaper	Benchtop; $\frac{1}{2}$-in. spindle; universal motor or $\frac{1}{2}$-hp induction motor or router table	$\frac{1}{2}$-in. to $\frac{3}{4}$-in. spindle with $\frac{1}{2}$-in. router bit collet; 1-hp to $1\frac{1}{2}$-hp motor	$\frac{3}{4}$-in. to $1\frac{1}{4}$-in. spindle (preferably tilting arbor); 3-hp to 5-hp motor

*Motor power, wheel sizes, and belt/disc sizes are approximate.

Despite their space-saving sizes, you can get big performance out of many benchtop stationary machines, such as the Bosch 4000® portable tablesaw (left), Delta® BOSS™ oscillating spindle sander (center), and Delta 22-560 portable thickness planer (right).

Router Tables vs. Shapers

Shapers have a reputation for being the shop's most dangerous machine. Used with appropriate guards and safety consciousness, they perform a wide variety of shop tasks efficiently and well. But many woodworkers choose a table-mounted router over a shaper for both safety and versatility. In fact, a router table fitted with a powerful router (preferably 13 amps to 15 amps) can perform most shaping functions nearly as well as a shaper can. Moreover, router bits are less expensive and more widely available than shaper cutters. And you can use the same router out of the table for freehand work as well.

afflicted, their homes, backyards, porches, and rented storage sheds as well). But the sheer quantity of tools and machines in your shop can quickly overwhelm the quality of working comfortably in that space. If you're short on space, there are some workable options.

Benchtop tools One way for the space challenged to save room is to buy benchtop-size machines, many of which are capable of doing nearly all the work of their full-size counterparts (see the photo above). While benchtops aren't as sturdy and vibration free as large, cast-iron floor models, they offer the advantage of portability. They're not only easy to cart around the shop but you can also tote them outdoors or to a job site if need be.

You'll get the best performance from these lighter-weight tools by mounting them to a sturdy benchtop, portable stand, or pedestal. Machines especially prone to vibration problems, such as wood lathes, are best served by a base that has lots of vibration-dampening weight. A simple boxlike stand, built from ¾-in.-thick plywood and filled with sand, gravel, or bricks, provides an inexpensive, sturdy base that can actually improve the performance of light benchtop models or bargain-quality machines that normally come with rickety sheet-metal bases. By making the weighted plywood base's top or side removable, you can empty it to make a major move a lighter proposition.

Combination machines Another option worthy of consideration for a cramped shop is to buy a combination machine. Very popular in Europe where workshop space is typically very limited (most Euro-garages are built to accommodate only one tiny car), combination machines integrate two, three, or more stationary power tools into one compact package. Popular combinations range from jointer/planers to tablesaw/shaper/horizontal mortiser/jointer/planers.

The disadvantage of these machines is the setup time that's needed when switching from one use to another. This requires careful planning of the machining steps needed to construct a project.

Three simple plywood boxes bolted together and filled with beach sand provide a heavy, stable base for this small wood lathe, actually improving its performance by dampening vibrations that occur during turning.

When workshop space is scarce, a combination machine can provide all the machinery you need in a very compact package. This Felder® machine integrates a big tablesaw (with a panel-cutting attachment) with a planer/jointer, shaper, and horizontal mortiser.

If you don't have room in your shop (or in your budget) for stationary machines, a full complement of portable power tools—including router; electric drill; circular/panel saw; jigsaw; and belt, random-orbit, and orbital sanders—can tackle just about any woodworking job.

The king of versatility among portable power tools is undoubtedly the router, which, in addition to a wide range of shaping operations, can handle joinery, mortising, edge jointing, pattern routing, and inlay work.

PORTABLE POWER TOOLS

There's certainly no shortage of types and models of portable power tools. These days you can find an electric motor attached to just about every kind of woodworking device. With all those options, where do you begin when even a basic complement of these portable powerhouses might set you back a wad of C notes? If you're just starting out, one approach is to buy super inexpensive Asian-made tools. This allows you to get the hang of woodworking and try different types of power tools without investing much money. Another strategy is to buy better-quality tools one at a time, starting with portables that are the most versatile. For example, a router performs an extensive array of shaping operations for joinery or decoration and, with the right jigs and accessories (mixed with a little ingenuity), can even slice, joint, and plane wood.

With no long power cords to untangle or have to plug in, battery-powered portable electric tools are among the handiest around. Keeping battery chargers in a drawer or on a rack makes recharges more convenient, especially if you own several cordless brands with non-interchangeable battery packs.

An electric hand drill—corded or cordless—is another versatile purchase that not only will bore holes but also, when fitted with the right cutter or device, will cut, shape, and sand wood and buff a finish.

Other tools that make up a basic complement of powered portables include:

• A jigsaw for trimming and crosscutting parts, cutting out curves and circles, and (with special blades) shaping and smoothing edges.

• A portable circular saw for ripping and crosscutting lumber and plywood.

• A belt sander for smoothing parts and large panels, flush-sanding edges and cabinet face frames, and shaping small parts.

• Orbital or random-orbit sanders for smoothing wood parts and panels, easing sharp edges, and rubbing out and buffing finishes.

• A plate joiner for cutting slots for biscuits used to reinforce joints in plywood and solid-wood projects and for edge-slotting stock.

Battery-powered portables Most corded portable power tools now have cordless twin siblings, starting with the handy cordless drill and including battery-powered panel saws, reciprocating saws, and sanders. When buying cordless tools, it's a good idea to match their battery voltage to the level of work you're doing: DIYers can get most home-improvement jobs done with lighter, less expensive low-voltage (9.6v and 12v) tools. More ambitious woodworkers will need the greater power and run times that 14.4v to 18v tools provide. Pros who typically push tools to their limits will demand the top performance of the biggest (and heaviest) 19.2v, 24v, and even the latest 28v or 36v cordless tools.

Because all brands and even some models are proprietary in both their battery packs and chargers, plan your purchases carefully so you don't end up with a cabinet full of different types of packs and chargers. It's much more practical to buy one brand and voltage so that batteries can be swapped between different tools, say, a drill and a jigsaw. And you'll definitely want to have more than one battery available for any cordless tool you use, so you can charge one pack while the other is in use. It's typically economical to buy new cordless tools in a kit that includes two or more batteries.

Air tools If you own an air compressor, you have access to another great alternative to buying electric portable power tools. In addition to powering spray equipment and lots of other stuff (see "Compressed-Air Systems," on p. 210), a compressor can run pneumatic tools, which are compact and lightweight. The prices of decent-size, 2-hp to 5-hp air compressors have plummeted in recent years, and small-shop-size pneumatic tools, such as random-orbit and in-line sanders, die grinders, and drills, have become readily available, typically for less than the cost of their electric counterparts. Portable pneumatic tools are very simply constructed and rarely require service: When they wear out, it's time to replace them.

HAND TOOLS

Chances are you already have a basic selection of hand tools in your house or shop that includes the most essential items: hammer, chisel, handplane, tape measure, square, screwdriver, and saw. A more complete list of recommended hand tools for a woodshop can be found in "Basic Woodshop Tool and Machine Purchases," on p. 102.

Layout tools are necessary for accurately executing just about any project.

Getting Enough Air

The ante for smooth sailing with pneumatic tools is having adequate air capacity. Most air-powered tools are very hungry for cubic feet per minute (cfm)—the volume of air put out by a compressor (see the chart on p. 212). Hence, you must connect them to a fairly large compressed-air system or be prepared to wait for a smaller compressor to recharge between work sessions.

As great alternative to electric portables, pneumatic tools, such as random-orbit and in-line sander and die grinders, are compact, lightweight, affordable, and rarely require service. All that's needed to run them is a compressor big enough to handle their often voracious appetite for air.

Hence this class of tools is not subject to scrimping: Buy the best layout tools you can afford, and they'll serve you for a lifetime. You'll want to buy basic hand woodworking tools—chisels, hand-planes, saws, and so on—because even in a world-class power-tool woodshop, it's sometimes faster and more efficient to cut a mortise or trim a tenon with a hand tool rather than take the time to set up a machine. Even if you never take a single shaving with a handplane, you'll need wrenches, screwdrivers, and pliers to keep your power tools shipshape and in good tune.

EQUIPPING A SPECIALTY SHOP

So far I've discussed tools and machines for a general woodshop. But if your only interest is carving, woodturning, scroll-saw work, or marquetry, you certainly won't need to buy an extensive array of equipment. For example, a carving shop can be equipped very simply: a work-bench or other steady surface to hold the work, a set of carving tools chosen for the type of work you do, and sharpening equipment chosen with carving in mind, including slipstones. The only power tools you may need are a bench grinder for regrinding your chisels and perhaps a power carving tool. A turner, on the other hand, needs a lathe, a bandsaw for roughing out turning blanks; turning tools; and a bench grinder and sharpen-ing equipment designed to shape and hone turning gouges, chisels, and scrap-ers. Those who wish to pursue scrollwork or marquetry can get by with a good scrollsaw, a few portable power tools, and a basic kit of hand tools.

Even the most fanatical power-tool woodworker needs good hand tools, including basic woodworking tools (chisels, hammers, handplanes, and saws); layout tools (squares, rulers, and marking gauges); and general-purpose tools (screwdrivers, wrenches, and pliers), the latter needed to keep tools adjusted and in good working order.

Stay within Your Means

Furniture maker extraordinaire Sam Maloof started his long and illustrious career with nothing more than a few hand tools and an 8-in. tablesaw borrowed from a friend. I once asked Sam for any advice he had to give a beginning woodworker. The first thing he said was "don't get into debt."

PLANNING FUTURE PURCHASES

It seems like you can never have too many woodworking tools. Just about the time you think you have one of everything, the tool companies come out with new kinds of tools, like rotary cutout tools and twin-blade circular saws. If you wisely plan your future acquisitions based on need and the kind of woodworking you do, you can develop a purchasing strategy that allows you to work within a budget and add new tools as you need them and as your skills and woodworking ambitions increase. Just remember that it doesn't take a complete shop full of all the latest techno marvels to do good woodworking.

Unfortunately, it seems that those woodworkers with the most disposable income have a greater tendency to do just that—dispose of their income on all kinds of gadgets, geegaws, and doodads. Consider that thirty $10 impulse purchases add up to a single $300 purchase—a single machine or portable power tool that's a solid lifetime purchase, instead of a shelf full of cool but relatively useless junk.

If your budget is really tight, it makes more sense to acquire most small tools and accessories on an as-needed basis, rather than to try to buy every imaginable tool at one time. Try not to get hooked on buying every size of chisel, shaper cutter, and drill bit known to humankind, only to discover that you end up using only a handful of them.

Buy Quality Tools or Bargains?

Once you have figured out which woodworking tools and machines you want for your shop, you still have to figure out exactly which tools to get. Should you splurge for the highest-quality or settle for bargain-basement models? Should you buy used machines? Ultimately, the tools you choose should suit your style of woodworking, whether you're looking to do home repairs and improvements or earn a professional's bread and butter. The idea is to minimize the frustration of making bad purchases and to get the right tools for the right job at the right price.

BUY THE BEST FOR DAILY USE

Things you use every day, such as a tape measure, tablesaw, layout tools, and any tool that must retain its precision to be good and accurate (square, rulers, calipers), should be the best you can afford. If you clock 8 hours a day doing woodworking, buying the best is an investment that's worthwhile, because it will not only give you heavy-duty tools that you can push hard day after day but also it will save on downtime that cuts into your paycheck. With portable power tools, more expensive models incorporate work-saving features and are often made of lighter alloys, so they save you sweat in the long run.

But the best tool doesn't always mean the most expensive. One way to economize is to look for models that are solid

RECOMMENDED SHOP ACCESSORIES

Personal protection devices*	Goggles or safety glasses Ear muffs or plugs Dust mask (disposable or replaceable filter model Cartridge-style respirator for use while applying finishes Work gloves
Clamping and assembly aids	Bench vises and hold-downs Assorted clamps: C-clamps, bar, pipe, quick-action Glue brushes and applicators
Machine-safety accessories	Guards, hold-downs, antikickback devices Push sticks and blocks
Machine adjustment and maintenance	Precision measuring tools; dial indicator, calipers, square, protractor Antirust sprays and treatments
Sharpening equipment and supplies	Whetstones or abrasive papers and glass plate Lubricating oils, sharpening aids, honing straps, compounds Bench grinder
Containers and organizers	Tool totes, boxes, chests, cabinets, racks Bins for small parts and supplies
Finishing accessories	Brushes Spray guns Filters Strainers
Sanding accessories	Sanding blocks Shaped rubber cauls Belt cleaning sticks

*See Chapter 10 for specific recommendations.

but lack unnecessary bells and whistles. For example, a good, basic cordless drill doesn't need a built-in level indicator or a removable stud finder to be useful. Examine features and decide which ones you need, but don't mistake essential things, like a good rip fence on a table-saw, as gadgetry.

BUY LESS-EXPENSIVE TOOLS FOR OCCASIONAL USE

Buying cheaper is a good thing if you want to expand your woodworking abilities but aren't sure if you'll like it. For example, it's unfortunate to buy an expensive lathe or scrollsaw only to discover later that you don't really like to turn spindles or cut out fretwork. Inexpensive

tools and machines can provide a great way to start out—even for trying out woodworking in the first place. You can always sell tools you outgrow and replace them with bigger, better models.

You can save money by purchasing lower-priced bargain and sale tools for one-time jobs or tasks you'll perform infrequently. For example, you don't need to buy the latest ultra-high-duty router bit if you're going to use it only to cut moldings for your own custom kitchen; chances are you'll never use that bit again. And it's worth putting up with the shortcomings of an inexpensive plate jointer machine if you rarely build plywood carcases.

Sharpening equipment, including a bench grinder, sharpening stones, hones, and accessories, is a necessary investment if you want to keep all your bladed hand tools razor sharp and performing at their best.

BUY USED EQUIPMENT

One woodworker's dream machine might be another's rusty hulk, taking up room in a corner of a shop. Even though dream deals have become few and far between, buying used tools and equipment can really stretch your budget.

Woodworking guilds and clubs provide a way to get to know lots of local woodworkers and keep tabs on who is about to sell what in your area. In lieu of that, you can regularly scour eBay[SM], Craigslist[SM] or if you're not computer savvy, your local newspaper's classified ads for used tools and equipment. If you're an adventurous sort, there's always the local flea market, but this provides only spotty results and you can't usually check out tools as thoroughly as you should before buying.

If you do find a tool that seems like a good deal, it's a great idea to take someone along with you who is an experienced tool mechanic or who at least can tell you what to check before deciding on a purchase. This will save the heartache of discovering you've just purchased a jointer with drooped tables or a shaper with a bent spindle, both of which work better as boat anchors than as woodworking machines.

If you like a tool but not the price, here's a bit of advice I learned from my mother, who is the best bargainer I know. Say you find a decent tablesaw at the local flea market, but the seller wants about twice as much as you're willing to spend. Instead of just making a verbal offer, try waving the cold, hard cash under his nose. All but the most hardened veteran dealer will be hard-pressed to pass on your offer. It seems the sight and smell of money is the proverbial "bird in the hand" which they'll take more often than not.

Which Add-Ons and Accessories Should I Buy?

I love those car commercials in which they show you a beautiful, elegant new automobile (typically being driven by an even more beautiful and elegant woman) and proudly announce the car's reasonable-sounding price tag. Unfortunately, the end of such commercials is punctuated by the rapid-fire voice of some speed reader, stating that the car as shown includes quite a few options and extras that cost considerably more.

Precision measuring tools, such as dial indicators and Vernier calipers, make setting up and adjusting power tools—and their fences, gauges, and jigs—much easier.

It's easy to forget the little things that are needed to run a woodshop, items without which woodworking is impractical, unsafe, or impossible. If you're just starting out, a list of possible accessories can be quite extensive. Even a basic list includes items such as personal safety gear and clamping and gluing supplies. Many of these things support tools you already own. For instance, having the best set of chisels or finest handplane ever seen by mortal men won't do you any good if you don't spring for the sharpening equipment necessary to keep its edges from turning as blunt as a well-licked Popsicle® stick. Precision tools, such as dial indicators, engineer's squares, and calipers, are extremely helpful for setting up and

adjusting stationary power tools (and their fences, gauges, and jigs) and for keeping them running smoothly and accurately.

In "Recommended Shop Accessories" on p. 113, I've listed what I consider to be some key workshop items worth adding to your wish list. Some accessories will be dictated by the kind of woodworking you wish to do.

There are other accessories not directly involved in woodworking that you shouldn't overlook. These will help make life in the shop more comfortable and convenient. For example, many woodworkers complain of not being able to hear the telephone ring when power tools are in operation. A phone flasher is a simple accessory that installs on your shop's

Buying the best-quality blades, cutters, bits, and abrasives that you can afford will provide the best performance from all your stationary and portable power tools—even if the tools themselves are economy rather than top-of-the-line models.

Jig accessories, such as the FastTrack extruded aluminum track and sliding flip-stop system on this cutoff saw fence, make woodworking machines more versatile, accurate, and quicker to use.

phone line and activates a bright strobe light to alert you to an incoming call.

HIGH-QUALITY BLADES, CUTTERS, BITS, AND ABRASIVES

It's a shame to spend a small fortune on a new tablesaw and then save a few bucks by fitting it with a cheap sawblade. Even the best tool will perform only as well as the component that actually does the sawing, planing, boring, or sanding. You'll never regret buying the best-quality blade, cutter, bit, and abrasive that you can afford.

For daily woodworking tasks, buying cheap bits and blades is an act of false economy since the ones made with better grades of steel and carbide typically last far longer, ultimately giving you more sawdust for the sawbuck over the life of the tool. Better performance can be coaxed out of even inexpensive tools and machines. I'd rather use a $79 belt sander fitted with a high-quality coated abrasive belt than a unit costing three times as much that is running a "bargain-bin" belt.

JIGS THAT EXPAND THE CAPACITY OF YOUR TOOLS

Experienced woodworkers know that you can coax a lot more work out of the machines and tools that you already have by using jigs and fixtures. Whether store bought or shopmade, devices such as

A Bandsaw Substitute

A router isn't the only portable power tool that can be adapted to table operation. If your shop lacks a bandsaw, a jigsaw can prove to be a reasonably useful substitute. You can even buy accessory tables designed to hold a jigsaw upside down, making it a stationary curve-cutting tool.

These template jigs—the Leigh Jigs® dovetail and joinery jig system and the Woodhaven® angle base—are only a couple of the dozens of valuable accessories that tap the vast shaping and joinery potential of a router.

tenoning jigs, templates, tilting tables, sliding carriages, and end stops allow a stationary or portable machine to perform many jobs it can't do when it comes from the factory.

Jigs can also bring speed and accuracy to everyday jobs. For example, adding a cutoff fence with a pivoting flip stop such as the FastTrack fence system to your cutoff saw makes trimming boards to precise length an effortless task.

There are many devices that attach to machines to expand their capacity. A sliding table enables a regular tablesaw to cut large panels easily and accurately.

Mounted to the saw table left of the blade, some sliding tables are big enough to allow you to crosscut a 4-ft. by 8-ft. sheet of plywood. And when it comes to the router, jigs like angle bases and dovetail templates allow you to create a staggering array of different shapes and joineries (see the photo below).

Portable power-tool tables Possibly the most popular accessory for a router is a router table, which transforms the portable tool into a small shaper. Whether you build one entirely from scratch or buy a commercially made model, a router

table helps you perform machining operations that are impossible with a hand-held router.

Feature-wise, a good router table should have a large, flat table; removable throat inserts to suit different sizes of bits; free access to the router underneath to allow bit changes; a fence that's easy to adjust with a guard that keeps fingers from contacting the bit; and a safe on/off switch that can be turned off easily in an emergency. If you build your own table, consider fitting it with a height-adjusting insert plate, such as the Rout-R-Lift™ (see the photo below). These devices use a removable crank to adjust the entire router up and down, which makes setting a bit's cutting depth easy and accurate.

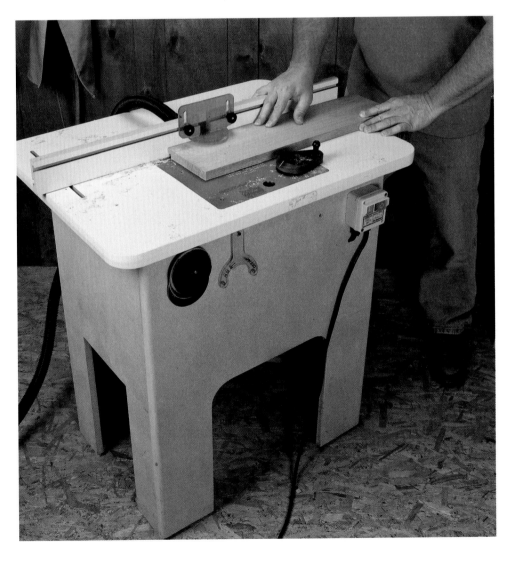

A good router table transforms a portable router into a stationary machine with all the versatility of a small shaper. The author's shopmade table features a Rout-R-Lift™ insert plate that allows rapid and accurate bit-height adjustments.

6 Shop Layout

"Planning the layout of your workshop early in its development . . . can keep you from spending years in an uncomfortable, poorly organized space."

The physical aspect of a shop is simply a space of some kind—a garage, a barn, a teepee—that keeps the rain, rust, and robbers away and houses a collection of implements needed to saw, plane, slice, sand, and pound raw wood into useful objects. But careful organization and layout can transform a building full of tools into a comfortable workshop that makes all your project-building tasks safer and easier.

Let's be clear about one thing: No workshop is perfect for everyone. If there were an ideal workshop, I could simply give you a precise plan to follow with clear dimensions. Every person who comes to the hobby, avocation, or profession of woodworking has his or her own particular collection of tools and unique work styles, skills, and desires pertaining to the kind of woodworking he or she wants to do. These personalized needs dictate a specialized approach as to how one will lay out a shop: where the tools should go, where lumber and supplies are stored, and how much bench area is needed.

Develop a Layout That Works for You

Because each woodworker is unique, one solution cannot work for all. Rather than offering you plans for the layout of a "perfect" shop, I can only alert you to the issues you should consider and offer guidelines, tools, and strategies for planning a shop that is efficient and comfortable—one that's, I hope, perfect for *you*.

Unless you're a big fan of frequent shop remodeling, planning the layout of your workshop early in its development will save you a lot of time and trouble and can keep you from spending years in an uncomfortable, poorly organized space. And if you already work in a shop that's as organized as a trailer park after a tornado, careful planning and a little remodeling is likely to help you make a quantum leap.

As Santa Rosa, Calif., woodworker David Marks applies gold leaf (a trademark of his work) to a sample, careful shop layout and planning ensure that he has most everything he needs within easy reach of his bench area.

Machine Placement

Some of the most important decisions in laying out a shop involve the placement of basic machines, such as the tablesaw and jointer. Deciding where to put them depends, in part, on the scale of woodworking you do, which then determines the necessary clearance area around these machines for handling long stock or large sheetgoods. You'll also want to consider work flow to avoid an excess amount of running around the shop to accomplish tasks, as well as how to power your machines without turning your shop into a snakepit of extension cords (see "Powering Machines away from Walls," on p. 54).

Tablesaw Layout

Option 1

Locate the saw in the middle of the shop, leaving maximum room for ripping and plywood cuts beyond the capacity of the fence.

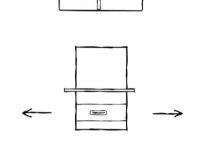

Option 2

Place the extension-table end of the saw near a long wall of the shop. This allows long rip cuts and plywood cuts up to the capacity of the fence.

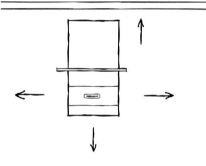

Option 3

Orient the saw diagonally in the shop, with the outfeed side facing doors or windows. This allows the ripping of long boards.

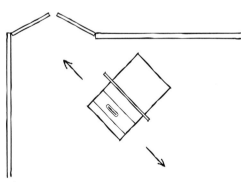

Option 4

By placing the saw on a mobile base located near a large doorway, the saw can be moved outside for long rip cuts and large plywood work.

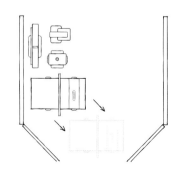

In this section, you'll read about the common issues you should take into account when planning machine placement. You'll find diagrams that illustrate some of the more common layouts that experienced woodworkers employ today.

TABLESAWS

First, let's take a look at four placement options for the tablesaw, the machine that is at the heart of most woodshops. The first option places it in the center of the shop (see "Tablesaw Layout" at left), which lends maximum space and flexibility for ripping and panel sawing as well as crosscutting long boards. The main requirement here is a shop that's at least long and wide enough to allow room for the workpiece, both on the infeed and the outfeed side.

If your shop is long and narrow, Option 2 in the drawing provides maximum space to the left of the fence for handling large sheets of plywood. If you often work with full sheets of plywood or other sheetgoods, you might want to build the tablesaw into an extension table surround, as San Diego woodworker Pat Curci did in his small shop (see the photo on the facing page). The surround offers support for large panels, as well as provides an ample work surface near the saw.

If you don't have enough room for ripping long boards, try orienting the saw diagonally in the shop. If that won't work, you can gain outfeed room by aiming the back of the saw toward an operable door, as shown in Option 3.

Finally, if your shop is in a garage where machines are stored compactly when not in use, keep the saw near the door, as shown in Option 4. You can then wheel or drag it outside when you need to saw stock too large for the garage.

JOINTERS AND PLANERS

Next come two options for the tablesaw's trusty sidekick, the jointer, as well as for the thickness planer. Because it's usual to work among all three tools when dressing lumber, Option 1 in "Jointer Layout," below, locates the jointer nearest the saw to the right of its extension table, with the planer nearby. As with the tablesaw, it always makes sense to align these tools with the shop's long axis.

An interesting variation of this layout is displayed in Jim Tolpin's shop, shown in the photo on p. 128. Tolpin located his jointer to the left of his tablesaw; its height is low enough to allow panels cut on the saw to pass over the jointer.

To save space, his portable planer lives beneath the saw. All three tools are oriented toward the garage-style door, which can be opened to allow long boards to be ripped, jointed, or thickness planed.

Building your tablesaw into an extension table that surrounds it on three sides, as woodworker Pat Curci did in his small San Diego shop, offers lots of support when cutting full sheets of plywood; it also provides a large work surface adjacent to the saw.

Jointer Layout

Option 1

To save space, group the jointer with the planer.

Locate the jointer mid-shop near the tablesaw with its axis in line with the shop's longer dimension.

Leave a minimum aof 24 in. between the jointer and the saw's extension table.

Option 2

Locate the jointer next to a wall, preferable a long one. If there's not enough room for jointing long boards, locate it one third of the length of the wall from a doorway, then open the door to clear long workpieces.

When Doug Warren rolls open the door to his long and narrow Port Townsend, WA, workshop, it isn't always to greet visitors. Having the jointer near the doorway allows him to face or edge-joint the very long planks often needed for the architectural woodworking that he does.

[Building a radial-arm saw or sliding compound-miter saw into its own long, narrow support table located against the shop's longest wall makes crosscutting or mitering long boards or heavy planks fast and easy.

If your tablesaw is near a wall and your shop is fairly narrow, positioning the jointer and planer against the opposite wall is reasonable, as shown in Option 2 in the drawing on p. 123. If the shop isn't long enough to accommodate long workpieces, try to put these machines near an operable doorway, as shown in the top photo at left.

CROSSCUT SAWS

Radial-arm saws, sliding compound-miter saws, and powered miter boxes (chop boxes) used for crosscutting long boards are best located against the longest wall of the shop, as shown in the Option 1 in "Crosscut Saw Layout" on p. 125. If the saw is to become a stationary machine, it's typical to mount or build it into a long, narrow support table fitted with a fence.

One useful idea for woodworkers who regularly must cut right- and left-handed workpieces, such as miters for picture framing, is to build two crosscut saws into a single cutoff bench. This way, they can share the same fence and stop system.

If your shop lacks wall space or doesn't have a long enough wall to accommodate long stock, another option is to place the crosscut saw near an operable doorway with the right-hand side closest to the door (see Option 2 in the drawing on p. 125). This leaves most of the length of the fence to the left of the blade (preferable if you're right-handed), allowing short and midsize parts to be cut to length or trimmed without your having to open the door.

OTHER MACHINES

In most small shops, once the key machines are in place, others are arranged wherever there is room for them. There typically isn't enough free space to put these tools in the middle of the floor area, although sometimes you can tuck a machine into an unused space. For example, in a shop where the tablesaw is in the center, a shaper (or a router table or spindle sander) with a table the same height as the saw can be put on the outfeed side of the extension table (see "Shaper or Spindle Sander Layout" on p. 129). Also, building a router table directly into the tablesaw's extension table is a great way to save space as well as make use of the saw's fence for routing operations.

Building a router table into your tablesaw's extension table not only saves shop space but allows your saw fence to handle double-duty.

Crosscut Saw Layout

Option 1   Most saws require little or no clearance against a wall.

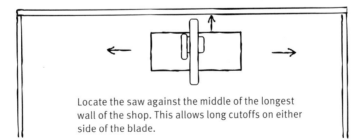

Locate the saw against the middle of the longest wall of the shop. This allows long cutoffs on either side of the blade.

Option 2

Locate the saw on a short wall of the shop near a doorway. The length of most stock will fit to the left of the saw; the door can be opened to provide clearance for longer boards.

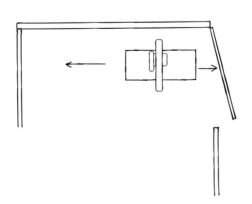

Use the corners Some machines are perfectly content to live in a corner, including the bandsaw, scrollsaw, disc or combination sander, and lathe (see "Corner Machine Layout" on p. 129). Orienting the lathe's tailstock end into a corner will leave room for outboard turning. Pulling the bandsaw away from the wall allows the necessary clearance for cutting large curved parts, while locating it near a doorway or window permits resawing of long planks.

Line 'em up Most other woodshop machines work harmoniously when lined up along the walls, where they are easy to power and connect to dust collection (see "Machine Layout against a Wall" on p. 127). The amount of space left between these tools depends on the amount of room you have, the size of the stock you work with, and whether adjacent tools have tables at the same height. You can always pull a machine away from the wall if additional space is needed.

Orienting Machines in a Line

BY CAREFULLY COORDINATING THE positions and table heights of stationary machines, you can reduce the amount of clearance between certain machines. For example, by placing machines such as a shaper/router table, oscillating-spindle sander or disc sander, and horizontal boring machine in line, then setting them up with all their tables level and at the same height, a long workpiece may rest or slide on an adjacent machine's table (as shown here). Such an arrangement allows you to handle large or long work without having to rely on outfeed tables or roller stands for support. For this same reason, it's a good idea to level the tabletops of benchtop tools that are in close proximity to one another.

By setting tables to the same height and leveling them, a workpiece can pass over any or all of these machines.

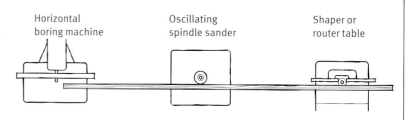

Horizontal boring machine

Oscillating spindle sander

Shaper or router table

Machine Layout against a Wall

Machines such as a bandsaw, drill press, router table, shaper, stationary sanders, lathe, joinery machines, and overarm routers are ideal to locate along a wall. Power and dust collection are easy to hook up.

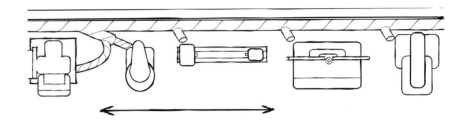

Clearly, these options are not the only possibilities and are contingent on the mix of machines you have, the shape and size of your shop, and the kind of work you do. The bottom line is if the layout works for you, then that's the best for your shop (and don't let anyone tell you any different!).

Machine and Workspace Proximity

If you've ever remodeled your kitchen, you've undoubtedly read about the ideal "work triangle"—a three-sided circuit among the refrigerator, sink, and stove/range with about 6 ft. between each. You can apply that same formula to your shop, say, for designing an efficient bench area or workstation (see "Workstations," on p. 155). But most woodshop tasks don't revolve around just three major work areas. Instead, it's more important to consider the proximity of machine tools (as well as lumber racks, storage cabinets, and workbenches) to one another and arrange them in ways that make sense for your work habits.

The bench area in Jim Casebolt's small shop is close to the drawers and shelves that hold his hand and portable power tools as well as to the glue and supplies he commonly uses for building furniture or doing boat work.

Closely grouping machines that are often used in concert, such as a tablesaw, jointer, and thickness planer, will save steps when repeatedly going back and forth among machines.

Space Needed around Shop Machines

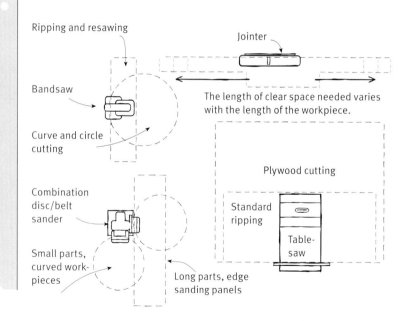

Ripping and resawing

Bandsaw

Curve and circle cutting

Jointer

The length of clear space needed varies with the length of the workpiece.

Plywood cutting

Combination disc/belt sander

Small parts, curved work-pieces

Standard ripping

Table-saw

Long parts, edge sanding panels

GROUP RELATED TOOLS AND MACHINES

It's most important to group together certain machines that are used in conjunction or in close order of one another for everyday tasks. For example, the tablesaw, jointer, and thickness planer should be located close together because the process of dressing lumber's edges and surfaces and ripping it to width often involves repeatedly going back and forth among these machines.

Likewise, a well laid out bench area should be in close proximity to hand and portable power tools as well as to other supplies that are commonly needed at that work area.

Carefully considering the proximity of these things when planning shop layout will pay off big in the long run. "Proximity of Shop Tools," on p. 132, shows some other machines and wood-shop elements that you should consider placing near each another in your shop.

SPACE NEEDED AROUND MACHINES

How much space is needed around a tablesaw or shaper? The Occupational Safety and Health Administration (OSHA) has its own ideas about how much clearance is needed around machines used in factories and commercial shops, but these don't necessarily apply to the small-shop woodworker.

The practical approach to machine ergonomics A more practical approach is to consider the space needed for the workpiece and how much elbow room you need when operating the machine. Jointers, tablesaws, and shapers require a corridor of open space left on the infeed and outfeed sides of the machine's table (see "Space Needed around Shop Machines" on the facing page). Of course, the proportions of that corridor can vary tremendously, depending on the size of the stock being machined.

In a small shop, you can fudge the amount of room needed when machining large workpieces by moving the machine outside or to a more spacious part of the shop when necessary.

If you work in a multiperson shop, safe space margins between machines are very important to ensure that no one gets bumped in the middle of an operation, a very dangerous event. Generally, you'll need to leave a lot more space around machines that are constantly in use, such as the tablesaw and the jointer, so that colleagues can work without being disturbed by those using other machines nearby.

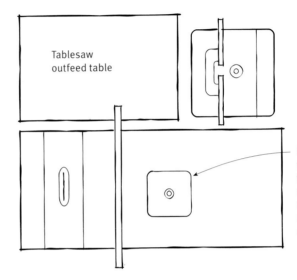

Shaper or Spindle Sander Layout

Locate a shaper or spindle sander behind the tablesaw and next to the outfeed table. (Tables must all be on the same level.) When the bit or drum is removed, the shaper or sander's table can support outfeed for wide tablesaw cuts.

Tablesaw outfeed table

Building a router table into the tablesaw's extension table saves space and uses the saw's existing fence.

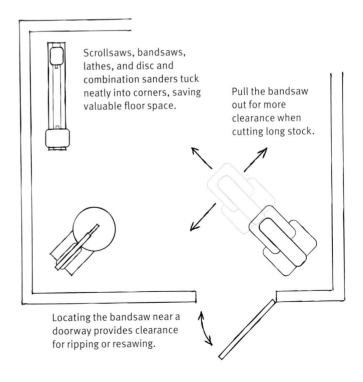

Corner Machine Layout

Scrollsaws, bandsaws, lathes, and disc and combination sanders tuck neatly into corners, saving valuable floor space.

Pull the bandsaw out for more clearance when cutting long stock.

Locating the bandsaw near a doorway provides clearance for ripping or resawing.

If your space is long and narrow, you'll achieve the smoothest work flow through the shop by orienting most machines in line with the shop's long axis, which provides the most clearance when machining long stock. Note the lumber storage on the right wall.

Accommodating Work Flow

If you find yourself running from one end of your shop to the other in the normal course of building a project (regardless of how leisurely the pace of work), you might consider revamping your shop layout to allow a more fluid work flow.

One area that warrants a look is where materials are stored relative to where they are used. For example, if lumber is stored in a shed at one end of your shop and the tablesaw and crosscut saw are at the other end, you're probably working a lot harder than you need to. Many woodworkers like to keep lumber on a rack

above or near a cutoff saw (see the photo above). Such an arrangement allows boards to be cut to rough length before edge jointing and ripping them to width. If you build cabinets and work with plywood, a well-situated sheet goods rack should allow you to remove sheets and lever them onto your panel saw or table saw without much of a hassle.

Multipurpose Shops

When a craftsman's interests and commitments extend beyond making saw dust, shop space must be shared with other pursuits. Some of these are more

Woodworkers should always use extreme caution when sharpening tools in the shop; all it takes is one stray spark from a grinding wheel or belt to start a dangerous shop fire.

compatible with woodworking than others. For example, a watch repairer would be foolish to practice in an environment as dusty as a woodshop. And welding or blacksmithing would be downright foolhardy when you consider the effect a spark could have on a pile of wood shavings. If you wish to lay out a shop that accommodates such activities, consider creating separate rooms, either with permanent walls or temporary dividers that allow you to create environments that are suitable for each activity.

DIVIDING SHOP SPACE

Just as it's hard to live in a single-room apartment, it can be very tiresome to perform all of woodworking's different operations in a single space. For example, it's a bad idea to apply a finish in the same room in which you've just sanded parts (unless, of course, you like a nubbly

Locating the Drill Press for Long Work

IF YOU COMMONLY MORTISE OR BORE LONG OR large workpieces on the drill press, consider locating the machine next to a workbench or between a pair of benches. Benches or tables can be useful for supporting big workpieces in lieu of having to set up outfeed supports to keep them level with the drill press's small worktable. On the downside, you'll have to clear the clutter before machining.

Locate a drill press in between workbenches. The benches help support long stock during boring or mortising.

PROXIMITY OF SHOP TOOLS

TOOLS TO LOCATE NEAR ONE ANOTHER	REASON TO KEEP THEM NEAR EACH OTHER
Wood lathe, bench grinder, sharpening equipment, and bandsaw	Keep sharpening and grinding tools nearby to service turning tools; a bandsaw is good to have close by to cut turning blanks from rough lumber or thick boards
Tablesaw, jointer, and thickness planer	Dressing lumber and ripping it to dimension involves moving repeatedly among these three machines
Assemble table, clamps, gluing supplies, fasteners, and hardware	Everything used in the process of assembling workpieces should be at close reach
Workbench, hand tools, layout tools, portable power tools, and shop vacuum	Tool storage cabinets should put tools within reach of your bench; a shop vacuum should be close by for collecting dust from portable power tools
Stationary sanders: disc, horizontal edge, oscillating spindle, flap, and drum	Abrasive shaping and smoothing often involve sanding different parts of a workpiece on different machines (for example, long, flat areas vs. concave curves)

varnished surface). If you have the space, dividing the shop into separate areas for different operations can save you time and trouble and simply make woodworking more enjoyable.

The most common division found in woodshops is a separate machine room and bench and assembly area. This allows you to do all the sawdust spewing you wish in one space and then to go into a cleaner, quieter space for hand-tool operations and assembly. Bench rooms are very popular in multiperson shops, where one person can run machines while the other works in peace. Unfortunately, the complexities of shop layout and work flow seem to multiply exponentially. Getting two people to successfully work in the same space is more than two times as difficult as it is for a single person.

FINISHING AREAS

If wood finishing is your specialty or a big part of your business, then creating a separate room or area for finishing is essential. The easiest way of creating a permanent finishing area that's properly ventilated and fire safe is to install a spray booth, as described in Chapter 4. Another way to add a permanent finishing room in your shop is to wall off a corner or section of the main shop or add a small addition off the back of the shop (see the bottom photo on the facing page). Adding a ventilation fan to the room will allow you to work inside without worrying about finish fumes harvesting your brain cells or knocking you out.

Temporary finishing areas For small-shop woodworkers, who must use the same benchtop where they cut, plane, and sand wood to also varnish their completed projects, a dedicated spray booth or finishing room is not a very practical use of space.

The easiest way to create a separate finishing area in a shop is to put up temporary dividers that separate the dusty part of the shop from a clean space in

Having separate workbenches in a clean bench room that's separate from a noisy, dusty machine-tool room helps keep ukulele and guitar builder Tony Graziano on good terms with the other woodworkers who share his shop.

If your main shop space lacks a clean finishing space, you might consider adding a small addition onto the back of your workshop. Installing a high-volume fan and filters allows you to apply finishes that will dry clean and smooth.

You can create a quick, temporary clean area inside an otherwise dusty shop by putting up a light, plastic dividing wall. The ZipWall® system, shown here, uses thin plastic sheeting and spring-loaded poles that expand to fit tightly from floor to ceiling to trap the edge of the sheeting.

which you can finish your work. You can make light dividers by covering a thin-wood framework with 4-mil or 6-mil polyethylene sheeting. By making the dividers fit floor to ceiling, you'll keep dust from wafting over the top (fine wood dust is so light that it floats on the electrical charge in air itself).

Another way of erecting a temporary divider is to use a system of spring-loaded poles and plastic sheeting, called ZipWall. The poles expand to fit tightly against the ceiling and trap the edge of the plastic sheeting. Unless you thoroughly ventilate this plastic-enclosed space, wear a respirator and don't spend too much time inside.

Even without a separate finishing area, you can still get good results by thoroughly vacuuming your bench area (preferably the day before finishing so fine dust has a chance to settle from the air) and wiping or brushing a quick-drying finish on your project. Another

alternative is to finish outdoors, provided that it's any cleaner out there than it is in your shop and the weather gods are smiling on you.

CREATING CONVERTIBLE SPACES

Not every woodworker is lucky enough to have a space to can call his or her own 24 hours a day. There are a great many woodworkers and DIY weekend warriors who share their shop space with the family car. Compactness and mobility are the key elements for keeping a shared space quick and easy to convert from one use to another. Benchtop machines, which can be mounted on hinged, swing-down platforms or pull-outs or simply lifted and stowed underneath benches, are a good choice, as are wheeled bases that allow benches or tool stands to be rolled around with ease.

If you install casters on heavy workbenches or stands that need to stay rock-solid during use, choose those that lock the swivel action of the caster as well as the rotation of the wheel. Alternatively, you could mount large plastic furniture glides on the feet to allow the bench to be dragged with relative ease across a smooth concrete or wood floor without leaving gouges. Very heavy benches with thick legs might need three or four glides on each foot.

Although folding tables can be tiresome to set up and break down, they can provide a substantial work surface that's great for project layout or assembly, yet they take up little room when they're folded and stowed away.

Careful layout and thorough organization are the keys to having an effective woodshop in a space that doubles as a home for an automobile. A model of efficiency, Joe O'Rendy's single-car-garage workshop has more than a half-dozen benchtop-size machines with shelved cabinets against one wall and a compact desk, bookshelf, and a pull-out clamp rack/storage space on the other side. His tablesaw, router table, and workbench can all be rolled to the back of the garage when it's time to move the car in.

A Smart Folding Table

SEATTLE-AREA FURNITURE MAKER CURTIS ERPELDING has done one better than a simple folding table. His large, vacuum-clamping worktable, built from a sheet of particleboard and four folding-leg assemblies, is hinged directly to a wall and tilts up and out of the way when not in use (as shown in the photo). Instead of relying on sheer brawn to wrestle with the heavy table, Erpelding rigged up a block and tackle, which allows him to lift and lower the brawny table with ease.

MOBILE MACHINES

Unless you're a former pro wrestling champion, manhandling heavy machines around the shop is a real bear. But fitting machines with wheeled bases will allow even the most muscularly challenged individual to reposition the heaviest cast-iron monster with ease.

Ready-made rolling bases are available for a wide variety of modern stationary machines. These steel-framed bases bolt to the bottom of the tool and rest on the floor when the tool is in use. Before the machine can be moved, the base's retracted wheels are engaged by either pressing a pedal or cranking down on handscrews, depending on the design of the base.

Build your own mobile bases Shop-built wheeled bases can be made for practically any type of machine. But un-less you're up to the task of constructing some kind of wheel-retraction mechanism, it's much easier to make a two-wheeled base that tips up for moving. "Shop-Built Mobile Machine Bases," on p. 138, shows two variations of this idea.

In the first design, a pair of wheels (mounted so they just make contact with the ground) are screwed to the edge of a plywood and lumber frame that is bolted to the machine's base. The machine rests firmly on the floor until it is tipped back onto the wheels.

In the second design, a pair of non-pivoting wheels are mounted at one side of the base, opposite heavy elevator bolts on the other. Tipping the machine up slightly allows it to be moved. Since one side of the machine always rests on the wheels, it's best to use this configuration on very heavy machines not prone to

A commercially made, steel-framed rolling base can be mounted to practically any heavy stationary machine, making it readily movable via a set of retracting wheels.

A small plywood base with locking wheels bolted to its underside allows you to easily move small machines, such as this scrollsaw, around the shop. (Note the shopmade rack for blades mounted to the stand.)

vibration and movement. If the machine has a table or motor that overhangs its base, mounting the wheels on that side of the mobile base will make tipping and moving the machine easier.

Lighter machines, such as scrollsaws and bench grinders, and benchtop machines can be mounted on shopmade platforms that ride on regular locking casters (the kind with rubber wheels, available at most hardware stores). Pat Curci's scrollsaw, shown in the photo at right is mounted on a simple plywood stand fitted with a trio of wheels that must be locked before the machine is ready for use. Using all pivoting-type wheels, instead of a combination of fixed and pivoting wheels, will allow you to move the machine in any direction.

If you're resourceful (or a flea-market scavenger), you might come up with an

If you're the resourceful type, you might be able to transform an old wheeled base or stand, such as this typing table complete with locking wheels that engage with a single foot pedal, into a handy mobile base for a woodworking machine.

old, wheeled stand that can be converted into a mobile machine stand. Take, for example, the old, metal typing table shown in the photo at left which serves as a perfectly serviceable portable stand for a combination sander.

Strategies for Gaining Space

Few woodworkers will ever get to build their dream shops. The majority of us who are working in small shops would probably rather buy a bigger and better tablesaw than foot the bill for a major shop renovation. But there are a few things you can do to get a lot of the clutter out of your shop and give you more elbowroom.

ADDING A LOFT

If you're blessed with a shop that has an open-vaulted roof or a high ceiling, one of the easiest ways to gain additional space is to add a loft. A loft doesn't have to have enough vertical clearance to stand up in to be useful. By building a loft high enough to leave ample headroom underneath, you can gain useful storage space for lumber, parts, tools, supplies, and finished workpieces while freeing up the shop's main floor space.

A loft typically can be added in a shop with a gable roof by fitting joists atop the wall plates. In a shop with attic space that's open on one end, you can create a loft by adding flooring atop existing ceiling joists. The length of the span and the amount of weight you want to put up

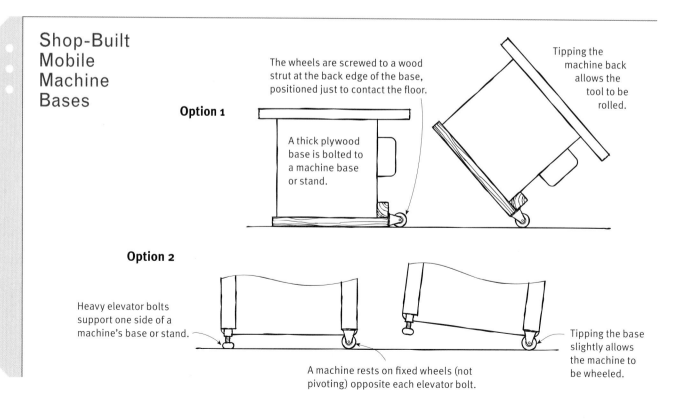

Shop-Built Mobile Machine Bases

Option 1

The wheels are screwed to a wood strut at the back edge of the base, positioned just to contact the floor.

A thick plywood base is bolted to a machine base or stand.

Tipping the machine back allows the tool to be rolled.

Option 2

Heavy elevator bolts support one side of a machine's base or stand.

A machine rests on fixed wheels (not pivoting) opposite each elevator bolt.

Tipping the base slightly allows the machine to be wheeled.

Storage Sheds and Truck Boxes

IF STORAGE FOR LUMBER AND SUPPLIES is a significant issue in your small shop, a neat and easy way to gain a little elbow room is to erect a shed nearby. You can buy ready-made wood or metal garden sheds, which are very easy to assemble, and install them in your backyard or next to your home or garage. Best of all, the vast majority of these sheds are small enough that no permit is required for erecting them.

Another terrific strategy for gaining shop storage is to buy a used truck box. By setting up a truck box next to his furniture and cabinet shop (see the photo), furniture artisan Roger Heitzman gained a clean, secure, and handy storage container in which to keep jigs and fixtures, lumber, sheetgoods, and other supplies.

A used truck box makes a handy storage container for lumber, sheetgoods, and other supplies.

Adding a loft to a shop with a tall, vaulted ceiling is one way to add storage in a small space. A sturdy ladder that engages hooks on the edge of the loft to keep it from sliding provides ready access to the lumber stored in this good-size loft.

Beware of Overhead Noise

Unless you like noise, don't move your compressor or dust collector into a loft space. A loft's wooden floor will amplify motor or fan vibrations, creating a thunderous din.

there will determine the size and spacing of these joists.

If you plan to use a loft for storing heavy lumber or supplies, it's always prudent to overbuild it because it isn't difficult to amass a stack of lumber that weighs half a ton or more. Play it safe and consult a contractor or builder before starting.

Loft access Unless your loft leaves you with enough headroom to create a second-story space, such as a finishing

room or office, it's more practical to leave a loft open to the shop on at least one side because that makes it easier to get stuff up and down from there. And unless you have room to build a proper stairway or folding stairs, you'll need to build or buy a sturdy ladder that lets you carry things up and down safely. A good loft ladder should have wide treads and some means of attachment at the top so it won't slide sideways just as you're carrying down that box of heavy rosewood scraps you couldn't bear to throw away.

Incidentally, a clever way of gaining space in a shop that has a second story with a built-in stairway is to move the stairs out of the shop entirely. Stairs, either a straight run or a double flight, can often be added to the outside of a shop building, provided there is room for a landing and a doorway to enable you to enter the loft from the outside.

RELOCATING DUST COLLECTORS AND COMPRESSORS

Another way to gain shop space is to move things that don't have to be in the shop somewhere else. A central dust-collection system's blower, cyclones, filter boxes, and dust bins or an air compressor and storage tank are good candidates for exile from the main shop.

To make more room inside this two-story barn-style woodshop, the owner moved the stairway outdoors, mounting it to the side of the building. The landing at the top and a dormer added to the roof makes upstairs access more convenient.

A simple shed-style roof keeps the rain off and provides all the protection the dust-collection system in this Northwest workshop needs. Building the shed adjacent to the shop keeps ductwork lengths short for better system efficiency.

To save room and cut down on noise inside the shop, the space underneath a stairway can be enclosed to form a small equipment room large enough to house an air compressor or a central dust collector, as shown here.

A small shed, closet, or adjacent building can easily house these pieces of support equipment. Such a relocation will help you gain usable space and will rid the shop of the excess decibels that these devices produce—a good enough reason alone for moving them.

Another good use of otherwise wasted space is to create a large closet under an exterior stairway, as Curtis Erpelding did to house his central dust collector (see the right photo above).

Insulation and noise control If you live in a very cold or hot climate, you'll want to enclose and insulate your equipment shed or closet to keep weather and temperature extremes from affecting the equipment. Doing this also keeps the noise level down outside the shop. In milder climates and in locations where outdoor noise isn't a problem, a simple shed-style roof may be all that's needed to house a compressor and dust collector.

7 Benches and Work Areas

"If for no other reason, you need a smooth, level surface to put your coffee cup on while you scratch your head and try to figure out what to build next."

Even if you have all the tools in the world, woodworking is not much fun if you don't have a comfortable place to work and a good surface to work on. Sure, you can always brush the sawdust off your tablesaw and do a stint of handplaning or glue up a drawer, but a cast-iron top is far from being an ideal work surface.

Ideal conditions depend, to a great extent, on the kind of woodworking you do and how and where you like to work. If you like to work outside on sunny days, a portable bench may be just right for you. Portability is essential if you often work at a job site away from your shop, requiring a bench that's easily transportable. If you have a woodworking specialty—such as carving—you may need a work surface with special vises or holding devices.

This chapter discusses work surfaces and workbenches and the advantages of integrating them into the rest of your shop by creating workstations—special areas designed and equipped to put all the tools and supplies you need for a specific job at finger's reach.

Workbenches

Unless you learned woodworking in a part of Asia where craftsmen work on the floor, (see the photo at right), you'll need an elevated workbench in your shop to help you perform such sundry tasks as trimming an edge with a hand-plane, routing an ogee on the edge of a board, and sanding a panel smooth. If for no other reason, you need a smooth, level surface to put your coffee cup on while you scratch your head and try to figure out what to build next.

If your shop is small, you might have room for only one workbench, which might have to fulfill multiple roles: workbench, drafting table, assembly surface, and outfeed table for a tablesaw or planer. In that case, you'd do best to be very thoughtful about the design and features of the bench so that it will fulfill all your needs.

BENCH DESIGN

Woodworkers tend to be as divided and opinionated about the design of their workbenches as they are about the cars

Unlike the Western practice of raising work up to the height of a workbench, craftsmen in Japan traditionally work wood at floor level. Here, master *shoji*-screen maker Toshio Odate saws a joint on the end of a frame member, supporting the work with on small sawhorses.

they drive. It's most important to focus on what's best for your kind of woodworking:

- Do you need a large surface that will handle large panels for cabinetwork that can double as an assembly table?

- What kinds of vises do you need to hold workpieces securely during machining or assembly operations?

- Do you need storage under the bench?

- How important is portability and ease of transport?

"Anatomy of a Traditional Workbench," on p. 145, shows some attributes of a good, basic workbench that you'll want to consider before building or buying one. Your own bench need not have all the features shown; but if you're currently working on a simple bench (such

A long built-in work table or counter built against the wall of a shop not only conserves valuable floor space but also provides plenty of space when working on large projects. By installing shelves above and cabinets below for tools and materials, a long counter becomes a very efficient work area.

With its versatile tail and face vises, a heavy, traditional-style workbench provides a sturdy means of supporting stock for sawing, planing, and more. Here California woodworker Om Anand is using his bench to scrape a panel, smoothing its surface.

as a door stretched across two sawhorses), you might want to consider adding things like a second vise or additional holes for bench dogs and hold-downs to make your bench more versatile.

If your current bench is rickety, the most important modification you may wish to add is bracing. Just a couple of wood struts, run diagonally in both directions and securely screwed at both ends, can prevent racking (back-and-forth motion) and restore the stability that's necessary for comfortable and accurate benchwork.

LOCATING THE BENCH IN THE SHOP

When deciding where to put your workbench, it's important to leave enough clearance around machines, cabinets, and so on to allow enough elbow room in which to work. But if your shop is small or crowded, your bench doesn't necessarily have to occupy valuable space in the middle of the floor.

Workbenches or counters built along walls are practical and, because they can be anchored to the wall, are sturdy (see

Anatomy of a Traditional Workbench

An end stop hold boards and panels for flat planing.

Thick, flat benchtop, heavy enough to take a pounding and daily abuse

Round or square holes in benchtop for bench dogs

Holes allow for the use of hold-downs and accessories.

A face vise on the side of the bench to hold work edge-wise for planing and general work.

A tail vise with a raised pin works with bench dogs to clamp work flat on the bench surface.

A shelf added atop stretchers provides storage under the bench.

Heavy, stable legs and base support the top without rocking. Wide stretchers tenoned into the legs (for crossbracing) prevent the bench from racking.

A board jack has an adjustable height pin to support long boards clamped in the side vise.

the top photo on the facing page). In addition, having shelves or racks on adjacent walls and cabinets or cubbies below the benchtop provides storage and ready access for tools and supplies.

A GENERAL-PURPOSE WORKBENCH

There are many ways to create a good, solid work surface in woodshop. One solution is to buy a heavy, European-made workbench—the woodworking status equivalent of having a Mercedes-Benz® parked in the driveway. It's true that a well-built traditional bench with a large, flat top can provide a terrific place to

perform all kinds of woodworking tasks, from laying out cuts to planing or routing, to finish-sanding (see "Make Sure the Top Is Flat," on p. 154). Unfortunately, such benches are costly to buy and, with the price of maple being what it is, are even expensive to build yourself. What's worse, many beginners end up with carver's-style benches, which have narrow tops and tool trays designed and sized to better fit the needs of a traditional hand-tool user than a modern power-tool woodworker.

A practical and economical alternative to traditional benches is a shop-built general-purpose bench, such as the one

This shop-built general-purpose workbench, made from a 5-ft. maple butcher-block countertop mounted to a pair of recycled lab cabinets, is inexpensive to build and provides a large, solid work surface with storage underneath for portable power tools.

shown in the photo at left. This bench features a large work surface combined with a tail vise and bench dogs, which make it practical for everyday hand-tool and power-tool operations.

I built this bench by mounting a 24-in. by 60-in. maple butcher-block countertop (available at any home-supply center) on a base made from a sturdy cabinet that I recycled from a photo lab that went out of business. The top could be 72 in. long, if needed, and an old kitchen base cabinet or a bathroom vanity would work just as well for the base. A second-hand cabinet with doors or drawers not only makes the bench cheaper to build but also provides ample, enclosed under-bench storage for portable power and hand tools and supplies.

How Tall Should Your Work Surface Be?

SOME SAY THE IDEAL BENCH HEIGHT is the distance between the floor and your hand (arm down, palm horizontal). But, depending on your height, strength, and work style, your bench might end up between 30 in. and 39 in. tall. Taller benches and work tables are great for doing carving or finer hand work without having to bend too far over, whereas lower-height benches are better suited for assembling cabinetry and furniture projects (see the bottom photo on p. 152).

Looking for a novel way to build a versatile bench that's readily adjustable to different heights? Consider the solution devised by California artist Michael Cooper,

who custom-built the 4-ft. by 10-ft. mobile work table shown here. The bench's heavy maple top raises and lowers via hydraulic cylinders powered by an electric pump.

Add your own features The great thing about building your own workbench is that you can add whatever vises, hold-downs, or other features you wish, customizing the bench to best suit your needs and work style. When I built my butcher-block-topped bench, I drilled two rows of bench dog holes and mounted an end vise on the top's left-hand end to make the best use of my shop space (end vises are typically mounted on the right end). I also added a cantilevered leaf, made from plastic laminate–covered medium-density fiberboard (MDF), on one side to serve as a small outfeed table for my tablesaw.

A great addition to any bench is a sliding end stop, shown in the drawing at right. The stop is made from a small strip of hardwood with two diagonal grooves routed through it. Two studded hand knobs with large washers screw into threaded inserts fitted into the end of the bench to hold the stop on. When not in use, the stop stays out of the way, but when you loosen the hand knobs, the stop quickly slides up and into action. Mounting the stop on the right end of the bench makes it great for keeping panels and stock from sliding during belt sanding. And mounted on the left, it will keep stock in place during handplaning operations.

Another feature of my workbench, which isn't visible in the top photo on the facing page, is a clamping groove on the underside of the top's long edge. The groove, shown in "Workbench Hold-Down Assortment," on p. 150, allows a long board to be C-clamped along the edge of the top for planing or mortising.

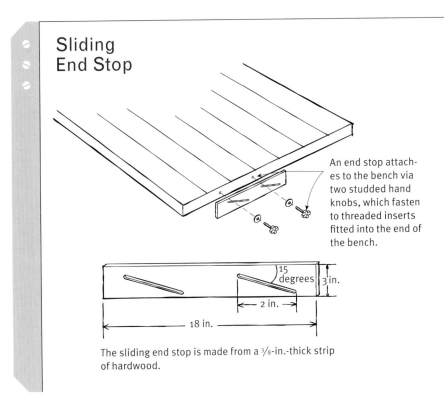

Sliding End Stop

An end stop attaches to the bench via two studded hand knobs, which fasten to threaded inserts fitted into the end of the bench.

15 degrees
3 in.
2 in.
18 in.

The sliding end stop is made from a ³⁄₈-in.-thick strip of hardwood.

Torsion-box top One alternative to fitting a shopmade workbench with a heavy solid-wood top is to build a hollow torsion-box top. The torsion-box design, shown in "Torsion-Box Benchtop," on p. 148, sheathes an inner gridwork between a plywood top and bottom. The result is a light, hollow structure, similar to the wing of an airplane, that is amazingly strong and very inexpensive to build (especially compared with the cost of a solid top made from hardwood).

Chances are you come in contact with torsion boxes everyday, since they are the basis for most hollow-core doors used in homes and offices. A hollow-core

Torsion-Box Benchtop

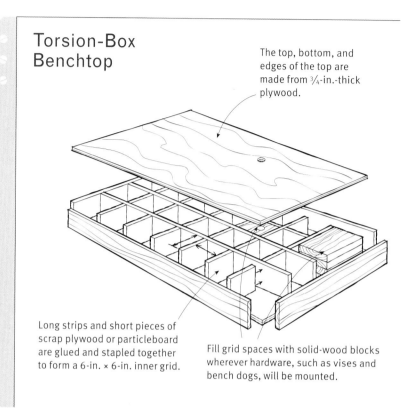

The top, bottom, and edges of the top are made from ¾-in.-thick plywood.

Long strips and short pieces of scrap plywood or particleboard are glued and stapled together to form a 6-in. × 6-in. inner grid.

Fill grid spaces with solid-wood blocks wherever hardware, such as vises and bench dogs, will be mounted.

Shop assistant Stu Sutcliffe uses glue and staples to assemble the ½-in. particleboard inner gridwork for a torsion-box worktable top. Despite its cheap inner construction, the tabletop—once skinned with ¾-in. plywood on both sides—will be light, flat, and incredibly rigid.

door has two extremely thin skins (⅛-in. ply, commonly called doorskin) glued to a wood framework with a paper honeycomb forming the grid that supports and strengthens the door in the middle.

Building a torsion box

1. Start by cutting out the top, bottom, and edge of the frame from good-quality, ¾-in. plywood (you could use MDF, but it would make the top much heavier).

2. Cut long and short members for a 6-in. by 6-in. inner grid to fit snugly into the edge frame. One of the beauties of the torsion-box design is that the inner-grid members need no special joinery to connect them. The only requirement is that each piece have clean, square edges and that it be glued thoroughly to adjacent members. Grid members may be cut from scraps of just about anything— ½-in.-thick plywood or particleboard or #3 pine.

3. Assemble the grid first, then glue on the edge, top, and bottom. It's important to assemble the grid on a flat surface, such as your tablesaw's cast-iron table, to ensure that the completed top will be dead flat. When gluing the short members to the long ones, staples are a handy way of holding the parts together while the adhesive dries.

4. Glue in solid-wood blocks wherever you'll want to mount hardware, such as vises or drill holes for bench dogs (see "Torsion-Box Benchtop" at left). You should do this before gluing and nailing the edge frame onto the gridwork.

5. Finally, glue and nail on the top and bottom "skins," making sure the top stays flat until the glue is dry. For long-term stability, it's best if the top and bottom are of the same thickness material.

VISES AND HOLD-DOWNS

Most woodworking jobs that take place at a bench—sawing, planing, pounding, sanding, chiseling—require the part to be held immobile. This is the job for vises and hold-downs.

Vises A good workbench should have at least one vise firmly mounted to its top. Among traditional-style vises, the most popular are the tail vise and the face vise. As shown in "Anatomy of a Traditional Workbench," on p. 145, a face vise mounts on one long side of the benchtop and allows the clamping of a wide variety of workpieces, horizontally or vertically. A tail vise, which mounts at the end of the bench, is used either to clamp work directly in its jaws or, with the aid of bench dogs, to hold it flat on top of the bench.

Wooden vises are integral to traditional benches, whereas metal "quick-action" vises, such as those made by Record and Veritas® (see the photo above), are favorite additions to many shop-built, general-purpose benches. A metal vise's raisable metal pin allows it to hold work flat on the benchtop, whether it's mounted on the side or at the end of the benchtop (I prefer the latter position because it lends more space for holding long workpieces).

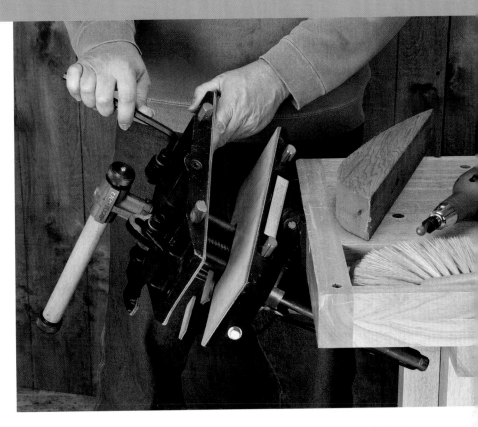

The extremely versatile Veritas Tucker vise has jaws that can rotate, tilt, and even be set out of parallel to hold irregular workpieces.

Bench dogs and hold-downs While a vise might be one of a workbench's key features, the dogs and hold-down devices do the lion's share of the work. Basic dogs that fit into square or round holes in the benchtop and, used in conjunction with a tail vise or metal vise, are everyday workers, holding panels and parts flat. There are even short bench dogs for cramped applications, appropriately called "bench puppies."

Some hold-downs are intended for special duties, such as clamping boards on edge for trimming or tapering and for clamping dowels or spindles for fluting or carving. Although you might not use these every day, they can be a godsend when you require them. You can buy a variety of commercial hold-downs, but there's no end to the clever and versatile designs that you can create for your

149

Workbench Hold-Down Assortment

Deep-Throated Hold-Down

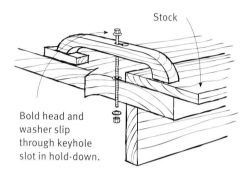

Stock

Bold head and washer slip through keyhole slot in hold-down.

Holdfast Yoke

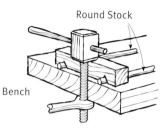

Round Stock

Bench

A long handle is threaded for a wooden screw.

Clamping Groove

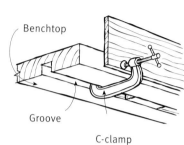

Benchtop

Groove

C-clamp

Side Dogs

Side dogs fit into the dog holes in the benchtop and front jaw of the tail vise.

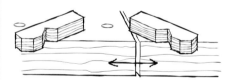

If your bench lacks a true tail vise you can add a jaw face with a dog hole in it to a regular bench vise.

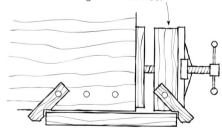

Handscrew Holdfast

Benchtop

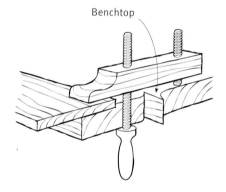

V-Blocks

Angled dowels may be used to secure a V-block on a benchtop.

TOP VIEW

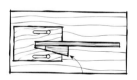

A wedge holds the block tight.

TOP VIEW

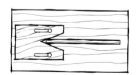

Thin stock is jammed in the mouth of the V-block.

own bench. "Workbench Hold-Down Assortment," on the facing page, shows a variety of useful hold-down designs that you can construct yourself.

Portable Work Surfaces

The biggest asset of a good workbench—its large size and heavy weight—can also be its greatest shortcoming. Dragging a bench around isn't always practical when you need a work surface outdoors or in another area of the shop.

If a small portable bench is what you're after, most hardware and tool stores carry folding portables, such as Black & Decker's® well-known Workmate®. These folding benches typically feature a built-in vise/clamping set-up, making them handy for holding small or medium workpieces or for clamping up small assemblies.

Wheeled workbenches require special attention (see "Mobile machines," on p. 136), unless you're resourceful enough to build something special, like Michael Cooper's amazing electric bench (see the bottom photo on p. 146).

SAWHORSES

In lieu of fancy contraptions, the favorite portable bench of many woodworkers is still the old carpenter's standby: the sawhorse. Sawhorses can be built plain, using 2×4s with simple metal hardware that allow them to fold or disassemble, or they can be made fancy, from hardwood designed with built-in features such as

Instant Outdoor Workbench

Sawhorses can provide the base for a decent portable work surface. Set them outside on a sunny day, throw a piece of sturdy plywood or an old hollow-core door on top and, voilà, you have a perfectly serviceable workbench.

The bigger the top (or length of workpiece), the farther apart you can set the sawhorses to accommodate even a full-size entry door for routing hinge mortises or trimming the bottom edge. And when the job is over, a pair of folding (or knock-down) sawhorses takes up no more room than a couple of folded cardtables.

Portable, versatile, and sturdy—a pair of good sawhorses can elevate and support workpieces in lieu of a worktable or bench. To make his beautiful walnut and maple sawhorses more versatile, Pat Curci added a wedge-locking adjustable-height mechanism.

This simple, adjustable-height horse serves as an outfeed support when cutting large panels on the tablesaw. By adding a roller, the same sawhorse can be used to support long stock run over the jointer or through the planer.

an adjustable top rail or perhaps a tool tray and a shelf.

A pair of sturdy sawhorses can be carried to a job site and set up in moments, and they're handy for getting work up to a height that's easier on your back.

By altering the basic design of a sawhorse and adding an adjustable-height rail or roller assembly, you can create an excellent outfeed support. Such supports are essential when planing or jointing long stock or when cutting large panels on a tablesaw.

Assembly Tables

In addition to a regular workbench that's used for everyday woodworking, it's handy to have a separate table that's just for assembly duties. Such a table should be lower than a standard 36-in.-tall workbench, which is too high for assembly tasks (putting clamps on a 48-in.-high cabinet that's on top of a regular bench means you have to reach up 7 ft.). Having a table with a top 14 in. to 18 in. high, such as the one shown in the bottom photo at left, makes it possible to glue up large carcases; install drawers, doors, and hardware; and handle other assembly and finishing tasks while working at a comfortable height.

A low, 14-in.- to 18-in.-high assembly table is terrific for gluing up large carcases, installing hardware, or doing finish work. In fact, cabinetmaker Cliff Friedlander, here installing hardware in a bank of kitchen drawers, prefers to do most of his cabinet-building work on this large-surfaced, low table.

KNOCKDOWN ASSEMBLY TABLES

Whereas a large, heavily constructed assembly table is a great asset, especially if you routinely put together big carcases and cabinets, such a table can take up an

California master woodworker Art Carpenter's versatile workbench serves multiple functions. With a particleboard cover, it becomes a work table for assembling projects, such as these walnut armchairs. With the cover removed, the thick subtop is riddled with holes used for positioning and clamping bent-wood laminations.

awful lot of free floor space. One solution is to build one that you can set up only when it's needed. Jim Tolpin has a great knockdown design for an assembly table, which is made of three interlocking pieces sawn out of ¾-in. particleboard. It takes only a few moments to put the table together, and it stores flat when it's not in use.

Veteran furniture maker Art Carpenter, whose pieces often incorporate bent-wood parts (see the photo above), has a different kind of assembly table in his shop. His large, solid-lumber-topped table is so full of holes, it looks as if it were made of Swiss cheese.

To save room in his small basement shop, woodworker and author Jim Tolpin built a pair of knockdown worktables, one tall and one low, from inexpensive particleboard. Each table's two-piece base interlocks for easy assembly and takedown.

Make Sure the Top Is Flat

IF YOU WANT TO END UP WITH CABINETS and furniture that are square and sit flat on the floor, the top of your assembly table should be absolutely flat and level. When he built the traditional-style cabinetmaker's workbench shown here, New Jersey cabinetmaker Frank Klausz took great pains to make sure that the bench's top surface was perfectly true and flat. Klausz routinely uses his benchtop to accurately align parts when assembling a project, such as this cherrywood Shaker step stool.

Another strategy for creating a flat-topped work surface is to build a torsion box (see "Torsion-Box Benchtop," on p. 148). A torsion box is strong and light and makes an excellent flat surface that's quite useful as an assembly table. And although it's less durable, a good-quality, hollow-core door can also be used.

Clamping Tabletop

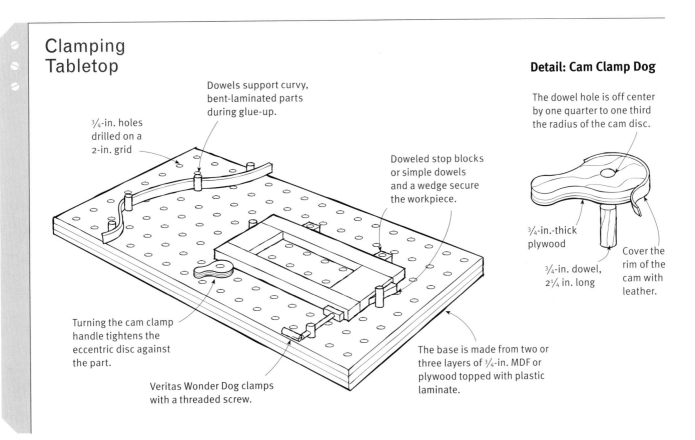

Dowels support curvy, bent-laminated parts during glue-up.

¾-in. holes drilled on a 2-in. grid

Doweled stop blocks or simple dowels and a wedge secure the workpiece.

The dowel hole is off center by one quarter to one third the radius of the cam disc.

¾-in.-thick plywood

¾-in. dowel, 2¼ in. long

Cover the rim of the cam with leather.

Turning the cam clamp handle tightens the eccentric disc against the part.

Veritas Wonder Dog clamps with a threaded screw.

The base is made from two or three layers of ¾-in. MDF or plywood topped with plastic laminate.

The holes are for dowels, which allow Carpenter to stake out the form of a bent-laminated part, such as a chair leg, then clamp the laminations together and hold them in place while the glue dries.

You can build your own version of this clamping tabletop from a couple of sheets of ¾-in. MDF or plywood (see the drawing above). Adding a layer of plastic laminate on top makes glue squeeze-out easy to clean off. By using both round dogs (made from dowels) and clamping devices, such as the Veritas Wonder Dog®, the top can handle other kinds of assembly tasks besides bent lamination,

such as gluing up face frames for cabinets and small carcases and boxes.

Workstations

Although most of us would scream at the thought of doing our woodworking in a factory, we can often better our small shops by borrowing the ideas and technologies used in the big wood industry. The workstation concept was developed on the factory assembly line, where special work areas were designed that had a workbench and all the tools, supplies, and support equipment needed for a worker to do a particular job with great efficiency, such as soldering a circuit board or torquing the head on a V-12 engine.

Even if you don't do (or want to do) repetitive, production woodworking, you can apply the workstation concept to your small shop to make any regular woodshop task—sanding, resawing, plate joining—quicker and easier to do.

SHARPENING STATION

You can create a simple workstation by dedicating a particular spot in the shop or patch of benchtop to a specific duty, such as sharpening. The area should be organized with shelves, drawers, and bins to keep all the things you need within arm's reach. Having a special area for sharpening tools that's equipped with

In the San Diego shop of marquetry and antique-restoration expert Pat Edwards, a small bench is dedicated to sharpening. In this area, all the tools and supplies that he needs to quickly retouch or hone the edge on a chisel, gouge, or plane blade are within easy reach.

a bench grinder, whetstones, strops, and paraphernalia you need to touch up an edge probably means you'll be less likely to put off sharpening (see the photo on the facing page).

SANDING STATION

To make a job like power sanding less messy and odious, a well-planned sanding workstation, such as the one shown in the photo at right, should have all the sanding tools and supplies on hand as well as provide a surface to sand on. In this case, the sanding station also includes downdraft dust collection to make the dirty job of sanding less dusty. For hand-sanding duties, an even simpler workstation, shown in the photo below, holds sanding blocks and supplies ready for use.

Hooked up to a central dust collector, a downdraft sanding table provides a clean work surface in the author's sanding workstation. Built from particleboard and hardwood, the unit features a sandpaper storage drawer and cubbies to keep a bevy of power sanders—all of which are plugged into a power strip on the side of the base—ready for action.

To make hand-sanding quicker and easier, this small wall-mounted workstation keeps a separate sanding block for every grit in use and sanding accessories and supplies are within an easy grab of the workbench where they're used.

With its large table and scores of different-style clamps and gluing supplies organized and readily at hand, Pat Curci's assembly area is a compact, comfortable place to glue and clamp up a project.

POWER-TOOL WORKSTATION

Workstations that use power tools should have an electrical power strip mounted nearby so that tools can be left plugged in for instant use without their cords getting in the way. For pneumatic tools, a compressed-air drop station can be built into the workstation or mounted nearby (see "Compressed-Air Systems," on p. 210). Task lighting, such as a gooseneck or adjustable-arm lamp fitted to the workstation, should be used to supplement general lighting and help you better see what you're doing. Finally, including things like a dedicated pair of goggles, a mask, and any specific wrenches needed to adjust tools or change bits, blades, and sandpaper will save steps and help you avoid frustrating searches.

ASSEMBLY WORKSTATION

Because of all the paraphernalia required, project assembly is another area of woodworking for which the workstation concept is useful. An assembly workstation need not be grand, it may be just a corner of the shop where there's room to stow clamps and gluing supplies within easy reach.

A workstation's bench or table area should be sized and set at a height that suits the task, for instance, a large, low table for furniture and cabinet assembly. An assembly table in the back corner of Pat Curci's rectangular shop has racks on an adjacent wall with a variety of pipe clamps, bar clamps, and handscrews within reach, while spring clamps are located on the supports of an overhead storage rack (see the photo on the facing page). Glue, hardware, and other assembly supplies are kept on shelves behind him.

Portable Work Centers

Like a workstation, a portable work center can organize and provide storage for a collection of tools and supplies as well as serve as a convenient surface on which to work. Wheels allow a portable work center to move around the shop easily or move out of the shop when you want to work outdoors. If built light and compact enough, it can be transported to job sites away from the shop when necessary.

Make Room for Accessories and Supplies

Ideally, a workstation should have built-in racks, drawers, or cubbies for the particular tools needed for the task as well as accessories and supplies germane to the operation. For example, a plate joinery workstation should house not only the slotting machine but also special fences or positioning devices, a supply of different sizes of biscuits (organized in separate bins, of course), and a glue dispenser.

Del Cover covered the top of a simple boxlike wood cabinet with carpeting and fitted locking wheels on the bottom to create a mobile workstation that he uses when assembling and completing projects, such as this handsome mahogany and ebony rocking chair.

The sturdy top with folding, hinged extensions on Jim Tolpin's mobile work center gives him room to spread out the tools and supplies stored inside the four-drawer wheeled chest. The compact cabinet stows away beneath a bench when not in use.

ROLLING CABINET WORK CENTER

A simple, portable work center can be made out of a box or cabinet fitted with locking wheels on the bottom (foot-activated locks are important because they keep the unit from moving around while you're working). Del Cover's rolling box, shown in the photo on p. 159, has a carpet-covered top that provides a low work surface to support a partially or fully assembled project for shaping or trimming, fitting of hardware, or sanding and finishing. The space inside the box provides storage for small power tools and supplies.

Adding a sturdy top with folding extensions to a rolling box, such as on Jim Tolpin's four-drawer work center, shown in the photo above, offers a bigger surface on which to set tools and do light work. With the extensions folded down, the cabinet is compact, easy to roll around a crowded shop, and stows neatly away beneath a bench or worktable.

PORTABLE MACHINE WORK CENTER

Small machines such as a benchtop tablesaw, jointer, or shaper can be integrated directly into a portable work center. Woodworker and teacher Carol Reed used this idea when she built a mobile work center around her 10-in. tablesaw (see the bottom photo on p. 162).

In addition to fold-down outfeed and side tables, Reed's creation includes a small workbench top, complete with vise, router table, storage drawers for router bits, cubbies for blades and saw accessories, and bin for tablesaw-dust collection. The wheeled unit is compact enough for Reed to load into the back of a pickup truck, so she can take her woodworking on the road.

EQUIPMENT CARTS

An extension of the concept of portable work centers, an equipment cart packs heavy or cumbersome woodshop equipment, such as an HVLP spray rig, compressor or vacuum pump, and accessories, into a compact, mobile unit. This allows you to quickly move equipment from a closet or corner storage area to the workbench when it's needed. With a couple of store-bought wheels and a little plywood and assorted hardware, you can build your own cart from scratch, or you can

Ingenious Workstations in a Luthier's Shop

NOT SURPRISINGLY, A GOOD WORKSTATION is invaluable for doing any kind of repetitive work, such as producing a line of craft items or building limited-production furniture. Luthiers, who build custom guitars and other stringed instruments, often use workstations for specific tasks, such as gluing up and trimming the body or shaping the neck because it makes operations more accurate and easier to perform.

Guitarmaker Jeff Traugott's shop, shown below, has a series of workstations set up along his benchtop. Special clamping fixtures, sanding and assembly jigs, and more can be attached or removed from the bench as needed. They're set in order along the bench as necessary, forming a sort of mini-assembly line in the production of the instrument.

Traugott's bench room also includes a very simple station: a freestanding holding fixture, which consists of a vise mounted on a heavy steel base. The vise holds a clamping fixture that secures a guitar top firmly yet allows it to be rotated and tilted to a comfortable working position when Traugott does the tedious job of shaving the braces on the underside of a guitar top.

Another kind of luthier's workstation that's very useful for clamping flat assemblies and small projects is the instrument-maker's "go bar deck." Commonly used to glue braces to the top and back of a guitar, the deck employs a flat surface positioned parallel to a worktable (see the photo above). Flexible wood sticks or fiberglass bars are flexed to a gentle bend and then inserted between the deck and the parts to be glued together, thus applying the clamping pressure needed to hold parts in place.

Resourceful woodworker and teacher Carol Reed used a hospital surplus I.V. cart as a mobile base for her vacuum clamping and veneering system, allowing her to easily wheel the heavy equipment wherever she wants to use it.

recycle an old hand truck, wagon, or library cart into a functional portable unit. By mounting wiring, switches, plumbing fixtures, piping, and hose reels directly to the cart, even an elaborate system can be easy to hook up and use.

For example, take a look at Carol Reed's vacuum setup shown in the photo at left, which is made from a hospital surplus I.V. cart (the kind used to suspend bags of blood plasma and saline). She transformed it into a mobile cart by mounting the pumping system she uses for vacuum clamping and veneering to the cart's frame.

Built around a 10-in. tablesaw, this compact, mobile workstation features fold-down outfeed tables; a small workbench top; a router table; and storage drawers for router bits, sawblades, and accessories.

Storing Tools, Lumber, and Supplies

"Having a home for each tool helps protect them from accidents . . . keeping sawteeth, plane blades, and chisels from being nicked and precision tools from getting knocked about."

Within that big container full of stuff that we call a shop, we need lots of little containers to keep our things organized, protected, and ready for use. Boxes, chests, cubbies, cabinets, shelves, bins, trays, racks, and totes all provide specific places to store tools as well as the multitude of accessories, supplies, and junk that seem to be needed for even the most basic of woodworking pursuits.

Temperature- and moisture-sensitive materials, such as glues, finishes, and sandpaper, require even more attention when stored if they are to remain usable.

Then there's the wood itself and all the forms it comes in, from green timbers to kiln-dried boards to veneers to dowels to turning blanks to sheet goods. Unless you like to scrounge through an unruly woodpile every time you need a board, it's a challenge to find a way to keep these materials organized yet accessible. And, finally, there's the waste of daily woodworking: scraps that are too big to throw out but too small to store with regular lumber not to mention the full-size sheetgoods.

Unless you like working in a cluttered, disorganized space, storage problems take some ingenuity to remedy. Not only do you have to come up with containers, racks, and shelves but you also have to find a place to put them where they'll be accessible but out of the way. For most small-shop craftsmen, this is a challenge akin to untying the Gordian knot. Well-organized, easy-to-access storage in a confined space requires lots of different strategies to suit the nature of the items stored and the space they're stored in. And that's just what I explore in this chapter: solutions for all your woodshop storage needs, starting with containers to keep your tools in.

Toolboxes and Chests

Even the most amped-up power-tool-equipped woodshop has some complement of basic hand tools, layout devices, and accessories that need a place to call home. A well-designed box or chest provides racks, compartments,

Swing the handle down and open the barrel lid on Pat Curci's personalized cherry and maple toolbox, and you'll find ample space for large handplanes, geared drills, and other bulky tools. A pair of long drawers in the lower section house chisels and other long-handled tools.

trays, drawers, and cubbies that keep tools organized and handy so you can find just the tool you need when you need it (if you're pretty good about putting your tools back where they belong). Having a home for each tool helps protect them from accidents too, keeping sawteeth, plane blades, and chisels from being nicked and precision tools from getting knocked about. A box or chest with a tight-fitting lid or doors will keep dust out, can help in reducing rust (see "Preventing Rust," on p. 98) and can even protect tools from flying droplets of finish if you apply varnish with excess zeal.

While you can buy a very serviceable and practical toolbox to house a few tools or even your whole collection, building your own box or chest is something that every woodworker should do once in his or her life. Plain or fancy, the box you build will likely be a major source of pride. A good-looking wall-mounted chest is often the centerpiece of a shop, something to be seen and admired by all who pay a visit. I recommend you check out *The Toolbox Book* by Jim Tolpin (The Taunton Press) for inspiration.

PORTABLE TOOLBOXES

The simplest home you can build for tools is a portable tote, box, or lidded chest. These keep your tools secure and at hand wherever you go, whether you're working in a corner of the shop away from your usual workbench or at a job site across the state. Small, open-topped totes or boxes are great for keeping a group of tools together that

You can create a handy and portable tool kit by putting related small tools and supplies in a plastic tote. This kit contains a cordless screwdriver and other tools and supplies used in mounting hardware.

Can You Lift Your Toolbox?

WHEN DESIGNING A PORTABLE TOOLBOX OF YOUR OWN, consider that the more tools it will house, the less portable it will be. A large box can contain an awful lot of tools (for centuries, journeymen carpenters and joiners have been building tool chests that held all their hand tools). However, you might need a forklift to move it. Experiment first by putting all the tools you've selected into a sturdy cardboard box and try lifting it and moving it around before you begin building your new mega-chest.

are used for a specific task, such as for veneering, precision layout, or machine maintenance. Most cabinetmakers who work on site have their own "installation" toolboxes that contain all the small hand and power tools and spare components that might be needed when setting up a kitchen's worth of cabinets or a library full of bookcases.

Use Strong Hinges for Doors

I f you plan to load the doors of your cabinet with heavy tools, be sure to use heavy strap hinges or full-length piano hinges.

LARGE TOOL CABINETS AND CHESTS

In most shops, there is at least one area that serves as the spot where most work with hand and portable power tools is done. Mounted near a workbench, a large tool cabinet or drawered chest provides storage for most of the implements you use every day and keeps them at hand. The biggest advantage of such a cabinet or chest is that it's big enough to hold items that won't fit into smaller boxes—things like socket slicks and larger portable power tools and their accessories (which sometimes take up as much room as the tools themselves).

A cabinet with lockable doors that's too big to move can protect your tools from thievery. Del Cover's clam-shell-style cabinet, shown in the photo on the facing page, has lockable doors that keep his tools from taking any unexpected trips to the local pawn shop when he's away from the shop.

Cabinet chests Whether free-standing or mounted to a wall, tool cabinets take up very little floor space. And unlike traditional-style tool chests with trays that must be lifted out to get to tools in compartments underneath, a large tool cabinet with boxlike doors has lots of

Special racks, drawers, and divided compartments give each tool in Jim Tolpin's small, wall-hung cabinet a space of its own, so he can tell at a glance if anything is missing. A pull-out tray at the bottom provides a handy shelf when removing small tools or parts from the cabinet.

To house and protect his extensive collection of new and vintage chisels, Pat Edwards built a large wall chest with a pair of shallow, full-size doors that swing open to reveal the entire contents of the chest.

surface area. This allows you to find, remove, and replace tools without hunting
for them. Depending on their sizes and
shapes, tools can be hung on hooks or
racks or housed in divided compartments,
drawers, shallow trays, or open cubbies.

A nice, extra feature for any tool cabinet is a simple, flat pull-out tray, as in Jim
Tolpin's small, wall-hung cabinet, shown
in the left photo on the facing page. The
tray provides a convenient place to temporarily park a tool (think of it as an "on-
deck" area for tools that are about to go
to bat), dump a handful of hardware, or
set a coffee cup.

While many tall tool cabinets have a
clamshell design with a single box door,
like Tolpin's, there are other possibilities. Making two narrower-hinged doors,
like on Del Cover's cabinet (shown in
the photo at right), covers less adjacent
wall space and doesn't stick out as far
when partially open. Alternatively, if you
have a lot of tools to house that don't
have much depth, such as layout tools,
handsaws, and chisels, you might want to
incorporate double fold-out doors, such
as the ones featured on Pat Edwards's
carving-chisel cabinet shown in the right
photo on the facing page.

The pair of shallow doors on this
cabinet are hinged so that one must be
swung most of the way open before the
other one can be opened (see "Twin-
Door Chisel Cabinet," p. 168).

Dresser-style chests Another approach to housing tools is to build a
dresser-style chest with drawers and

Del Cover's floor-to-ceiling tool
cabinet provides storage for
virtually his entire collection of
hand and portable power tools.
The sturdy clamshell cabinet
keeps his tools organized,
readily accessible, and, by
locking the doors when he
leaves the shop, safe.

pull-outs (see the photo on p. 168).
Similar tools and accessories can be
kept in the same drawer, which is a good
scheme for keeping things organized
yet readily accessible. You can store long
tools such as handsaws, adzes, and socket
slicks in a pull-out, which is essentially
a tall drawer that's minus one side to
allow for side loading and access. Unlike

A multidrawered, dresser-style tool chest allows you to keep like tools or supplies organized by putting them in the same drawer. A tall, pull-out drawer that's open on one side has plenty of room for handsaws, socket slicks, and other long tools.

a tool cabinet, which remains open during work, the drawers of a dresser-style chest are opened only when tools are taken out or replaced, so tools aren't showered with dust and will stay cleaner (at least in theory).

An alternative to building this kind of chest yourself is simply to use an existing bedroom dresser, kitchen drawer bank, or other chest of drawers. Make sure to check the integrity of the drawers before you load one up with tools, as you'll likely want to beef up their typically all-too-thin bottoms or replace them with sturdier, thicker plywood.

Lining the insides of the drawers keeps loose tools from rattling around and bumping into one another (just be sure not to use materials that encourage rust; (see "Preventing Rust," on p. 98). Adding thin plywood dividers can help further organize drawers as well as protect delicate tools and instruments. Labeling drawers with their contents will prevent excessive rummaging when trying to find the tool you need.

Twin-Door Chisel Cabinet

Backs are rabbeted into a wall-mounted cabinet, as well as to both doors, for strength and to prevent the doors from racking under load.

This side of the wall cabinet is more than twice as deep as the other side to provide clearance for the right-opening door.

Heavy-duty piano hinges run the full length of both doors to carry weight of the tools without sagging.

RACKS

Tools aren't very useful if you can't grab them when you need them. If you don't mind getting a little dust on your tools, you can make it much easier to get your hands on them in a hurry by putting them in a rack. A tool rack gives every tool a place to call home without enclosing it inside a box. Racks, trays, and specially built tool holders can help any job go more quickly and efficiently, and they help cut down on time spent looking for tools by making it harder to misplace them. (Shelves also provide good open storage for some tools; see the photo on p. 182).

It's easy to make a simple rack; simply drive a few nails into a wall to hang up a hammer or saw. And then there's good old pegboard, with all those little holes and a wide variety of little metal hooks and hangers. Judging from photographs of old shops, I think that before about 1960, there must have been a pegboard tool rack in every woodworking shop in America.

With a little more effort than it takes to drive a few nails or hang a sheet of pegboard, you can create a much nicer wall rack for your tools, which will display them with enough flair to make them inspirational.

Specialty racks Small racks built to hold specific tools can be mounted wherever

As much a wall sculpture as a means of organizing tools, racks and hangers support tools and keep them on display, ready for use.

A traditional shop organizer, a pegboard nailed to the wall and fitted with all manner of hooks, loops, and racks is a flexible system for storing tools large and small. Holes bored directly into a post next to the drill press in this shop store dozens of drill and auger bits.

they are needed. This can make shop life a lot easier when performing specific tasks such as lathe turning, for which a number of different tools (bowl gouges, skews, parting tools) are used in succession; yet individual tools need to be kept safely stowed when not in use to prevent damage to sharp edges—or to human flesh. Mounting a tool rack directly next to the lathe puts the tools only an arm's length away when you need them.

Most portable power tools are too big to be hung from a rack (and they don't like to be hung by their tail-like cords). Housing them in open pigeonhole-style cubbies mounted above or below a bench or workstation, keeps them ready for immediate use.

If you're really into organizing your tools, you'll enjoy building racks for specific groups of tools and their accessories. For example, the rack shown in the top left the photo on the facing page has customized holders for both corded and cordless drills. The rack also has storage for drills, driver bits, extra batteries, and accessories. The battery chargers mounted to the wall and the screw storage bins mounted above the rack effectively create a fastener workstation.

Mounted directly to the lathe near the headstock, this small woodturning-tool rack has holes to keep tools from bumping against one another and to keep their razor-honed edges pointing safely downward.

Not unlike pigeonholes in a writing desk, cubbies large enough for portable power tools keep them stored and ready above the benchtop where they'll be used. Keeping power tools in separate compartments prevents their cords from tangling together.

Specially built racks are not only good for regular hand and power tools but can also provide a handy way of organizing and storing supplies and other shop necessities, such as clamps and spray-finishing guns. For example, a custom tray will keep all of your sanding blocks and sandpaper ready to go and it will prevent different grits from getting mixed up.

Clamp racks Glue-up can be an especially stressful time, particularly when things aren't going well and you find yourself scrambling for extra clamps only moments before the glue sets. Building wall or floor racks for pipe, bar, and C-clamps will keep them handy and will get them out of your way when they're not needed. If you do your assembly and glue-up in different areas of the shop,

A shopmade electric drill rack, with separate slots for corded and battery-powered drills, keeps the tools and their accessories handy. Colored bins above the rack hold different-size screws—a size for practically every occasion.

A simple wood tray keeps sanding blocks and various grits of sandpaper from getting mixed up as well as provides an easy way to move all these hand-sanding supplies to wherever they're needed in the shop.

Magnetic Bar Strips

ANOTHER KIND OF RACK that can be used to store chisels, knives, and any tool that has a metal shaft or body is a magnetic bar strip. This is the same kind that you might already use to keep knives safely stowed near your kitchen counter.

Making any clamp you're likely to need easily available when assembling a big cabinet or piece of furniture helps prevent glue-up from being a stressful time. This sturdy, wheeled clamp rack, welded up from tubular steel, can handle a lumberjack-size stack of steel clamps, allowing them to be rolled across the shop with ease.

This pull-out-style wheeled clamp rack stores long, heavy bar and pipe clamps out of the way when they're not in use. A pair of full-extension drawer glides mounted to the top of the rack control travel in and out of the rack's narrow storage space.

depending on the size of the project, a rolling clamp rack allows you to move a whole stack of weighty steel clamps around to where you need them.

In a small or crowded shop, getting bulky clamps out of the way when they're not in use is a good idea. You can fit a lot of clamps into a fairly small space by hanging them from a pull-out rack, such as the one shown in the bottom photo at left. The tall rack frame has wheels on the bottom to handle the weight of long pipe or bar clamps as well as shelves to store small power tools and supplies. A pair of heavy-duty, full-extension drawer glides fitted at the top guide the rack in and out of the narrow space it occupies.

Stock Storage

Depending on what kind of woodworking projects you build, materials you use may include lumber (rough or planed), plywood and other sheetgoods, veneer, and maybe even branches, twigs, burls, and whole logs. Here are some suggestions for storing wood and composite materials so they remain in good condition and ready for use.

STORING LUMBER

Unlike other stored equipment or supplies, lumber doesn't come in absolute sizes. You might buy narrow, long boards of one species today and wide, short planks of another wood next month. Further, as wood is cut up for projects, large boards leave the rack and end up as smaller pieces, which, unless they're scrap, will require storage as well. This is also true with sheetgoods, such as plywood and medium-density fiberboard (MDF). Therefore, any shop's lumber storage should be designed to accommodate not only full-size stock in a variety of lengths and widths but also the smaller pieces and scraps.

VERTICAL STORAGE

If your ceiling is high enough, one of the easiest ways to store boards and cutoffs of various lengths is to store them vertically. Because vertical-storage bays don't have to support the weight of the lumber, they are easy to build, don't occupy too much space, and make it relatively easy to rummage through 100 bd. ft. of walnut to find a stick with just the right color or figure without having to restack the pile. Vertical racks are also terrific for storing moldings and narrow strips of wood, as well as metal stock, pipe and long clamps. You can even use one of the racks' divider struts to hang a ladder or push broom.

From a construction standpoint, a vertical-storage rack couldn't be simpler. You need only a wall or other vertical surface to lean lumber against and enough horizontal struts to keep the lumber from falling over. The struts can be 2×4s or lengths of pipe fastened to a frame or directly to the wall. If your rack must hold cutoffs of various lengths, add enough struts to your rack to keep them in order (see "Vertical Lumber Rack" on p. 174).

If your shop ceiling is high enough to allow it, storing lumber and cutoffs vertically can be very space efficient and allow you to root through your stash without having to stack and unstack a big pile.

A wall-mounted vertical lumber rack is a handy place to securely store narrow strips and moldings as well as pipe clamps, ladders, and more.

Vertical Lumber Rack

Wall-mounted standard with short removable struts keeps lumber in order.

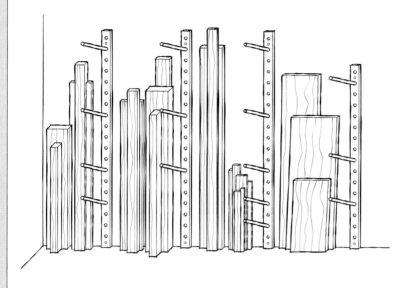

HORIZONTAL STORAGE

Unfortunately, unless you restrict your lumber purchases to short boards (or don't mind cutting long boards in half before they come inside the shop), most small shops don't have adequate ceiling height for vertical racks. Although not as handy as vertical racks, horizontal-storage racks provide the most practical option for the majority of woodworkers who have "ceiling-challenged" shops.

Design-wise, there is no limit to the types and kinds of lumber storage racks you can build or buy. Wall-mounted racks are most popular because they save precious floor space, although freestanding racks offer better access to lumber, if you have the room for them.

Wall-mounted lumber racks can be made using store-bought metal-shelf standards, or you can make your own brackets from just about any sturdy material: construction lumber, plywood, heavy dowels, or pipe. See "Three Shopmade Lumber Rack Designs" on the facing page for some design ideas.

In addition to being strong enough to hold heavy lumber, a good wall rack should have brackets placed at intervals close enough together to support long boards and heavy stock without sagging. An interval of 2 ft. to 3 ft. is about right for most racks. Bolting brackets directly to wall studs is convenient, although it may limit your choice of spacing. To mount brackets between studs, sheath the wall with ¾-in. plywood, then screw the brackets to it.

A commercially made rack with height-adjustable brackets, such as Lee Valley's lumber storage system, offers great flexibility because you can change the number and size of brackets to suit your current lumber storage needs.

The most important thing to remember when mounting any lumber rack to a wall is that the longer the bracket arms are, the greater the leverage they can exert on the standards mounted to the wall. Hence be very conservative when installing the standards. Attach them directly to wall studs with long, thick lag bolts.

If the integrity of the wall is in question, you might want to strengthen the connection of each stud at the floor and top plate with a metal tee strap or reinforcing plate. Alternatively, you could add new studs and brackets between existing ones so that the load is carried by more brackets and standards. For a concrete or brick wall, attach standards with heavy expanding bolts, such as Hilti® bolts, and install each fastener carefully, making sure it is fully seated in the wall and that the nut that secures the standard is not overtightened.

LOCATING LUMBER STORAGE

A popular place to put a lumber rack in an average woodshop is above a

With an adjustable lumber rack mounted to the wall, such as this sturdily made Lee Valley rack system, you can add or remove supports to create just the number of storage levels you need to accommodate the size of your lumber supply.

Three Shopmade Lumber Rack Designs

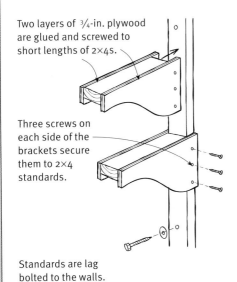

Two layers of ¾-in. plywood are glued and screwed to short lengths of 2×4s.

Three screws on each side of the brackets secure them to 2×4 standards.

Standards are lag bolted to the walls.

Brackets can be relocated on the standards as necessary.

Brackets are made from two layers of ¾-in. plywood sandwiched together or cut from 2×6 lumber.

Lag bolts mount brackets to 2×4 wall studs of unpaneled walls.

Brackets are cut lengths or ¾-in. pipe.

Dadoes are cut into the faces of a pair of 2×6s to make the rack standards.

Pocket holes bored into the edge of an assembled 2×6 sandwich allow the standards to be mounted to the wall with lag bolts.

radial-arm saw or cutoff saw bench. This allows you to pull long boards off the rack as they are needed and cut them to length before they are ripped and machined into parts. (See also "Accommodating Work Flow," on p. 130.)

When planning your lumber storage, you might also want to designate separate areas for short-term and long-term lumber storage. Short-term storage is for

wood that will soon be used for a project, so it should provide ready access and make it easy to pull boards from the stack as they are needed. Long-term storage is for wood that's stashed away for "someday." These are the boards and planks you buy because, even though you didn't have a particular need for that 6/4 flame-grained bubinga, it was just too beautiful to pass up (most woodworkers I know are tree-huggers at heart). You might even want to consider displaying these boards instead of hiding them away because chances are you'll never develop the nerve to actually cut up such treasures, so you might as well enjoy seeing them.

Green lumber If you're a woodturner, chair bodger, rustic furniture maker, or just like to save money by cutting and drying your own lumber, you can save space inside your shop by storing green lumber outside. Rough burls, logs and

Mounting a lumber rack directly above a cutoff saw bench lets you pull boards off and cut them to length as they're needed. This unique rack has supports that attach directly to the shop's frame members with strong mortise-and-tenon joinery.

English woodworker Alec McCurdy stickered and dried the stash of locally cut lumber he used for building cabinets and musical instruments under an open, metal-roofed shed next to his small country shop.

branches, and freshly cut roughsawn lumber can be stacked outdoors to dry in most climates. They need to be stacked off the ground and stickered properly for good air circulation. They should also be covered to keep the rain off and to prevent direct sunlight from causing cracks and checks. While a sturdy tarp can provide adequate coverage, building a small lean-to-style shed near or beside your shop will provide a safe place to store green lumber.

VENEER STORAGE

Because it is thin and fragile, sliced or sawn wood veneers need to be stored differently from regular lumber. Veneer sheets (called leaves) and flitches (stacks of consecutively cut leaves) need to be completely supported to prevent them from curling and buckling. One strategy is to stack all of your veneers on a piece of plywood that's slightly longer and wider than the largest leaf. Set another piece of plywood atop the stack and flatten the entire bundle using twine or tape. Store your veneer "sandwich" on a horizontal rack, shelf, or other cool, dry place—veneers are subject to cracking and splitting if exposed to excessive heat or dryness. Marquetry expert Pat Edwards created a cool, dry storage space next to his shop in which he keeps his stock of expensive and rare veneers (see the bottom photo at right). Edward's home-made "veneer cave" is built from stacks of concrete blocks, with the veneer flitches set atop a layer of clean, dry sand.

Protect expensive veneers from damage during storage by sandwiching them between a pair of plywood panels slightly larger than the veneer leaves.

Built from dry-stacked concrete blocks filled with sand, Pat Edwards's 16-ft.-long "veneer cave" provides safe storage for the dozens of flitches of rare and expensive veneers it contains (security is provided by shop dog, Nikki).

A Portable Lumber Scrap Bin

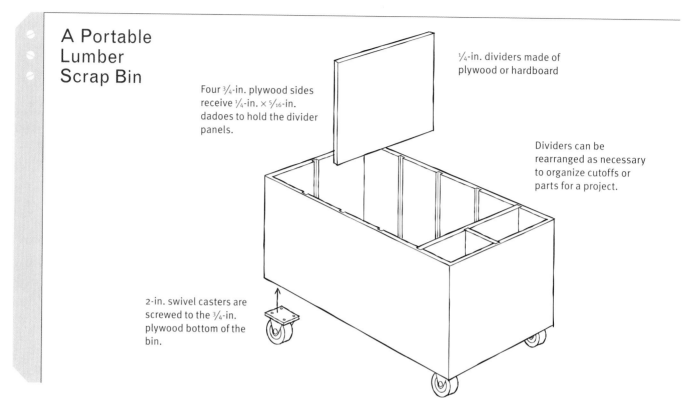

Four ¾-in. plywood sides receive ¼-in. × ⁵⁄₁₆-in. dadoes to hold the divider panels.

¼-in. dividers made of plywood or hardboard

Dividers can be rearranged as necessary to organize cutoffs or parts for a project.

2-in. swivel casters are screwed to the ¾-in. plywood bottom of the bin.

Nailing narrow strips perpendicularly on the undersides of ceiling joists provides an ideal location to stash spindles, moldings, and long, narrow scraps in a spot where they're accessible yet out of the way.

STORING CUTOFFS AND SCRAPS

Truly one of the most difficult storage problems in most shops is what to do with wood pieces that fall into the "too small for most parts but too big to get rid of" size range. As wood gets more and more expensive to buy, woodworkers are compelled to save little offcuts and trimmings, which are difficult to store in a way that keeps them organized and neat and allows you to find just the right piece when you want it.

Portable scrap bin Bins and cubbies for cutoffs can be built into any available nook or cranny in the shop: under counters and benches, in corners and closets, and in attics and lofts. If you want to

keep your scraps organized yet portable, consider building a mobile container, such as the one shown in "A Portable Lumber Scrap Bin," above. Basically an open-topped plywood box with dividers inside and wheels on the bottom, this mobile bin can be wheeled out of the way or rolled right up to a bench when you need to rummage through bits and pieces to find something that's just right for your project. Some woodworkers even use such bins for storing furniture or cabinet parts. For example, a large bin could hold all the plywood panels and face-frame members for a run of kitchen cabinets, keeping them organized and protected while they are machined in preparation for assembly and finishing.

Use ceiling space In a small and crowded woodshop where space is at a premium, the spaces between ceiling joists can provide valuable storage space for thin cutoffs as well as for dowels and moldings. Cross supports made from 1×2s or narrow strips of plywood can be nailed or, even better, screwed across the undersides of the joists at regular intervals. Space them close together for short scraps and stored furniture parts and farther apart for long strips and sticks.

STORING SHEETGOODS

Plywood sheets can be a real bear to wrestle around the shop, and even storing them can present a big problem. Delicate edges and corners are susceptible to dings, and thin face veneers scratch or tear easily. A sturdy rack can keep plywood and other sheetgoods—particleboard, MDF, Masonite®, Melamine®,—organized and protected from damage. Such a rack, made from scrap sheetgoods or construction lumber, can be a freestanding structure against a wall or built into a corner or closet space in the shop. Adding dividers on one side of the rack creates smaller compartments that keep partial sheets and cutoffs organized and easy to find when they're needed.

General Storage

How do you deal with all the little extras—hardware, fasteners, and sundry supplies and accouterments—that it takes to do woodworking? You can just stuff it all into a cardboard box or pile it up in some corner of the floor and try

A good plywood rack keeps valuable sheetgoods flat and protected from accidental damage to delicate face veneers and corners. Divided compartments provide a place to put usable-size scraps and cutoffs, and a Bungee cord keeps tall, narrow pieces from falling out.

Sheetgoods Safety

It can be dangerous to have a sheet of plywood or MDF fall out of a rack or come flipping out of a bin when you don't expect it. Heavy-duty Bungee® cords or chains hooked into screw eyes driven into the edge of a rack keep large, narrow panels from accidentally toppling.

to live with it—a system that seems to be employed in many shops I've visited. But you can save yourself from pulling out your hair every time you need to find a drawer pull or washer-head screw by taking the time to carefully store all your shop supplies. But before stashing stuff away, it's a great idea to develop a thoughtful organization strategy for all of your shop stuff.

GETTING ORGANIZED

How do you know how much storage space you need and what kind of containers to buy or build? You can start by doing an inventory of all your shop supplies, accessories, and assorted flotsam and jetsam (doing just one area of the shop at a time is less intimidating than trying to tackle the whole mess at once). Next, consider how often you use the various types of items, and prioritize

them on a scale of your own choosing from "most often used" to "probably should have been thrown out years ago."

Here's a three-tier approach that works for me.

1. The items that are most often needed should be kept the most accessible, located close to where you most often need them, such as the workbench, assembly area, or finishing room.

2. The next category are items I call "used infrequently, but when I need them, I want them now." This might include jigs, special tools for adjusting a machine, or spare furniture parts. When designating storage for stuff in this category, location is everything. It takes much less time to grab something that's stowed under a nearby counter than it does to climb into the attic.

Tubes for Thin Parts

TUBES ARE A GOOD STORAGE DEVICE for narrow, thin wood scraps and parts as well as dowels. Sturdy cardboard tubes, readily available from carpet stores (they're typically sticking out of Dumpsters® behind the stores), can provide a neat place to keep dowels, short lengths of moldings, and other thin scraps. Tubes can be nailed to a wall individually or glued together to form a freestanding rack. All kinds of cylindrical containers can be pressed into service as storage: large tins and dry goods canisters, plastic trash cans, even old coil springs and World War II brass shell casings.

3. Finally, there's the stuff that you use infrequently enough to put in boxes or containers, then secret in the shed, attic, or rented storage unit, where they're far less convenient to get to.

You can free up a major amount of shop space by "downgrading" items you have hanging around the shop but aren't using frequently. Just remember that putting things into boxes that aren't well labeled is pretty much like throwing them away. If you can't remember where something is, you might as well not have it at all. Therefore, if you bother saving and storing something, label the box clearly or use clear-plastic boxes that allow you to quickly survey their contents.

Getting shop clutter out of your way is a wonderful feeling. But before you haul all those boxes of odds and ends into the attic, remember that what goes up doesn't always come down. If you have pack-rat tendencies, try to make friends with your trash can. Decide which items should be thrown out rather than stored (do you really need that box of ½-in. by ¾ -in. plywood squares?), or you'll quickly fill up your storage space with junk.

OPEN SHELVES

Probably the quickest and least expensive way to add useful storage in your shop is to put up a set of shelves. Whether they are held by brackets attached directly to the wall, are part of an adjustable system, or are built into a freestanding unit (like

If your shop has an attic or loft, you can keep the main shop space less cluttered by moving infrequently used items upstairs. In this small shop loft, plastic buckets and a wire rack are used to keep wood scraps and chair parts orderly.

ORGANIZE STORAGE TO BE KIND TO YOUR BACK

HEIGHT OF SHELF OR CABINET ABOVE THE FLOOR	RECOMMENDED MAXIMUM WEIGHT OF BOX OR STORED ITEM AT THE HEIGHT
64 in.–74 in.	10 lb.
45 in.–64 in.	25 lb.
29 in.–45 in.	50 lb.
10 in.–29 in.	25 lb.
6 in.–15 in.	15 lb.

The Ergonomics of Shop Storage

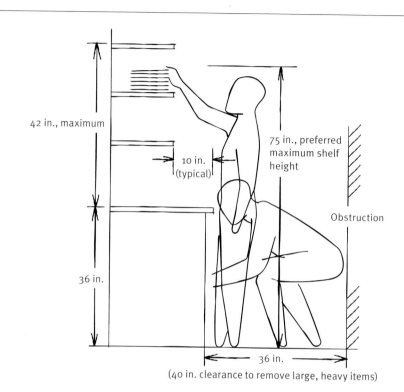

42 in., maximum

10 in. (typical)

75 in., preferred maximum shelf height

Obstruction

36 in.

36 in.
(40 in. clearance to remove large, heavy items)

See "Organize Storage to Be Kind to Your Back," on p. 181, for more information.

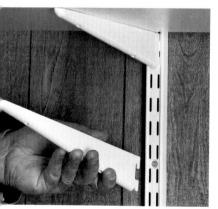

Adjustable workshop shelving systems with steel components and four locking lobes per standard can handle the weight of workshop tools and heavy supplies.

a bookcase), shelves take up little space for the amount of storage surface they provide. While open shelves do collect dust, they give you free access to whatever they hold, whether glue bottles or handplanes.

Building shelves If you build your own bookcase-style shelf unit, err toward the side of overbuilding it. Dado the sides for shelves instead of just nailing or screwing them together, or use dowels or plate joinery biscuits (the latter is best for plywood construction). Add at least a ¼-in. plywood back to help the unit resist racking. You'll be thankful if you ever decide to use the shelf unit you originally built to hold sandpaper and dowels for storing 1,000 lb. of exotic

wood scraps along with your treasured collection of old, metal-plane parts.

COMMERCIAL SHELVING

The aisles of a home-supply store offer boundless opportunities for strong, yet simple shelving. Adjustable wall systems offer flexible shelf spacing, which can be changed to suit future storage needs. Before selecting a system (standards and brackets come in aluminum, steel, or wood), check how much weight it's rated to handle, then use the most secure means possible to attach it to the wall. For shelves that must bear heavy loads, I strongly recommend heavy-duty steel wall shelf systems that feature standards that connect with each shelf bracket via four interlocking lobes—much sturdier than the aluminum, two-lobe bracket and standard systems typically used for household shelving (see the photo on the facing page).

If you buy a commercially made freestanding shelf unit, check its rated weight capacity before you load it with heavy stuff. Inexpensive units made of Melamine or vinyl-covered particleboard are all too easy to overload.

It's generally worthwhile to spend a few more bucks to buy a sturdy, well-designed unit rather than the cheapest variety-store bargain because the more costly unit will have a higher weight capacity and will resist abuse. Just be sure to assemble such shelves with all the supplied screws and hardware.

If you live in an earthquake zone, one thing to remember about shelves is that they don't do a particularly good job at keeping stuff from tumbling down during a ground swell. This might make you think twice before putting all your old cast-iron parts on high shelves directly above the workbench where you stand every day. Adding a lip to the front edge of shelves can help keep things from falling (see the bottom photo at right). Also, be sure to tether freestanding shelf units to the wall with hooks and cable to keep them from toppling during a shaker.

STORAGE CABINETS

If you want to keep tools and supplies close to where the action is but want to keep them clean and protected, cabinets with closable doors and drawers are the way to go. While a coating of dust and chips is only a nuisance for most tools

You can cram a lot of stuff—supplies, tools, wood scraps, and parts—onto the shelves of a metal storage rack. These chair and furniture parts are a portion of the inventory that furniture maker Sam Maloof keeps ready to use for commissioned work.

If your shop is in earthquake country (or directly above a subway tunnel), nailing a small wood strip near the front edges of shelves on which you store paint and finishes can prevent cans from vibrating off during a tremor (or when the E train comes barreling through).

Map It Out

If you end up with a lot of boxes stored on numerous shelves or in a crowded basement, a roughly sketched map of where various boxes are located will keep your blood pressure lower the next time you need to find that odd widget in a hurry.

and supplies, it can ruin some things, such as precision-dial calipers and gauges and sticky-backed sandpaper.

Unless you're lucky enough to occupy a shop that already has built-in cabinets, you'll need to acquire some form of storage cabinetry. One way to save time and expense is to pick up a set of recycled kitchen cabinets from a local cabinet installer. Just offer to pick up the old cabinets they're tearing out on a job, and they'll probably let you have them for next to nothing. Kitchen uppers often have adjustable shelves that are adaptable for storing containers of various heights, whereas kitchen lowers, in addition to storage, can provide a sturdy base for a bench or work

counter (see "Workbenches," on p. 143). Just don't let a set of "free" cabinets compromise your space. If your shop is already crowded with tools, counters, and benches, you'll gain the most additional storage space by adapting cabinets to fit into unused nooks and crannies: in corners, along an upper wall, or behind where a passage door opens.

Machine stands Machines with stands, such as lathes and jointers, often have open space below them where a cabinet can be fitted to house blades, bits, and supplies. And don't overlook the possibility of adding a cabinet or drawer underneath a bench or tool table. For example, a drawer underneath a tablesaw's extension table can hold sawblades, throat plates, and safety devices (see the top photo on p. 183), and a cabinet under a router table or shaper could hold bits, cutters, bearings, and wrenches. Using full-extension glides allows you to pull drawers all the way out for maximum access to contents.

Building and organizing cabinets
If you're ambitious and want to give your shop a hand-crafted look, nothing beats building your own tool and supply storage cabinets. Not only can custom shop cabinets enhance your pride but, by designing from scratch, you can create storage that suits your work type precisely while making maximum use of your space.

When designing storage cabinets, be kind to your back by avoiding putting storage areas for heavy items either too

A drawer mounted on full-extension glides beneath the extension table of this tablesaw has divided compartments that hold extra sawblades safely and has room to store saw accessories—throat plates, push sticks, and safety devices—right next to the machine.

high or too low. Cabinets, shelves, and cubbies are all more user friendly if you leave enough room around them to allow for comfortable use (see "The Ergonomics of Shop Storage," on p. 182). It's wise to build lower cabinets at the same height as other shop work surfaces. This gives you the option of using the cabinet top as an outfeed table or to support large or long work at the bench when necessary.

Adding commercially made divider trays, racks, and pull outs will help keep tools from bumping around as well as make finding hardware and smaller items easier. It's wise to buy any such organizers before you build, so that you can size the cabinets' interior dimensions to fit them with the least wasted space.

STASHING THE LITTLE STUFF

Like an army of ants, all the small stuff—nails, brads, tacks, screws, bolts, nuts, washers, hinges, latches, hooks, dowels, biscuits, pins, springs, grommets—that's necessary for building most anything can quickly overrun your woodworking picnic. Trying to keep all the minutiae sorted, organized, and identified is like trying to maintain your own mini hardware store.

Fortunately, there is no shortage of tried-and-true small storage solutions available. If you're looking to gain the maximum amount of storage for the least coin, plan to take a visit to the housewares section of your local variety store. There you'll see the most remarkable collection of molded plastic

IKEA's® Trofast system features three sizes of plastic tubs, ideal for storing all manner of shop supplies, hardware, and small tools. With a little ingenuity, you can make a shopmade cabinet for them to slide in and out.

Locking-Lid Fastener Box

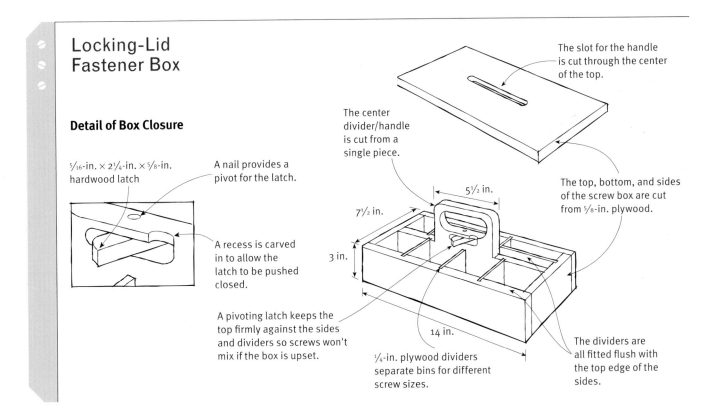

Detail of Box Closure

$5/16$-in. × $2\frac{1}{4}$-in. × $5/8$-in. hardwood latch

A nail provides a pivot for the latch.

A recess is carved in to allow the latch to be pushed closed.

A pivoting latch keeps the top firmly against the sides and dividers so screws won't mix if the box is upset.

The slot for the handle is cut through the center of the top.

The center divider/handle is cut from a single piece.

The top, bottom, and sides of the screw box are cut from $5/8$-in. plywood.

$5\frac{1}{2}$ in.

$7\frac{1}{2}$ in.

3 in.

14 in.

$1/4$-in. plywood dividers separate bins for different screw sizes.

The dividers are all fitted flush with the top edge of the sides.

Not only does this shopmade plywood screw box house and organize nine different sizes of screws but its locking lid keeps them from spilling or getting mixed up if the box is dropped or inverted.

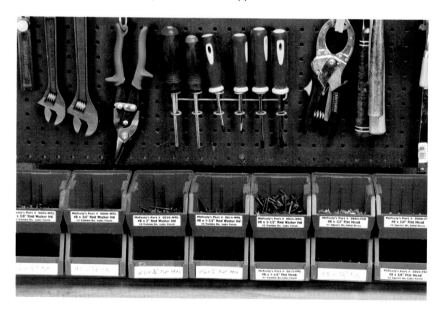

Ideal for organizing and storing screws, nails, and other small hardware items, small plastic bins can be mounted to wall racks or stacked on a bench or countertop.

items ever to inspire a blue-light special: rolling shelf units, corner cabinets, divider trays, trunks, interlocking bins, wheeled trunks, lidded and hinged-topped boxes, and much more. These containers that were designed to organize and store your household goods can also help you organize your shop stuff and store it safely and conveniently.

One particularly handy storage system sold by the Scandinavian furnishings company IKEA® is called "Trofast." Actually developed for storing children's toys, the Trofast system features inexpensive, yet sturdy, slide-out plastic bins that come in several different sizes. You can slide the bins into one of IKEA's quick-assembly wood cabinets or build your own—a good idea because you can customize the cabinet to suit the number and size of bins you need as well as the shop space it'll occupy. To keep dust from collecting in the Trofast bins, it's best to incorporate dust panels into your custom cabinets.

Here are several other tried-and-true approaches for storing hardware and small stuff, using a variety of containers, either store bought, recycled, or shopmade:

• Organizer cabinets with dozens of small, clear-plastic drawers or tilt-out trays are great for small quantities of screws or other fasteners that you want to stock in lots of sizes and lengths. When closed, the clear-plastic drawers keep dust out and allow you to see what's inside. Units are portable, although some can't be inverted without the contents mixing.

- Stackable plastic bins come in many sizes and colors. Most styles can be wall mounted or stacked on a counter. Larger sizes are good for bulky storage items, such as cabinet hardware, heavy fasteners, and spools of cable or twine. The open-bin design makes items quick to grab. If bins are mounted too high to view the contents, add labels or glue a sample of the item to the front of the bin. Just be sure to locate these bins where they'll be clear of sawdust thrown up by machine tools. If you want to keep them dust-free, put them inside a drawer or cabinet.

- Adding dividers to a drawer creates separate compartments for all kinds of items, from small tools and clamps to hardware, spare parts and accessories for machines, dowels, and sandpaper sheets or discs. Hot-glue thin dividers directly into the drawer or, for more rugged uses, dado the drawer sides to receive dividers.

- A shopmade, locking-lidded screw or nail box keeps fasteners organized and ready to take wherever needed. Made from scraps of ½-in. to ¾-in. plywood (see "Locking-Lid Fastener Box," on p. 185), the box's tight-fitting lid keeps fasteners of the same size separated— even if the box turns over.

- Screw-lidded jars attached to a board or beam/joist hung overhead, to wall

A Heated Storage Area

IF YOUR SHOP BECOMES an overnight icebox every winter, you'll save yourself a lot of grief by building an insulated/heated finish storage cabinet, as shown in the drawing.

A single 60w light bulb protected by a wire bulb guard provides the necessary heat, while a thermostat wired into the circuit, set for a maximum temperature of about 75°F, keeps the box from overheating. If your shop gets particularly frosty in midwinter (or in places like Fairbanks, mid-spring for that matter), it's not a bad idea to line the inside of the finish cabinet and its doors with some ½ -in.- to 1-in.-thick rigid foam insulation, which can be glued on with construction adhesive. This is an especially good idea if the cabinet will be located close to the floor or in an uninsulated part of the shop.

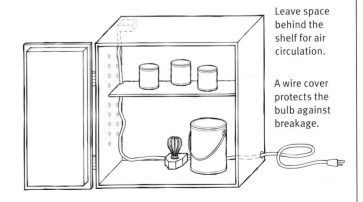

A thermostat mounted at the top of the cabinet controls temperature.

An adjustable shelf allows the cabinet to accommodate cans of different heights.

Leave space behind the shelf for air circulation.

A wire cover protects the bulb against breakage.

The doors, interior sides, top, and back of the cabinet may be lined with thin rigid-foam insulation for use in very cold climates.

A 60w light bulb supplies the necessary heat to keep water-based finishes and glues from freezing

brackets, or in a rack are an old-fashioned but efficient solution for storing nails and screws. Make sure to use jars with deep threads that screw securely to their lids to prevent jars from falling—newer baby-food jars have shallow lids and tight seals that make them poor candidates for this. Plastic film containers are good for ultra-small parts, and they're free for the asking at most film-processing shops.

- Old muffin pans, bread pans, and cafeteria trays (flea markets are a great source) can be used to hold all kinds of fasteners or parts small and large. Build a rack for them to slide in and out of by dadoing grooves that fit the edges of the pan or tray in the sides of a box or cabinet (see the photo on p. 184).

Special Storage

Some woodworking materials such as finishes and adhesives have special temperature and humidity requirements. Others such as abrasives need to be stored carefully or they'll lose the very qualities that make them useful. Here is how to manage these special storage needs.

STORING GLUES AND FINISHES

Adhesive products and finishing materials aren't like other supplies in your shop. They are chemical soups, some of which are flammable, toxic, and quite complex (see "Storing Flammable Liquids," on p. 225). Even inside a sealed can or bottle, glues and finishes respond to changes in temperature to the point

Protecting Shop Electronics

ELECTRONIC DEVICES, such as calculators, computers, and stereo components, all are sensitive to dust. Zipper-locking plastic bags can provide a safe haven for small calculators or MP3 players (such as iPods™). To protect a shop stereo or a computer system, build a dust-tight cabinet, such as the one shown here.

A clear plastic door lets you see the stereo's lighted display readouts and control most stereo functions with the remote control, which should also be kept in a sealed plastic bag. A similar cabinet could house a shop computer's CPU and monitor with the plastic-bagged keyboard sitting on the benchtop in front of it.

that very cold or very hot conditions can ruin or shorten their useful life. This is important to remember when choosing a spot to store them. For example, keeping a bottle of yellow glue in a hot attic will shorten its shelf life, sometimes significantly. It's always a good idea to write the date of purchase on any can of finish or bottle of glue. Finishes like liquid shellac last only 6 months to 12 months before they're unusable and should be disposed of properly (see "Keeping Your Woodshop Clean," on p. 224).

Beware of cold temperatures

Storing finishes in exposed sheds or near a frigid concrete floor often makes them too cold for use without preheating (remember that for best results the work-piece, finish, and air temperature should all be about the same). Worse, water-based glues and finishes are ruined if they are allowed to freeze—a definite possibility because most shops are un-heated at night.

If freezing temperatures are a fre-quent occurrence in your area, consider building a heated finish storage cabinet, as discussed on p. 187. An easy way to temporarily prevent ruined finishes is by placing a heating pad (the same one you used to soothe your aching back after installing kitchen cabinets) inside your finish storage cabinet. A low setting is all it takes to keep your water-based prod-ucts safe.

If you live in earthquake country and store your finishes in high upper cabinets, it's a good idea to install locking latches

on all doors. Easier still, nailing ½-in. by ½-in. wood strips on the top front edge of each shelf will prevent cans of stain and finish from creating a Jackson Pollock design on the floor dur-ing a mild tremor (see the bottom right photo on p. 183).

Extending finish shelf life

Another good idea when storing oil/solvent-based clear finishes, stains, paints, and wood fillers is to fill the can or container with inert gas (bought at a wine store and used to extend an open bottle's shelf life). The gas displaces the air that causes

Placing an ordinary drugstore-variety heating blanket inside a cabinet keeps temperature-sensitive water-based glues and finishes, which can be ruined by freezing, warm during spells of cold weather.

To prevent paper- and cloth-backed sandpaper sheets, discs, belts, and drums from curling due to humidity or moisture, store your extras in a plastic box or chest with a closable lid.

air-drying finishes to skin over and eventually become unusable. Unfortunately, it doesn't prolong the life of water-based finishes and glues.

STORING SANDPAPER

Like finishes, sandpaper is a woodworking supply that can be easily ruined by improper storage. Just dumping a pile of sanding sheets in a drawer can tear edges or rub off the abrasive grit. Even bent corners and haphazard folds can make it difficult to use sanding discs, belts, and partial sheets in various power sanders.

Keeping sandpaper sheets and discs separated and neatly stacked, either in an open rack or in divided drawers, can keep them flat, clean, and ready for use. Preferably, each grit should be kept separately. Small sanding belts can be kept in boxes or hung up. Large belts should be hung on a large-diameter hanger, such as a tube; stacking them or hanging them on a narrow rod or stick can cause creases that make belts difficult to track.

Keep abrasives protected But even if you've neatly stacked all your sandpaper, you're still not out of the woods if your shop has moisture problems. Moisture is an enemy of most sandpaper. It causes paper-backed sheets and discs to curl up and be difficult or impossible to use (you can't iron them out because most sandpapers these days have stearated coatings that will melt). Dampness can even warp cloth-backed sanding belts, causing them to track poorly.

About the best you can do in a damp shop environment is to leave out only as much sandpaper as you will use in a short period of time, keeping it as far from a moist floor or wall as possible. Store the rest of your supply in a sealable plastic box or tub. If your shop is in the tropics, you might want to keep a desiccant container inside your sandpaper storage box (see "Preventing Rust," on p. 98).

Yet another enemy of some sandpaper is dust. It's the despoiler of adhesive-backed sandpaper products, such as PSA discs and sticky-backed rolls. To avoid ruination, these should be stored in plastic bags or boxes when not in use. When switching between grits, temporarily stick discs to clean waxed paper between uses.

Dust Collection and Compressed Air

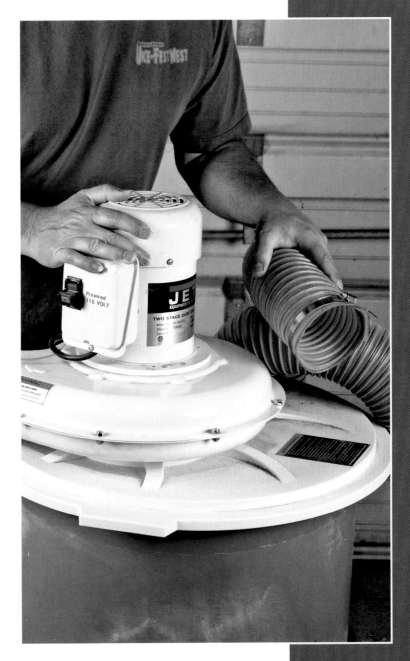

9

"If you're concerned about fire safety or for your respiratory health, it's important to develop a strategy for dealing with sawdust—regardless of the size of your shop."

In addition to all the great machines, tools, and devices that equip a good woodworking shop, every shop should have a means to control dust. Wood waste ranges in size from the chips generated during cutting, planing, and routing to the fine dust created from both hand and power sanding. Controlling dust not only helps keep the shop relatively clean but also makes for a healthier woodworking environment.

Another great addition to any serious shop is compressed air, which affords a woodworker a means to access an extensive and versatile collection of pneumatic devices for machining, sanding, cleaning, clamping, and finishing wood. In this chapter, I'll look at both kinds of air systems in the woodshop—sucking up dust and blowing pressurized air.

Dust-Control Methods

If you look back over the last few decades, the only dust collection that was available to small-shop woodworkers was a broom and dust pan. But in earlier times, when woodworking was mostly or entirely done with hand tools, cleaning up the shop was a matter of scooping up piles of shavings and sweeping a little dust off the floor. Absent then were significant amounts of fine dust because wood surfaces were typically smoothed by planing or scraping—not sanding.

Enter a modern woodshop and you're likely to find a full complement of stationary machines and portable electric power tools capable of producing mountains of wood chips and clouds of fine dust. Without some means of collection, chips pile up quickly and can easily ignite, and the air fills with particles fine enough to enter the human nasal passages and lungs, causing any number of health issues. If you're concerned about fire safety or for your respiratory health, it's important to develop a strategy for dealing with sawdust—regardless of the size of your shop.

TWO KINDS OF SHOP WASTE

Any shop dust-control strategy must address two kinds of shop waste: the shavings and large sawdust and the fine wood powder.

Getting rid of the big stuff is important because wood chips of various sizes are untidy and a hazard underfoot. They clog our machines, and at worst, they combust with little encouragement (if you're a woodturner, there's an additional concern: Big piles of green-wood shavings create heat as they dry out, and can actually combust). Gathering the big chips and shavings can be as simple as shoveling them up—if you're a neat person who remembers to tidy up the shop often. (I heard one guy say, "I sweep out my shop once a year, whether it needs it or not.") But installing some kind of dust-collection system is much better because, when well implemented, it will gather chips and sawdust as fast as you can make them, which beats sweeping any day.

Fine dust is another issue. The high-speed blades and cutters of modern power tools do a lot more than generate sawdust; they also produce a very fine dust. And more and more machines are finding their way into woodshops that use abrasive belts, discs, flaps, and sheets instead of knives to trim and smooth wood, churning out enormous quantities of fine dust in the process. Sawdust might get in your eyes, but fine powder gets into your nose and travels down into your lungs, where it can serve up all kinds of grief, from allergic reactions to bronchitis and emphysema to cancer.

SIX STRATEGIES FOR CONTROLLING AND COLLECTING WOODSHOP SAWDUST

METHOD	ADVANTAGES	DISADVANTAGES
Personal respiratory protection via disposable mask, reusable respirator, or powered air-purifying respirator (commonly called an "air helmet" or "dust helmet")	Disposable masks and respirators are inexpensive and readily available. They provide decent respiratory protection when other means are not available. Dust helmets provide thorough protection for users with severe allergies to wood dust.	Disposables that don't seal well against the face compromise respiratory protection (they don't work well on bearded users). Reusable respirators can be uncomfortable to wear for extended periods. Dust helmets can be expensive.
Shop ventilation	Ventilating your shop is an easy, inexpensive way to remove fine, dust-laden air from the shop.	Heated or cooled air is also blown out of the shop along with dust. This method only deals with very fine sanding dust.
Air-filtration devices	Air-filtration devices can remove the fine dust particles from the air without exhausting shop air. Units can be shop built, and they're easy to install.	These devices only deal with very fine sanding dust; they don't replace primary collection. Fans in units are often noisy. Prefilters may need cleaning often in dusty shops.
Shop vacuums	Shop vacuums are compact, portable, and relatively inexpensive. They're an effective means of shop cleanup and collection from portable power tools and small benchtop machines.	Shop vacuums are not effective for collecting shavings and large chips from full-size woodworking machines. Most units have small drums or bags that don't hold much. Many units are very noisy.
Portable chip and dust collectors	Portables are less expensive than installing a central dust-collection system. Even compact units can handle large shavings from full-size woodworking machines.	Portables are typically not powerful enough to be used with long hoses or ductwork, so they take up room on the shop floor. Some chip collectors come with poor-quality filter bags.
Central dust-collection system	A central system is the most powerful, effective way of collecting large chips to fine dust from stationary machines and other sources. The unit can be installed outside the shop to save space.	A central system is expensive and can be complicated to install properly (it requires additional purchase of ductwork, fittings, and hardware). It takes up more physical space than portable units.

Unfortunately, controlling this fine dust is much more difficult than just scooping it off the floor. Respirable dust particles are so light they can float for hours, held aloft by the static charge in the air. And they're so small, the biggest particles that you can breathe in are about 100 times smaller than the smallest thing you can see with a well-trained eye. Since what you can't see *can* hurt you, working without protection or not implementing dust control properly can put you at serious risk.

Primary and secondary dust collection The difference between large wood chips and ultra-fine wood dust accounts for the many different means there are for collecting and controlling them, as summed up in

"Six Strategies for Controlling and Collecting Woodshop Sawdust," on p. 193.

Primary collection, via central and portable collectors and shop vacuums, traps chips and dust as close to where they originate as possible. Secondary collection methods, such as air filtration and ventilation, trap or exhaust fine dust that's laying or floating around in the shop. And protection devices, such as masks and respirators (which are discussed in detail in Chapter 10) control fine dust by keeping it from entering your respiratory system.

The amount of chips and dust your shop generates and the degree to which you want to protect your respiratory health will dictate which one of these collection and control strategies—or

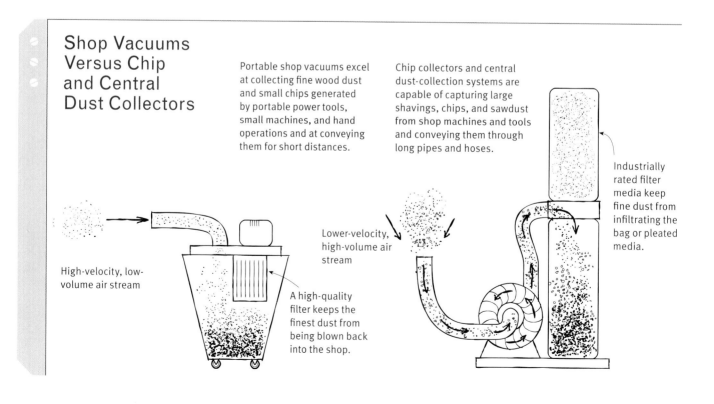

Shop Vacuums Versus Chip and Central Dust Collectors

Portable shop vacuums excel at collecting fine wood dust and small chips generated by portable power tools, small machines, and hand operations and at conveying them for short distances.

Chip collectors and central dust-collection systems are capable of capturing large shavings, chips, and sawdust from shop machines and tools and conveying them through long pipes and hoses.

Industrially rated filter media keep fine dust from infiltrating the bag or pleated media.

High-velocity, low-volume air stream

A high-quality filter keeps the finest dust from being blown back into the shop.

Lower-velocity, high-volume air stream

A good shop vacuum is a good investment for any size shop. Some models are capable of switching on and off automatically when used to collect dust from portable power tools, a time-saving convenience.

combination of strategies—is right for your shop. The average power tool–equipped woodshop does best by using a combination of primary and secondary control methods. For example, a central dust-collection system will gather shavings and chips, whereas an air-filtration device traps fine dust that escapes collection or is generated by hand-sanding.

In a shop with portable power tools and a few benchtop machines, a shop vacuum can handle the sawdust while ventilation exhausts fine dust. Let's look at each of the methods in more detail, starting with primary collection solutions and moving from least to most complicated.

SHOP VACUUMS

One of the most inexpensive means of capturing dust and chips in a woodshop is to use a shop vacuum. Made like your home vacuum cleaner but with a bigger motor and dust bin, most shop vacuums have wheeled bases for good portability,

yet they are compact enough to stow under a bench or in a closet. But if you have full-size machines, don't expect even the biggest shop vacuum to handle all your shop's collection needs.

Where shop vacuums really shine is in handling dust produced by portable power tools and benchtop stationary tools, most of which come with built-in dust ports or bags that can be removed for hose connection to a vacuum (see the photo above). Of course, they're also handy for secondary collection of dust and chips strewn across floors and workbenches.

Shop vacuum features It used to be that the only way to get good fine-dust filtration from a shop vacuum was to buy a high-quality unit that used high-efficiency filtration, such as European models. But today, even less-expensive models made by Sears® (Craftsman® brand), Hoover™, Shop Vac®, and Genie® can be retrofitted with high-efficiency CleanStream® filters (made of Gore® fabric), which trap fine dust particles down to 0.3 microns rather than blowing them around the shop.

More sophisticated shop vacuums, such as the Festool® CT-Mini, even have built-in automatic switches. When a power tool is plugged into a special outlet on the vacuum and switched on, the vacuum automatically comes on and stays on for a short time after the tool is turned off to clear dust from the hose.

PORTABLE COLLECTORS

Buying and installing a central dust-collection system is an awfully big investment of time and money for many small shops, where machines are run on occasion or generate only modest amounts of dust and chips. And then there are those of us who don't actually own our shops and want to take our dust collection with us when we move. Fortunately, you can keep sawdust at bay just as well with a portable collector as you can with a central system, provided that you choose the right unit and hook it up properly.

Why a Shop Vacuum May Not Be Enough

A shop vacuum pulls a small volume of air at a high velocity through a small-diameter hose (1 in. to 2¼ in.), compared to portable and central collectors, which pull a large volume of air at a lower velocity through a big duct or hose (at least 4 in. in diameter). This means that, while a shop vacuum can grab and gobble up fine dust and even sizable shavings, it can't handle the volume of air usually needed to entrain large shavings from machines like planers and shapers.

Connecting Multiple Machines to a Single Collector

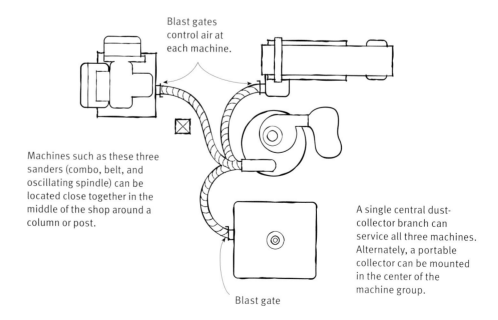

Blast gates control air at each machine.

Machines such as these three sanders (combo, belt, and oscillating spindle) can be located close together in the middle of the shop around a column or post.

A single central dust-collector branch can service all three machines. Alternately, a portable collector can be mounted in the center of the machine group.

Blast gate

An Upgrade to Two-Stage Collection

ALTHOUGH IT WON'T BE AS PORTABLE, you can effectively transform a single-stage collector into a two-stage unit by connecting a preseparator device in between the dust source and the collector. Plastic lids designed for this purpose, such as the Veritas cyclonic lid, have ports for attaching flexible hoses and mount atop a trash can or drum. You do lose some suction power with this configuration, but it's more than worth it in terms of convenience because the collector's bags have to handle only very fine dust and don't need emptying as often.

Portable collectors are wheeled devices that are not only more powerful than shop vacuums but also have fans and large-diameter hoses capable of handling the large volume of chips and dust produced by full-size shop machines. By wheeling a portable collector around and hooking it up to machines with a flexible hose, you get high-performance chip collection without the need to install permanent ductwork, which is required for a central system.

You can service quite a few machines with a single portable collector by grouping the machines around the unit and connecting each with a hose and the necessary fittings (see the photo at right), and "Connecting Multiple Machines to a Single Collector," on the facing page).

You can use a portable chip collector to gather sawdust from a group of machines by connecting them with flexible hose branched with Y connectors. Blast gates direct suction to only the machine in use.

Single- and double-stage collectors

Before you run out and buy a portable collector, you should be aware that the various makes and models aren't all alike. They fall into two basic types: single-stage and two-stage collectors.

Older-style *single-stage collectors*, known as chip collectors, are basic two- and four-bag units in which chips are drawn through the fan and blown directly into the filter bags, the lower bag serving as the collection bin.

In contrast, a *two-stage portable collector* pulls dust-laden air into a separation chamber first, so all the heavy chips and dust settle out before passing through the fan and into a filter bag or cartridge, where fine dust is strained out. This has several advantages. First, larger chips and objects don't pass through the fan. A single, large woodscrew can ruin the fan in a single-stage collector or bounce around its blower's sheet-metal housing and cause sparks that can start a fire, or rarely, an explosion. Second, the greatest volume of dust and chips ends up in a drum, which is much easier to empty than a single-stage collector's filter bag. Further, as the filter bag of a single-stage collector fills with chips, it doesn't pass air through as easily, thus cutting down the vacuum power of the unit (that's why it's important to empty bags often).

Changing the constructs of portable dust collectors are a new breed of single- and two-stage models that employ canister filtration. Resembling an oversize pleated vacuum cleaner filter, a canister-equipped portable collector does a better job of filtering out fine dust than a portable with canvas or synthetic fabric bags; plus the canister's pleats lend more surface area, resulting in higher airflow and better collector performance. Also, the lower bags on single-stage units, like the Jet 1100 CK, are replaced by disposable plastic bags, making dust disposal a cleaner job.

CENTRAL DUST-COLLECTION SYSTEMS

When most woodworkers think of dust collection, they think of a central system. A well-designed, properly installed

A two-stage dust collector, such as this drum-style portable, deposits most chips and dust in a separation chamber, here the drum, where they are easy to dump out. The unit's fine-dust-filtering canister needs only occasional cleaning, by blowing from the outside with compressed air.

central system can keep your shop amazingly free of wood chips and shavings, as well as significantly reduce the amount of fine dust in the air. The only catch is that there's a lot that goes into a good system—it's about the most complicated element of infrastructure that a woodshop is likely to have.

In this section, I give an overview of just what's involved, so that you can figure out if a central system is right for your shop and, if so, what you'll be getting into if you decide to put in a system yourself. The 10 most important steps to follow when creating a decent system are detailed on pp. 201–202. For a complete rundown on installing a central system, pick up a copy of my book *Woodshop Dust Control* (The Taunton Press).

System anatomy

Fundamentally, a central system uses a vacuum-like fan (blower) to pull air through a system of pipes (ductwork) that collects chips from woodworking machines and other sources (sanding tables, floor sweeps, etc.) around the shop and deposits them in a bin or bag, where they can be disposed of. Two-stage units, which are recommended for central collection, remove the majority of chips and particles in a preseparator, such as a cyclone or drop box, before the chip-laden air reaches the blower. The air that passes through the blower carries very fine dust that either goes into a filter bag (or a series of bags, called a "bag house"), filter cartridge, or is expelled outside the shop. When clean, filtered air goes back into the shop, it's known as a "return-air

Taming Vacuum Noise

Because shop vacuums use the same kinds of universal motors found in routers and other portable power tools, they are noisy at best. If you don't mind losing a little of their portability, you can house them in a sound-deadening enclosure, such as the one shown in "Smart Ways to Reduce Machinery Noise," on p. 43. A shop vacuum that I use exclusively for collecting from portable power tools lives in an enclosure underneath my tablesaw's outfeed table.

The funnel-shaped cyclone on this 3-hp central collector separates out chips and larger dust particles, depositing them in a drum under the unit for easy disposal.

The essential components of a return-air central dust-collection system—preseparator cyclone, blower, and filter bags—are mounted inside the shop in a corner where ductwork brings chip-laden air from machines all around the shop.

and even the filters into a compact unit. The power and air-moving capacity of these units also vary considerably, with motors in the 1½-hp to 5-hp range being most appropriate for small- to medium-size shops.

Before selecting a unit, add up the air requirements of all the machines that you want to collect from at once, referring to "Cfm and Duct Diameter Requirements for Woodshop Machines," on p. 205. For best system performance, choose a collector that's rated to handle 30 percent to 50 percent more cubic feet per minute (cfm) than your calculated maximum. Why? When a collector is hooked up to ductwork, it typically moves less air (lower cfm) than it's rated for (this is especially true of fabric bag–equipped single-stage models).

In a return-air system, mounting the collector and filters inside the shop reduces the length of ductwork needed to connect it to machines. Alternatively, you can save space by mounting the collector's blower and preseparator in a closet or adjacent shed and by putting only the filters inside the shop.

A downside of having filter bags inside the shop is that static electricity tends to attract fine dust, which settles on the bags or canisters. Starting up the system then sends clouds of dust around the shop. To overcome this, mount the entire system, filters and all, in an enclosed shed attached to the shop and cut an opening in the wall for filtered air to return through (see "Sample Ductwork Layout for a Central Dust-Collection System," on p. 206).

system" (see "Return-Air Versus Air-Exhaust Collection System," p. 203).

Designing a central system Central collector units vary considerably in design. Some have components (blower, cyclone, filters) that mount separately and connect with a hose or pipe. Other systems, such as the collector shown in the photo above and in the top photo on the facing page, integrate a cyclone, blower,

Installing a central dust-collection system

1. Plan the layout of pipes, being sure to lay out the main duct so as to keep the branches reasonably short.

2. Using the chart on p. 205, calculate the cfm requirements and branch-duct diameters to each machine. Then obtain the main-duct diameter from the chart on p. 204, based on the total cfm needs of the system.

3. Buy a central dust-collector unit that has a cfm rating one third to one half higher than the highest cfm needs of your system. A 1¼-hp to 3-hp collector that delivers at least 600 cfm to 800 cfm should be adequate to handle a system with a single machine running at a time, with the largest air requirement being for a thickness planer or shaper.

4. If you're planning a return-air system (see "Designing a Central System," on the facing page), fit the collector with filter bags made of 12-oz. or 16-oz. felted-polyester filter fabric. The bags should have 1 sq. ft. of surface area for every 10 cfm (based on the system's highest cfm needs). Alternatively, install cartridge filters with this amount of surface area.

5. Decide where to put the collector, keeping it close to the machines with the highest cfm requirements if possible. Install the unit, making sure the frame and motor of the collector are grounded.

6. Cut and fit sections of metal pipe for the main duct, assembling them on the ground using pop rivets and working out from the collector. Next, assemble and

Integrating the fine-dust filtering cartridge into the cyclone itself makes this Oneida® central collector more compact and thus easier to mount in a cramped shop.

To save space, Curtis Erpelding located the central dust collector outside his shop yet mounted the filter bag house inside to maintain a return-air system that doesn't waste heated or cooled air by blowing it outside.

install the branch ducts. Use large-radius elbows to turn corners and 45-degree lateral tee fittings to join the branches to the main duct (see the photo below). Use metal pipe tape to hang ductwork as necessary.

7. Connect the branches to machines with short lengths (2½ ft. or less) of flexible hose, fitting a blast gate at each branch end. Use each flex hose's spiral wire to complete the ground connection between the branch pipe and the frame/motor of each machine.

8. For best results, make sure the hood around the blade, bit, or sanding belt contains chips being thrown during machining. But the hood shouldn't restrict airflow excessively. A good volume of airflow is necessary to catch sawdust and transport it through the ductwork for collection.

9. Seal all pipe joints with silicone caulk or duct tape.

10. Wire remote switches for turning the collector on and off.

Planning the ductwork Your central collector will do the best job of capturing dust and chips if you use the right size pipe and configuration of ductwork to connect them to the machines and devices they service. Like a tree, branch ducts from each source converge with the "trunk," a main duct that carries chips in a stream of air back to the collector.

Before deciding on the design of the ductwork, carefully consider the layout

For best airflow in a collection ductwork system, branch ducts should join the main duct at a 45-degree angle with pipe fittings called 45-degree lateral tees.

of the machines in your shop. The system will perform best if machines that produce the largest chips (planers, shapers) and machines with high cfm requirements are placed closer to the collector than machines that have low cfm needs. Benchtop machines and stationary sanders can be on branches that connect farther out on the main duct. Try to keep branch ducts from being excessively long by running the main duct straight across the shop, diagonally across, or around the perimeter of the shop as necessary.

Sizing the ductwork Properly sizing ductwork can involve some intense calculations, including factors such as the length of the run and static-pressure

Plastic Versus Metal Ductwork

CHOOSING WHAT KIND OF PIPE to use for the ductwork has become one of the most controversial aspects of installing a central system. Plastic pipe is inexpensive and easy to work with, but it is flammable and difficult to ground properly, so it is not officially recommended for woodshop dust-collection piping. Metal spiral pipe provides industrial-strength piping but at a high cost of materials and installation time.

I recommend metal snap-lock HVAC pipe (24-gauge or 26-gauge, *not* the thinner 30-gauge stovepipe), which is easy to ground, much less expensive than spiral pipe, and easier to install. Lengths of snap-lock pipe and special fittings pop-rivet together for easy assembly.

Return-Air Versus Air-Exhaust Dust-Collection Systems

Air-Return System

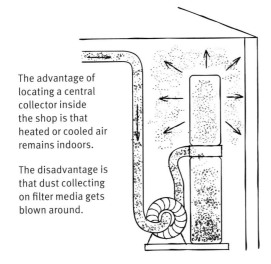

The advantage of locating a central collector inside the shop is that heated or cooled air remains indoors.

The disadvantage is that dust collecting on filter media gets blown around.

Air-Exhaust System

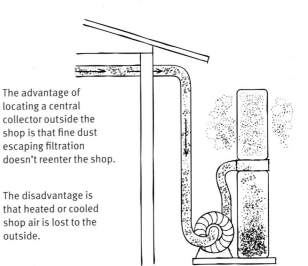

The advantage of locating a central collector outside the shop is that fine dust escaping filtration doesn't reenter the shop.

The disadvantage is that heated or cooled shop air is lost to the outside.

DETERMINING THE MAIN-DUCT DIAMETER

LARGEST CFM REQUIREMENT	MAIN-DUCT DIAMETER (IN.)
Up to 300	4
Up to 475	5
Up to 675	6
Up to 925	7
Up to 1,200	8

losses. However, in a small shop, you can get decent results by following a few simple shop layout recommendations and simplified duct-sizing guidelines, as follows.

1. Find the size of pipe needed for each branch duct according to the machine it serves, using the chart on p. 205.

2. Next, add up the cfm requirements of all machines that will be used at one time (which shouldn't exceed the capacity of your collector).

3. Use this number to find the main-duct diameter, gleaned from the chart at left.

Connecting the Ducts

The way that ducts connect to one another is as important as their proper diameter for good airflow. For the most air-efficient connections between the main and branch ducts, they should join at a 45-degree angle (rather than at 90 degrees) by using fittings called 45-degree lateral tees. Be sure to turn corners in the main and branch ducts gradually, not sharply, by using either "long-radius" elbows or a pair of 45-degree elbows with a short length of pipe in between. When connecting two machines at the end of a branch duct, use fittings called Y branches.

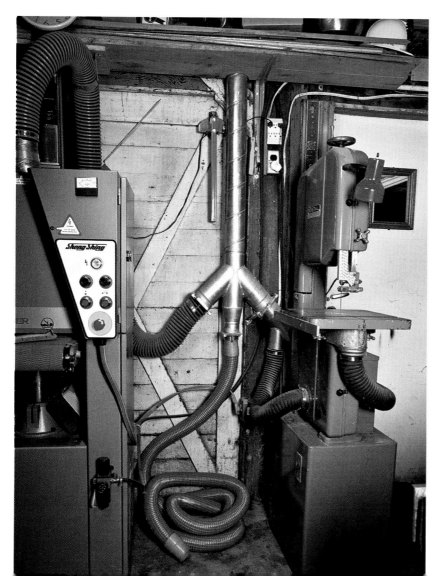

A properly sized and laid-out system of main and branch ducts carries sawdust from machines and other sources back to the central collector. To economize on the number of ductwork branches, various pipe fittings, such as this custom Y branch, allow several sources to be connected to a single branch duct.

Installing the ductwork When you're ready to install the ductwork, assemble the main duct on the ground first, then mount it. It is common to run the main duct around or across the shop at ceiling level or, in vaulted-ceiling shops, at a height where it's out of the way. The main duct, as well as suspended branch ducts, is hung with metal hangers or pipe strapping.

If your shop has a wood floor with enough space, running the main duct underneath can provide a convenient means of reaching machines located at the center of the floor. Ductwork can even be run in concrete slabs but must be set in before the slab is poured.

After the ductwork is assembled, all joints should be sealed with silicone caulking or duct tape to minimize air losses that can zap system efficiency.

Blast gates and flexible hoses In most small central dust-collection systems, the collector isn't powerful enough to service all the machines at once. To limit airflow to only machines that are in use, blast gates are installed at the end of each branch duct.

Opening only one gate at a time reduces the size of the blower needed to power the system (for convenience, the bigger the blower, the better; with a higher air-moving capacity, you can leave two or three blast gates open at once at machines you use most often).

Although automated gates are available (see "Switching Options" later in this chapter), most blast gates are manually operated via a sliding plate that pulls

CFM AND DUCT DIAMETER REQUIREMENTS FOR WOODSHOP MACHINES

MACHINE/DUST SOURCE	CFM REQUIREMENT	RECOMMENDED BRANCH DUCT SIZE (IN.)
• Router table • Scrollsaw • Narrow-belt sander	150–350	2¼–4
• Tablesaw or panel saw (10 in.–12 in.) • Sliding compound miter saw, or other cutoff saw (10 in.–12 in.) • Bandsaw (14 in.–16 in.) • Jointer (up to 8 in. wide) • Oscillating spindle sander • Spindle shaper (up to ¾-in. arbor) • Drill press • Disc sander (12 in.) • Cleanup hose	350 – 400	4
• Wood lathe (small)	400–550	4 or 5
• Combination sander (48-in. belt, 8-in.- to 9-in. disc) • Drum thicknessing sander (12-in.- to 24-in.-wide drum)	550–600	5

• Thickness planer
  10 in.–12 in.
  15 in.–20 in.
	500
	600–800
		5
		5 or 6

• Wide-belt sander
  12-in.-wide belt
  15-in.- to 24-in.-wide belt
	500–750
	800–1200
		5 or 6
		6 to 8

To help a central collector provide the strongest suction, airflow can be limited to machines that are in use via blast gates installed at the end of branch ducts. A short length of flexible hose connects the end of the branch to each machine.

out to open airflow in the branch. Gates should be located within easy reach of the machines they serve, pop-riveted to the end of the branch. Flexible hose that is the same diameter as the branch connects the machine's dust port to the system. The ribbed hose creates a lot of air resistance, so it should be kept as short as possible.

If the machine has a dust port that's smaller than the duct diameter, use a reduction fitting at the port itself (don't downsize the hose to match). If the

Sample Ductwork Layout for a Central Dust-Collection System

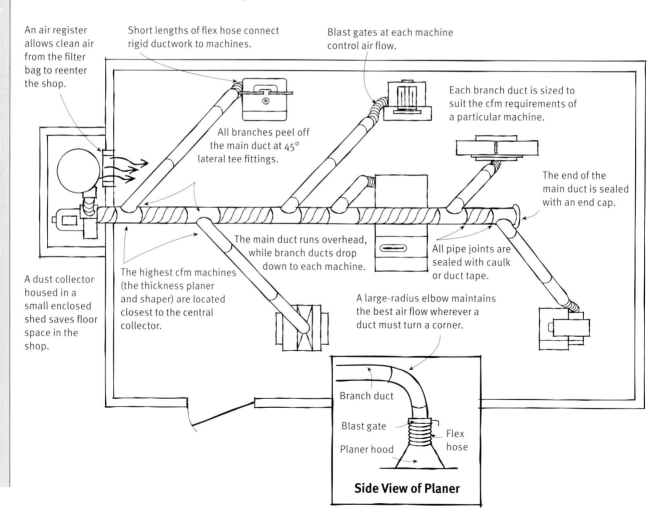

An air register allows clean air from the filter bag to reenter the shop.

Short lengths of flex hose connect rigid ductwork to machines.

Blast gates at each machine control air flow.

Each branch duct is sized to suit the cfm requirements of a particular machine.

All branches peel off the main duct at 45° lateral tee fittings.

The end of the main duct is sealed with an end cap.

A dust collector housed in a small enclosed shed saves floor space in the shop.

The highest cfm machines (the thickness planer and shaper) are located closest to the central collector.

The main duct runs overhead, while branch ducts drop down to each machine.

All pipe joints are sealed with caulk or duct tape.

A large-radius elbow maintains the best air flow wherever a duct must turn a corner.

Branch duct

Blast gate

Planer hood

Flex hose

Side View of Planer

machine lacks a ready dust port, a collection hood is needed to contain and direct the stream of sawdust coming off the blade or cutter into the ductwork. But take care not to constrict the airflow. For example, sealing up every nook and cranny of an enclosed-base tool, such as a tablesaw, can cut airflow to the point that dust collection is practically nil.

Grounding the system One of the reasons that metal pipe is preferable to plastic is that it is easy to ground, which is necessary for safe operation. Start by making sure all machine frames and motors are grounded, as well as all components of the collector. To connect the machine ground to the ductwork, peel the rubber or plastic coating from the helical wire in the flexible hose and make sure it touches bare metal at both ends. For added security against a fine-dust explosion, which is rare but possible, add a ground strap to the filter bag house or metal drums or bins that collect fine dust.

Switching options Because the central collector is usually switched on and off concurrently with machines, putting it on its own dedicated circuit will avoid thrown breakers (see "New Circuits for Machine Tools," on p. 52). To make switching the collector on and off easier, many woodworkers use a remote switch or automatic switching system to control the collector. Remote-control systems are available that work with either 110v or 220v circuits and have a small transmitter that will operate the collector from anywhere in the shop.

The EcoGate system uses a sensor mounted to a machine's motor housing both to automatically open the dust gate and to switch the central collector on when the tool is in use.

If you really want to automate your shop, you can fit your ductwork with an automatic blast gate system. For example, the EcoGate® system uses solenoid-operated gates (see the photo above) that automatically open and close whenever a machine is turned on or off. The system uses a small sensor to pick up machine vibration that sends a signal to operate the gate as well as to automatically switch the central collector on and off—how convenient!

Using a downdraft sanding table is a great way to capture fine dust produced by hand or power sanding. This shopmade portable sanding table has a slotted table that's connected to a central collection system.

Sanding tables Central systems typically collect chips only from machines and aren't well suited to connecting directly to portable power tools. But because fine sanding dust is one of the worst sources of lung pollution in the shop, it pays to take extra care in controlling the dust produced by sanding operations—especially power sanding using portable tools—by working atop a sanding table connected to dust collection.

A sanding table uses downdraft air to suck fine particles away from you, collecting them in your shop vacuum

or central system. To contain dust generated by belt sanders and random-orbit sanders, which tend to throw dust horizontally with quite a bit of force, it's best for a sanding table to have a raised back and sides, as shown in the photo, at left.

Checking your collection system's efficiency If your dust collector or vacuum doesn't have the oomph to suck up the chips produced by your thickness planer, the piles of chips around the machine provide a pretty good indication. But how is your system handling the fine dust that's the cause of respiratory problems?

Unfortunately, your eyes can't tell you whether or not your dust-collection system is doing a good job of collecting respirable dust (remember, such dust is imperceptibly small). You can get a pretty good idea though by cleaning up your bench and toolbox tops thoroughly after an afternoon of power-tool use. If those surfaces are covered with a fine layer of dust the next morning, you can be pretty sure that your system isn't up to snuff (no pun intended).

Unless your typical day of woodworking produces tremendous amounts of fine dust or your collector is seriously undersize, the usual culprits for poor fine-dust control are the filter bags. A single- or two-stage collector is likely to come with inexpensive cloth filter bags that do a poor job of removing respirable dust. The best bet is to replace them with thick felt polyester bags that are made from an industrially rated fabric that filters out a large percentage of respirable particles. Pleated canisters are also very effective.

There's always going to be some dust that evades collection, even in shops with a terrific central system and a good shop vacuum servicing portable power tools. Add to that dust that's created by hand-sanding and portables that don't easily hook up to dust collection, and you can end up with a lot of fine dust floating around the shop.

VENTILATION AND AIR FILTRATION

Besides wearing a mask or respirator for protection, you can deal with errant fine dust by using ventilation or air-filtration methods. Ventilation relies on a strong fan to suck dusty air out of the shop and expel it outdoors. Simply installing a

single fan in a window opening provides an inexpensive and effective way of keeping small shop spaces from being filled with choking dust. As in a spray-finishing booth, it is best to set up ventilation so that the source of the dust is between you and the fan and that fresh air is coming into the shop from behind you. You can further enhance the airflow by placing a second fan upwind of you to blow fresh air toward you. Just don't let it blow so hard as to churn up settled dust and whisk it around the shop.

In hot or cold climates, blowing heated or cooled air out of the shop doesn't make sense, so using ventilation for clearing dust is limited. In such circumstances, it's better to keep the shop

Sizing and Installing an Air-Filtration Device

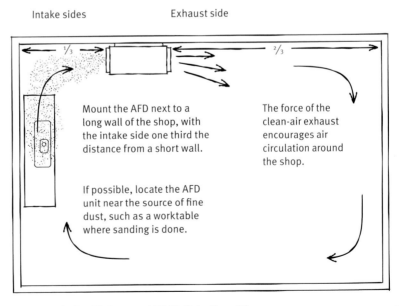

Intake sides

Exhaust side

Mount the AFD next to a long wall of the shop, with the intake side one third the distance from a short wall.

The force of the clean-air exhaust encourages air circulation around the shop.

If possible, locate the AFD unit near the source of fine dust, such as a worktable where sanding is done.

Formula for Sizing an AFD Unit to Your Shop

Cubic-foot volume of shop (length × width × height) × Number of air changes per hour (6 for hobby use; 8 for full-time use)

= air-moving capacity (cfm) of AFD

60

Don't Rely on Air Filtration Alone

It's important to note that an AFD is not a good substitute for primary collection, which traps the lion's share of the dust and chips produced at the source. If you regularly use power tools and machines in your shop, don't bother with an AFD until you have installed a central dust-collection system or portable collector to your machines.

Although it's no substitute for a central dust-collection system, an air-filtration device can remove fine dust from the air without exhausting the air outdoors.

closed and filter fine particles out of the air with an air-filtration device (AFD).

Air-filtration devices An AFD is basically a cabinet with a motorized fan and filters that capture airborne dust as it circulates around the shop (see the photo below). If you put your hand over the intake of a running AFD, you'll immediately notice that even a big unit generates very little suction. Most fine-dust particles find their way to an AFD only if they are carried there on an air current. Fortunately, an AFD's exhaust air is powerful enough to create air movement in the shop, but careful placement is crucial to develop the necessary circular air current. "Sizing and Installing an Air-Filtration Device," on p. 209, shows the best placement for an AFD unit in a typical rectangular shop to encourage air movement. The drawing also contains the formula to use for sizing an AFD unit to the cubic footage of your shop.

Compressed-Air Systems

Because of the great variety of jobs that can be accomplished with compressed air, many regard a compressor system to be as much of a "luxury" in a woodshop as electricity. But clean, high-pressure air provides many conveniences, which many modern woodworkers call necessities, such as the following:

• Blow guns for dusting off workpieces and benchtops. They're also great for cooling off tools that get hot during use, such as drill bits and hollow-chisel mortisers.

• Spray guns for applying finish, using either standard guns or more-efficient HVLP (high-volume, low-pressure) conversion guns that run on compressed air in lieu of a turbine. Compressed air provides a very fast and effective way of coating large surfaces of cabinets, big furniture pieces, and complex sculptural work with surfaces that are difficult to finish by hand.

• Nail guns that drive brads, staples, and finish or construction nails. Even if you make only fine furniture, nail guns provide a rapid means of building jigs, fixtures, and shop cabinetry and accessories. If you build cabinetry, inner carcases or subassemblies can be nailed without the fasteners showing on finished surfaces. And pneumatically driven brads are absolutely the easiest way that I know of to mount prefinished moldings.

- Sanders, handheld drills/drivers, die grinders, and other portable power tools that come in pneumatic models. These tools are lighter in weight, more compact, and often more affordable than their electric counterparts (see "Air Tools," on p. 110).

- Air clamps for clamping parts during machining or glue-up. An air clamp uses a pressurized cylinder to hold parts firmly during machining or assembly.

- Vacuum valves, which use compressed air to produce suction to hold parts on work surfaces, machine tables, or in custom-built fixtures. These are especially useful for operations for which regular clamps get in the way of machining and when parts must be loaded and removed from production jigs very quickly.

- Sand blasting, caulking, and more. These jobs can be done economically and efficiently with compressed air. It's likely that once you install a compressor system in your shop, you'll wonder how you ever lived without it!

To get satisfactory performance from your air-powered devices, your shop must have a compressed-air system that's correctly set up. First, your compressor must be powerful enough and have enough capacity to run the various devices you wish to use. Second, the air should be cooled and filtered so that it is free of oil and water. Third, the pipes and hoses used to convey the air around your shop should be convenient to use and allow rapid change of air tools and

A compressed-air system in the shop is your gateway to a thousand tasks, from everyday jobs like blowing chips out of chiseled mortises, spray finishing, and running air tools and nail guns to advanced uses like air clamping and vacuum veneering.

Improving Collector Performance

You'll improve the performance of a dust collector by retrofitting it with either oversize filter bags or canister filter(s). Doing this increases the amount of area that escaping air has to get through, thus reducing air resistance, just like a hot rodder soups up a car by fitting a "free-flowing" exhaust system.

devices. Start by selecting a compressor that suits your needs.

CHOOSING A COMPRESSOR

The compressor is the heart of any shop's air system. It is the pump that presses the air molecules together and traps

them inside a storage container so that their stored energy can be used to do the work you need to do. Compressors come in a befuddling assortment of sizes and types, which makes choosing one all the more daunting. The motor that drives the pump on most woodshop compressors is electric, but gasoline engine–driven compressors are also available if your shop is well beyond where the power poles end.

The importance of compressor size The basic rule when it comes to choosing a compressor is "bigger is better." I have yet to hear a woodworker complain about his or her compressor being too big; but if yours is inadequate in size, it'll make your life miserable.

Calculating the air volume you need Even though compressors are sized by the rated amperage and/or horsepower output of it's motor, air output is what you should be most concerned with. This output—stated in standard cubic feet per minute (scfm), the industry rating standard—is the volume of air the compressor is capable of putting out (smaller, less-expensive compressors are often rated in cfm, which is 10 percent to 20 percent less than scfm). The air volume that you'll need depends on what you want to run on your air system. "Average Air Consumption of Pneumatic Tools and Devices," at right, shows some air requirements of common woodshop air tools.

There's more to a compressor's scfm output than just motor horsepower. The

AVERAGE AIR CONSUMPTION OF PNEUMATIC TOOLS AND DEVICES

DEVICE	PSI	SCFM
7-in. body grinder	90	7.5; 30*
Blow gun	100	2.5
3/8-in drill	90	6; 24*
Finish sander, random orbit	90	4; 16*
Jigsaw	90	7; 27*
Router (with 1/2-in. collet)	90	7; 28*
Nail gun (up to 2-in. nails)	100	2.2
Stapler (1/4-in. by 1 1/2-in staples)	100	1.8
Spray gun (with general-purpose nozzle)	30–50	7.8–11.5‡
Touch-up spray gun	30-50	4.2–6.9‡
Vacuum valve	80	1.8
Air-cylinder clamp	40–100	1–5†

* The first number indicates the scfm with intermittent use. The second number is the scfm with constant use.
‡ Actual scfm usage depends on air pressure and the gun's nozzle and air-cap selection.
† Varies, depending on how often the clamp is cycled (opened and closed).

capacity of the air-storage tank that the compressor's pump feeds affects air output in a big way.

It's air volume that limits the work that you can do with a tool or device. What this means given a compressor of any size, say 3 hp, is that a unit with a 60-gal. tank will output more air and have to run less often to recharge its tank than a like-powered unit connected to only a 20-gal. tank. The bottom line is once you've decided on motor size, choose the unit with the largest tank you have room for. As a guideline, most professional finishers I know regard a 5-hp compressor with a 60-gal. tank as the minimum they would work with. Many modern compressors further increase their air-storage capacity by compressing air up to 175 psi, rather than just 125 psi, which was most common for consumer-quality compressors in years past.

If your air needs are more modest and your space more limited, you'll likely end up with a portable compressor (shown in the top left photo on p. 218). A 1-hp to 3-hp portable can be hooked up in lieu of an elaborate plumbing system and still supply clean, dry air.

The catch is that once the compressed air stored in the tank has been exhausted, the running compressor may be unable to keep pace with the air requirements of the tool, meaning that you'll have to wait until the compressor recharges before work can resume. (This is more than just an inconvenience if you're in the middle of spray finishing a big tabletop or panel.)

Improving compressor performance To bolster its scfm capacity, smaller compressors can be connected to larger storage tanks. Such tanks can be purchased from suppliers, such as Northern Tool & Equipment Company^SM (www.NorthernTool.com), and hooked up as a replacement for the unit's existing tank or as an auxiliary tank.

If you're working with a small portable unit, say a 2-hp compressor with a 20-gal. storage tank, you can gain air capacity by adding an auxiliary air-storage tank. Purchasable as a "portable air tank," this small 10-gal. to 20-gal. tank acts as an additional reservoir connected downstream from the compressor's regular storage tank. The compressor still has to run to fill the auxiliary tank, but the additional air capacity gives you more air volume to work with between recharges.

Connecting a portable air tank downstream from a small compressor can temporarily boost its air capacity and increase the amount of time you can work with air-hungry devices, such as this pneumatic die grinder, before the compressor must recharge.

Oil-less Compressors

MANY NEWER COMPRESSORS sold at building-supply stores and home centers have pumps that are of an oil-less design. This is an advantage over oil-lubricated pumps, which require more maintenance (pump oil must be changed regularly) and tend to spew some oil into the air that must be filtered out completely before using spray-finishing equipment. On the downside, oil-less compressors are definitely noisier than conventional models and usually have a slightly lower cfm output.

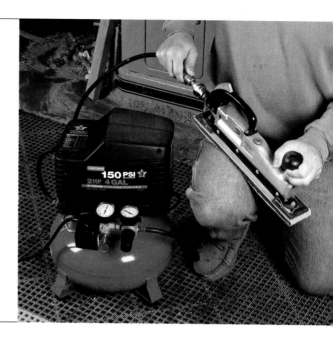

In a stationary system, you can gain additional air capacity by installing a manifold—basically a length of large-diameter pipe—downstream from the unit's air tank. The manifold, which can double as an air system's condenser pipe (described in the next section) acts like a long, skinny auxiliary storage cylinder.

INSTALLING A COMPRESSED-AIR SYSTEM

Although you can just run a hose directly from your compressor to an air tool or device, installing an air-piping system in your shop will make using compressed air a lot more convenient.

If installed correctly, a pipe system will also help overcome one of compressed air's biggest problems: condensed moisture collecting in the lines. Such moisture can be a nuisance if it mists moisture when blowing off dry wood

surfaces or an absolute nightmare if it contaminates a sprayed finish. If your compressor isn't the oil-less variety, the risks of contamination run even higher because most spray finishes can be ruined by fine oil droplets that come through the air lines.

Dealing with condensation As you can see in "Anatomy of a Compressed-Air System," on p. 216, a shop air system starts with a short section of flexible hose that connects the compressor's air tank to the rigid pipe. The first section of pipe should be at least 25 ft. long to act as a condenser that helps remove moisture from the plumbing. This is needed because air heats up as it is compressed (if you don't believe me, just hold your hand close to the compressor pump's outlet pipe). As the heated air cools, it loses moisture, the lion's share of which accumulates in the bottom of the compressor's air tank. This moisture should be drained off by opening the petcock at the bottom of the tank at least once every week and more often in humid weather.

The air carries some moisture with it into the pipe or hose that leaves the air tank, which is why a condenser pipe should be installed. If you lack room for a long pipe, you can simply run shorter lengths back and forth in a zigzag (see the photo on p. 217).

A drain valve at the condenser pipe's lowest point allows any collected liquid to be purged. It's especially important to run a condenser pipe if your compressor is located outdoors because the temperature difference inside and outside the shop can create even greater condensation in your compressed-air piping.

Configuring the system The main pipe that runs from the condenser to the various points where air is used around the shop is typically ½-in. galvanized pipe, which is adequate for runs of up to 100 ft. in a system with a compressor of up to 5 hp. (Larger systems with longer runs require larger pipe; consult a compressed-air systems supplier for more information.)

One practical configuration for small, one-man shops is to run the pipe around the perimeter of the shop high along the ceiling with short drop lines sprouting off wherever compressed air is needed.

A good design for the main line for a larger, multiperson shop is a loop; the line starting and ending at the condenser

Choose Steel Pipe for Compressed Air

Although you'll sometimes see compressed-air systems in small shops run in plastic PVC pipe, it is a practice that's thoroughly discouraged by air-system professionals. The reason is that in a cold shop, a sudden impact, say the accidental bump of a metal tool or pipe clamp, can shatter the PVC pipe and have possibly disastrous consequences. When you consider the ready availability and relatively low price of standard steel galvanized pipe, it's a small price to pay for a safe, long-lasting air system.

Even the largest, professional-model compressors condense moisture from the air they pressurize. Hence moisture must be drained from the compressor regularly via a valve or petcock at the base of the tank.

For Air Tools Only

If you use air tools, dedicate one or more hoses just for this purpose. Mark them as "for air tools only," and do not use them for spray finishing because lubricating oil in the hose can contaminate and ruin most finishes.

pipe. This keeps air pressure more constant at all the drop lines. Otherwise, the person working off the drop line located at the end of the main line will have poor pressure if others are using air farther upstream.

To help drain any residual moisture that may accumulate in the piping, the horizontally run main line should have a slight slope: A 1-in. drop every 10 ft. is ideal. One or both ends of the run should have a drop pipe with a valve or petcock for draining condensed moisture. All pipe should be secured to wall studs and

ceiling joists with U-brackets or perforated metal pipe tape.

For a ½-in. main line, use ⅜-in. pipe for the drop lines. Just above where each drop line terminates, a shut-off valve should be fitted so that line can be turned off for filter cleaning or replacement or in case there's a leak or other problem with the system.

FILTRATING AND REGULATING AIR

Although a condenser pipe and drain remove most of the moisture from your

Anatomy of a Compressed-Air System

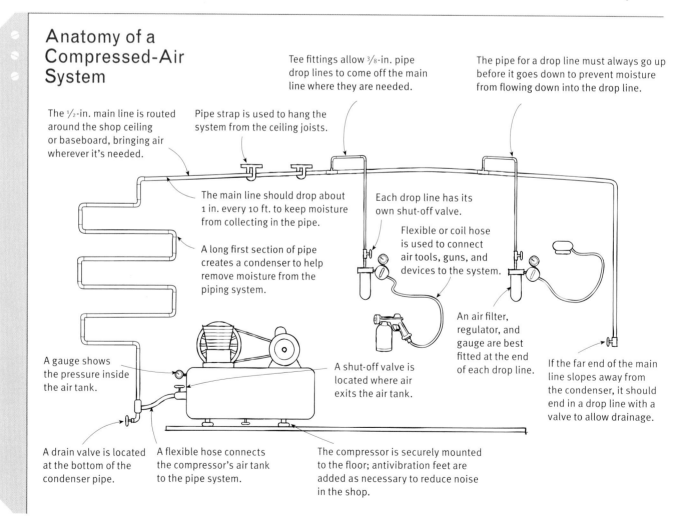

The ½-in. main line is routed around the shop ceiling or baseboard, bringing air wherever it's needed.

Pipe strap is used to hang the system from the ceiling joists.

Tee fittings allow ⅜-in. pipe drop lines to come off the main line where they are needed.

The pipe for a drop line must always go up before it goes down to prevent moisture from flowing down into the drop line.

The main line should drop about 1 in. every 10 ft. to keep moisture from collecting in the pipe.

A long first section of pipe creates a condenser to help remove moisture from the piping system.

Each drop line has its own shut-off valve.

Flexible or coil hose is used to connect air tools, guns, and devices to the system.

An air filter, regulator, and gauge are best fitted at the end of each drop line.

A gauge shows the pressure inside the air tank.

A shut-off valve is located where air exits the air tank.

If the far end of the main line slopes away from the condenser, it should end in a drop line with a valve to allow drainage.

A drain valve is located at the bottom of the condenser pipe.

A flexible hose connects the compressor's air tank to the pipe system.

The compressor is securely mounted to the floor; antivibration feet are added as necessary to reduce noise in the shop.

air system, it's still a good idea to install filtration devices. These will remove any contaminants, including fine oil droplets, dirt, and dust particles as well as any residual moisture from the air. This is most important if the system will feed spray-finishing guns and equipment, which are quite sensitive to contaminants.

If you can afford it, it's best to fit filters at the end of each drop line, closest to where the spray gun or air device is used. On a portable compressor, a filter/regulator unit can be mounted at the air tank or the unit, fed by a flexible hose, can be temporarily mounted on the wall above where the compressor is located so moisture will drain back down into the air tank. This is your best assurance that only the driest, cleanest air will get to your hose and spray gun or tool.

To drain condensed moisture from the pipe in a permanently installed compressed-air system, a long condenser pipe (run back and forth to save room) with a drain valve at the bottom is installed just after the compressor's air tank.

Sample Pipe Installation for a Compressed-Air System

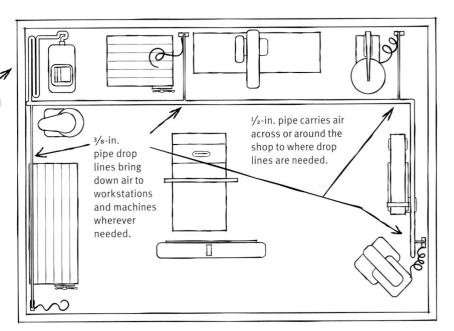

The compressor and condenser pipe are tucked into a corner of the shop.

3/8-in. pipe drop lines bring down air to workstations and machines wherever needed.

1/2-in. pipe carries air across or around the shop to where drop lines are needed.

Drop lines bring pressurized air from a main pipe, run around the shop ceiling, down to where it's used. Each drop line terminates in a shutoff valve and filter unit, in this case a filter with a built-in oiler designed to service pneumatic tools.

Even a portable compressor should have an air filter and moisture and oil trap fitted to keep its air output clean and dry. Here, the author uses flexible coil hose to connect the compressor to a filter/regulator unit temporarily hung on the wall.

Regulators and gauges, the final items added at the end of each drop line, are necessary to reduce the air pressure in the main pipe down to the pressure that's desired for the device in use. A convenient but more costly alternative is to fit each device with its own regulator, which allows you to change pressure whenever needed without having to walk back to the drop line. This is especially useful with spray guns because fine adjustment of the air pressure is often required during spraying.

CHOOSING AIR HOSES

Woodworkers seem to be split on which type of air hose is most practical in the shop. A coiled air hose is the least bulky and its self-retracting nature keeps it out of the way, but it is more susceptible to kinking. Also, some people don't like the tugging feeling on the end of their hose while they're working. I like to use a coiled air hose at workstations where the tool or device doesn't require much of a range of motion during use, such as for blow guns at the drill press or for air-clamping devices.

Regular straight air hose is readily available in 25-ft., 50-ft., and 100-ft. lengths, but it tends to get tangled and become a nuisance under foot. The best way to tame long air hoses is to mount them on an automatic reel. You can pull out only the length that's needed, and the spring-loaded retractor gets it out of the way fast when the job's done. Using ¼-in.-dia. hose is good for most small-

An automatically retracting hose reel installed overhead in the author's shop provides all the air hose needed to reach work areas in and around the shop while preventing hose tangles that quickly become a nuisance under foot.

Quick-release air-hose fittings are a blessing for rapid changes of hoses and pneumatic tools. But a plethora of noninterchangeable brands and sizes make it essential that you choose one particular model for your entire system.

shop jobs; but whenever you need a long air hose with an air-hungry tool or device, a ⅜-in.-dia. hose will result in less pressure loss via air friction.

Air hoses come in a variety of materials, including rubber and various synthetics. Better-quality hoses are made of reinforced polyethylene, which is more durable and less subject to kinks than cheaper rubber or inexpensive plastic hoses.

INSTALLING QUICK-RELEASE FITTINGS

Just as electrical plugs and outlets allow you to connect power tools to electricity without having to splice wires each time, quick-release fittings provide a valuable means of rapidly switching between de-

vices on the end of your air hose. There are just about as many different fittings as there are models of automobiles. Each manufacturer has its own quick release, which, of course, does not mate with other manufacturers' fittings.

When installing fittings, the female quick-release coupler fittings go on the ends of your pipes and far ends of your hoses, and the simpler (and cheaper) male nipple ends mount to all your air tools, guns, and devices. Both male and female quick releases come with either male or female mounting threads. Make sure you note which you need for each tool or device before you buy them.

Shop Safety

10

"Knowing what can hurt you is the first step toward preventing slight inconveniences . . . as well as the possibility of tragedy."

It's inviting to think of your woodshop as a sort of sanctuary for creativity, a safe place for expressing yourself and building the objects of your dreams. But taking a careful look at the contents of your shop should awaken you to the fact that woodworking is a dangerous business: blades and cutters that can cut flesh, lumber and dust that can ignite, finishing materials that can burn or explode, and electrical cords and machines that can electrocute.

Fortunately, knowledge and careful planning can keep the woodshop a safe haven. Knowing what can hurt you is the first step

Get Out First

Your first concern should be making sure you can safely get out of the structure, then call 911 to alert the fire department. You should always call, even if you think you can put the fire out yourself.

A fire extinguisher's label clearly shows the types of fires it is designed to effectively handle. An extinguisher with an "A-B-C" designation is best for putting out all kinds of woodshop fires.

toward preventing slight inconveniences, such as minor cuts and splinters, as well as the possibility of a tragedy, such as a shop fire.

Fire Safety

Just about every material and byproduct connected with woodworking could double as an excellent fuel. Lumber, shavings and chips; dust; finishing materials; adhesives; rags; sandpaper; and even books, paper plans, and drawings are easily ignited by the tiniest spark and can quickly burn your shop to the ground.

Even the sparks and heat produced by sharpening chisels, switching electrical devices on or off, and mixing volatile catalyzed glues and finishes can cause shop fires. If you want to protect your investment and preserve your woodworking shop, it pays to know what causes shop fires and how they can be

prevented or extinguished before they require fire department intervention.

FIRE EXTINGUISHERS

Most woodshop blazes start small: a spark that ignites a small pile of shavings or a smoldering ash thrown into a trash can filled with paper. To prevent a tiny flame from becoming a full-blown conflagration, every shop should have a means of controlling small fires. While large commercial shops often have full sprinkler systems installed, every workshop should have at least a portable fire extinguisher on hand.

A decent extinguisher will only set you back $25 to $75 and can quickly put out a trash can fire before it escalates. An extinguisher is especially important if your shop is near your home, attached to it, or inside it because woodshop fires can spread with alarming rapidity.

Choosing an extinguisher There are two things you should look for when purchasing a fire extinguisher for your shop. First, make sure the model is rated for A, B, and C class fires. Class A fires involve combustibles like wood, cloth, paper, rubber, and plastic. Class B fires involve flammable liquids like gasoline, paints, and solvents. Class C fires involve electrical sources such as wires, cords, and outlets. Obviously most woodshops contain all three sources of combustion, so an A-B-C extinguisher will be effective, regardless of a fire's fuel source.

The second important purchase consideration is the unit's capacity. A shop

extinguisher should be rated at least size II for class A fires and size I for class B and C fires. Such extinguishers, which stand about 20 in. tall, have enough capacity to handle many small shop fires (see the photo on the facing page). Smaller units, such as the Thermos®-size extinguishers that many people keep in their cars, may not have enough fire-retardant material to put out even a minor blaze.

Locating extinguishers To be useful, a fire extinguisher needs to be within easy reach, such as near a doorway, where you can access it safely. An extinguisher that's stashed under a workbench or in a far corner of the shop is dangerous if you have to brave life and limb just to get to it.

The extinguisher should be mounted on a quick-release bracket (included at time of purchase), which can be screwed to the wall or door frame. Be sure to check the unit's gauge every few months and replace or recharge the extinguisher if the gauge indicates it is necessary.

Using a fire extinguisher If the fire seems confinable, easily accessible, and isn't near volatile combustibles, such as flammable liquids or gas pipes and if the shop is not filled with smoke, grab your extinguisher, pull the pin that locks its trigger, and apply short bursts of flame-extinguishing chemical aimed at the base of the fire. Squirting a steady stream will exhaust the extinguisher's small capacity very quickly.

SMOKE DETECTORS

Since fires don't always happen when you're in the shop, early warning is needed when something starts to smolder. If you have a shop that's within earshot of your home, install an electronic smoke detector and alarm. Inexpensive models are available that are powered by batteries as well as models that wire directly to 110v power.

Most units have a loud siren that can be heard for some distance (do a test to see if a shop-mounted alarm can indeed be heard inside your bedroom in case of a night fire). You can evade false alarms by avoiding these mounting locations: at the peak of a vaulted ceiling, directly in front of air vents or near wood-burning stoves, and near fluorescent lights.

Try to keep the alarm from getting too dusty. Dust can cause false alarms as well as disable the unit, so regular dusting and testing is in order for any woodshop installation.

Always within safe reach, a fire extinguisher mounted near your shop entrance allows you to quickly douse a pile of smoldering rags or burning wood shavings before it becomes an inferno that destroys your entire shop.

The author wired a non-battery-powered 110v smoke alarm in his home shop to provide early warning in case a blaze starts when he isn't inside.

By occasionally vacuuming the tops of all shop fluorescent light fixtures, the author prevents fine dust that accumulates there from being ignited by an overheated light ballast.

An oily waste can with a foot lever–operated lid that keeps the can sealed provides a fire-safe way of temporarily disposing of finishing- and solvent-soaked rags in the woodshop.

KEEPING YOUR WOODSHOP CLEAN

To prevent the day from ever coming when you'll have to employ the procedures outlined above, keep your shop clean of wood chips that accumulate—and combust—so easily and quickly. Surprisingly, even heavy chips produced during green-wood turning or planing can generate enough heat for combustion, so don't let big piles build up. Vacuum wood chips that pile up in corners and against walls as well as fine the dust that builds up on and inside electrical outlets and junction boxes that can be sparked into combustion. If your shop has fluorescent lights, vacuum the top of the light housings occasionally because fine dust built up there can be ignited by an overheated light ballast.

Empty shop trash cans often, as well as your dust collector's bags or sawdust catch bin. Avoid piling lumber or other combustibles up against the outside of your workshop, especially if the area is accessible to alleys or public areas where a stray cigarette butt could be flicked.

Oily waste hazards A very easy way of preventing one of the most common sources of woodshop fires is not to leave oily, dirty, and dusty rags around the shop. They are just begging for a stray spark, a light bulb that's too close, or an overheated motor to ignite them. Keep all workshop rags that you wish to reuse in a metal can with a tight-fitting lid. A special "oily waste" can with a foot-operated lid that works like a kitchen trash receptacle can be found in any safety-supply catalog.

Rags soaked with finishing materials need to be spread out to dry before disposal, preferably outside the shop. Never keep rags that are soaked with oil finishes, such as Danish oil, sitting around

Be Kind to the Environment

EARNING "GOOD WOODCHUCK" STATUS requires that you be environmentally responsible. Dispose of hazardous materials properly, including many woodshop finishes and adhesives. In most cities, this means transporting these materials to a local dump or landfill that has a hazardous-materials reclamation center. Even environmentally friendly materials, such as water-based lacquers and glues, should not be thrown into regular trash in liquid form. Instead, spread them out on scrap cardboard or paper and allow them to dry before disposing.

the shop or in any of your shop trash cans. These are a four-alarm fires waiting to happen because they can create self heat as they dry and spontaneously combust—no kidding!

STORING FLAMMABLE LIQUIDS

If you work with solvent-based polyurethanes, NGR stains, or varnishes and nitrocellulose lacquers (an increasingly endangered class of finishes), you'll sleep more soundly knowing that these highly flammable substances are stored properly in a metal locker or a flammable-liquid safety cabinet.

Double-wall-constructed metal safety cabinets, often with self-closing doors, are designed to reduce the fire danger of keeping highly flammable liquids inside the shop. They prevent volatile finishes and solvents from being exposed to heat or other external sources of combustion.

If a shop fire does occur, a sealed finish cabinet helps prevent the fire from consuming the materials stored inside;

An old metal locker or cabinet with tightly closing doors can provide a safe way to store flammable finishes by containing spills and minimizing fire danger. Locking the doors will keep small children away from toxic solvents.

Storing Reactive Materials

One important consideration when storing finishes and other shop chemicals: Don't store reactive materials, such as A/B bleach, oxalic acid, and peroxides, in the same cabinet with flammable finishes like lacquers and varnishes (and even some water-based finishes). If they accidentally mix, it could cause a violent reaction.

To protect vulnerable shop fluorescent fixtures from taking a direct hit that results in a shower of glass shards, the author mounts a grating, cut from a length of hardware cloth, to the underside of each fixture.

a good thing, since most solvents and spray finishes can explode when burned. A vent pipe from the cabinet to the outdoors prevents explosive fumes from accumulating inside, in case finishes are spilled or their lids come off.

LIGHTING YOUR SHOP SAFELY

While not as apt to start a fire as a combusting rag or a portable heater that's tipped over, incandescent light bulbs can start fires if they end up too close to flammable substances. High-wattage (100w and above) tungsten, heat lamp, and halogen bulbs are the worst culprits: They generate searing heat along with the light they produce. To be safe, never exceed the highest wattage specified on a fixture.

Be especially careful if you leave lights on when you lock up, such as when you want to provide heat for a small project you've finished or glued up. Position lights so that they'll not end up falling into combustibles if they're disturbed by an earthquake (or workshop gremlins).

Preventing breakage Another important consideration with exposed light fixtures in the shop that isn't fire related is their vulnerability to breakage. Long fluorescent bulbs in overhead fixtures can easily shatter when accidentally struck with a long board or pipe clamp; being showered with fine glass and the powder that coats the inside of the tube (which is harmful to inhale) is particularly unpleasant.

You can protect vulnerable fluorescents by installing special polycarbonate plastic sleeves over the bulbs. This won't prevent breakage in the event of a direct hit, but it will contain glass shards and keep them from raining down. An even better means of protection is to mount wire grates or stiff hardware cloth mesh over light fixtures. Ready-to-mount wire cages are available for incandescent fixtures to protect their bulbs from trauma.

Personal Safety

While worn safety items, such as goggles, gloves, earplugs, and masks, aren't a guarantee against power tool–related accidents (nor are they a substitute for diligence and good safety habits when operating machines), they provide a great deal of protection from the everyday assault of dust, noise, splinters, and the occasional accident. But should misfortune beset you, being prepared by keeping emergency first-aid supplies on hand will help make the best of a bad situation (see "Contents of a Woodshop First-Aid Kit," on p. 230).

PERSONAL PROTECTIVE GEAR

Your eyes and ears are your portals to the outside world, and I have met few individuals who don't dread the possibility of losing their sight or hearing. But I have met plenty of woodworkers who feel inconvenienced by having to wear protective gear when doing machine woodworking. I won't strike fear in your hearts with horror stories. All I can do is encourage you to protect yourself by wearing good safety glasses; ear protectors; and when necessary, a mask or respirator.

Eye protection If you already wear eyeglasses, safe eye protection requires only a request for prescription safety glasses. Nowadays, safety lenses are available to fit even the most fashionable frame styles, so you don't have to look like a vo-tech school dropout to protect your peepers. And don't forget to don a full face mask for machining operations

Seeing through the Fog

If you wear eyeglasses and are plagued with fogging problems while wearing a mask, try one that has an exhaust valve (disposable models are also available). Your moist exhalation will be blown out the valve and have much less of an effect on your eyewear. Not as effective, but a help, are solutions applied to the eyeglass lens that inhibit fogging. These are available in many ski shops.

such as lathe turning that could send more hurtling toward your head than just sawdust.

Hearing protection Ear protection runs the gamut from disposable foam ear plugs to large, well-cushioned ear muffs. The important thing to look for is the protector's noise-reduction rating (NRR) in decibels (dB). This ranges from only 17 dB up to 30 dB and higher for the best muffs and compressible-foam

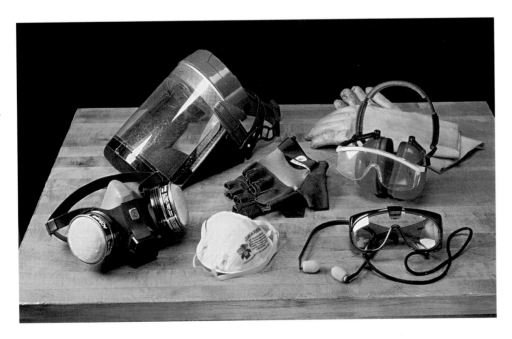

When working with power tools, keep eyes, ears, nose, lungs, and hands from harm by using safety glasses, goggles, or a face mask; ear muffs or plugs; a dust mask; respirator or air helmet; and gloves.

LIMITS OF DAILY NOISE EXPOSURE PERMITTED BY OSHA

DURATION OF SOUND	SOUND LEVEL (DB)*
8 hours †	90
4 hours	95
2 hours	100
1 hour	105
30 minutes	110
15 minutes	115

* Sound level permitted without ear protection.
† Permissible 8-hour exposure goes up to 112 dB when you wear earplugs and 120dB when you wear high-attenuation ear muffs.

Filter Ratings

THERE ARE NINE PARTICULATE-FILTER SERIES specifications issued by the National Institute for Occupational Safety and Health (NIOSH), which include N, R, and P series filters, each available in 100 percent, 99 percent, and 95 percent efficiency. N 95 disposable masks and respirator cartridges, which filter up to 95 percent of respirable particles down to 0.3 micron, are the least expensive filters that provide good protection from wood dust and other floating particles you're likely to encounter in a woodshop. N 100 filters are equivalent to HEPA filters, removing up to 99.97 percent of particles, and they are the best choice if you have severe allergies or other respiratory problems related to breathing wood dust.

earplugs. You'll need the most protection from very noisy tools, such as routers, shapers, and portable planers, because the longer you are exposed to high levels of noise, the more likely you are to sustain some level of hearing damage.

Even the loudest woodshop machine isn't loud enough to deafen you from a single exposure, but continued exposure will, over time, result in irreversible hearing loss. "Limits of Daily Noise Exposure Permitted by OSHA" at left gives you an idea of the maximum amounts of machine noise unprotected ears can tolerate without sustaining hearing damage.

Respiratory protection Protecting your lungs is a good idea for the average woodworker who sands wood, machines composite materials such as MDF and plastic laminates, and applies wood finishes (even water-based finishes contain small amounts of toxic solvents). Disposable dust masks will protect you against limited exposure to fine wood dust but are still best used in conjunction with some form of dust collection (see Chapter 9).

Don't waste your time with cheap, single-strap disposable "nuisance dust" masks; buy either double-strapped disposable masks or a good-fitting rubber face mask that takes replaceable filter elements (see "Filter Ratings" at left).

If you work full-time in a commercial shop and are exposed to wood dust, your employer should help you determine which filter is best for you. Any disposable mask or cartridge should be replaced when it becomes damaged or soiled and when there's a noticeable increase in resistance when breathing through them.

Remember that if you're sanding wood—especially with power tools—you'll need to wear a mask or respirator both during and after sanding because lung-damaging fine wood dust can remain aloft for hours.

For spray finishing and working with toxic finishing materials such as solvent-based lacquers or catalyzed polyurethanes, you'll need to wear a respirator that is fitted with organic vapor filters that remove harmful fumes with a charcoal element. These filters provide protection from the majority of woodworking finishes and are typically color-coded with a black band. Because the active charcoal elements continue to work even when the mask isn't used, they should be kept in a sealed plastic bag or container between uses to extend their life.

Air helmets If you're particularly sensitive to dust or finishes, you might need to wear a powered air-purifying respirator (PAPR), commonly known as an air helmet or dust helmet. These units have built-in fans that blow filtered air into a clear shield that's sealed around your face. Many models can be fitted with either N-series cartridges for dust protection or with organic vapor cartridges for use when applying finishes.

It's vitally important to remember when applying caustic or toxic finishes that a mask or PAPR will only prevent you from inhaling harmful fumes: They

do not supply the necessary oxygen to dilute the chemicals. Always ventilate your finishing area so that plenty of fresh air is circulating around you (see "Ventilating Your Finishing Area" on p. 90).

FIRST-AID KITS

A good first-aid kit is a convenience if you cut your finger or get a splinter. But if you have a catastrophic accident, such as severing a finger or being run through by a nail, a well-stocked first-aid kit can be a lifesaver.

You can buy a ready-made first-aid kit, such as the one shown in the photo below, which comes in a wall-mountable metal box. Or you can assemble one yourself by placing the items listed in "Contents of a Woodshop First-Aid Kit," on p. 230, in a clean box that has a tight-fitting lid that will keep out dust and moisture. In addition to basic supplies, there are some other things worth having in your first-aid kit. If you are prone to getting sawdust in your eyes,

Keeping a well-stocked first-aid kit in your woodshop can provide comfort if you get a splinter or a small cut and it can save your life in the unhappy event of a severe accident.

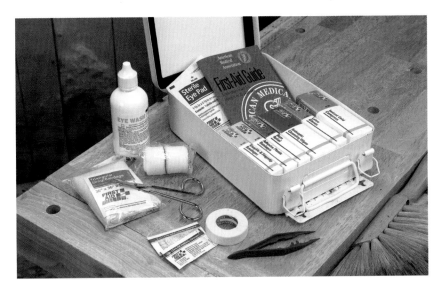

CONTENTS OF A
WOODSHOP FIRST-AID KIT

ESSENTIAL ITEMS	WHAT IT'S USED FOR
Band-aid® assortment	To cover small cuts, blisters, and assorted small injuries
Sterile gauze roll	To cover burns and wounds and to apply pressure to deep wounds to control bleeding
Triangular bandage or 4-in. x 4-in. gauze pads	To bandage larger wounds
Adhesive tape	To hold gauze and large bandages in place
Small, sharp scissors	To cut bandages, gauze, and tape
Disinfectant ointment or solution (Mycitracin® or Betadine®)	To disinfect small cuts and wounds
Clean, sealable plastic bag	To keep amputated parts clean en route to the emergency room
Antiseptic wipes	To clean dirt from abrasions and lacerations
Fine-point tweezers	To remove splinters
RECOMMENDED ITEMS	**WHAT IT'S USED FOR**
Eye cup, boric-acid solution	To flush sawdust particles from eyes
Small mirror	To aid self-inspection of eyes for foreign objects
First-aid guide	To provide instructions on how to handle medical emergencies
Antiseptic/anesthetic cream or lotion	To soothe burns
Butterfly bandages	To close up large lacerations
Rescue blanket	To cover up and to help retain body heat in case of shock
Instant cold compress	To reduce pain and swelling of injuries and to keep amputated parts cool en route to the emergency room
ITEMS TO INCLUDE AS NECESSARY	**WHAT IT'S USED FOR**
Asthma inhaler	To counteract allergic reactions to toxic wood dust, smoke, or solvent fumes
Prescription medications	To remedy an unexpected, sudden onset of symptoms that the medication is prescribed for

it might be a good idea to include eye drops and an eye wash cup in your kit so you can flush out irritating particles. You may also wish to keep prescription medications in your kit in case you need them in a hurry.

Power-Tool Safety

It's easy to forget how dangerous the tools of a woodworker's trade are. A modern shop is filled with wickedly sharp blades, bits, and cutters that can slice through skin at the slightest contact, not to mention the damage they can inflict when running at full power. Even a machine's means of propulsion—electricity—can pose a threat to human safety if power tools are not used with the proper precautions. This section provides an overview of some things you can, and should, do to make working with portable power tools and machines a safer practice.

SAFETY ACCESSORIES

Among the safety gear that every power-machine woodshop should have are devices that help keep your hands out of the path of flesh-hungry blades, bits, and cutters. Some of such safety gear includes push sticks, push blocks, featherboards, and wheeled hold-downs.

Whether purchased or shopmade, push sticks allow you to propel and guide a board past a tablesaw blade or shaper cutter without having to get your fingers near the blade. A push stick can be custom made to specifically handle narrow or small workpieces—the most dangerous items to push with bare hands. Push

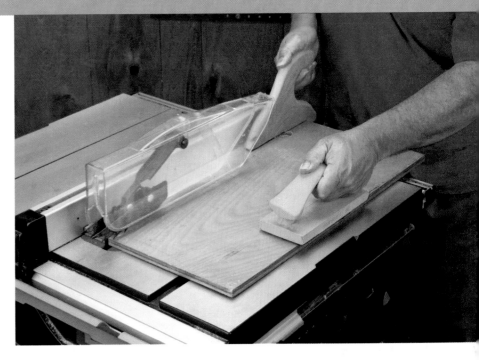

blocks help you keep a workpiece flat on a jointer or other power-tool table and apply pressure to the work with a margin of safety in case something goes wrong.

A featherboard is basically a piece of wood or plastic with thin fingers that deflect slightly as they hold a workpiece firmly against a fence as it is pushed through a blade or cutter. Some featherboards are made to be mounted to a tool table, in a miter-gauge slot, or even to part of a jig. A handheld featherboard can be used to safely hold a workpiece against a fence in the proximity of the blade, as well as to assist pushing it through the cut.

SAFELY POWERING TOOLS AND MACHINES

When things go wrong with power tools, they happen very quickly. And the last thing in the world you want to do is get into trouble and be fumbling around underneath a tablesaw or router table for the off switch. Whether shopmade or

Any device—blade guard, push stick, push block, featherboard, or wheeled hold-down— that helps keep your fingers clear of flesh-ripping blades, bits, and cutters is definitely worth the investment.

A shopmade paddle or push bar, hinged to make contact with a machine tool's on/off button, allows you to turn the machine off quickly in an emergency with your knee or thigh without having to fumble for the switch.

store-bought, a valuable safety accessory for machines is an emergency off switch. These replace or augment a machine's standard on/off switch and allow a runaway tool to be stopped in a heartbeat by simply bumping the oversize off button, paddle, or push bar, such as the one shown in the photo above.

Magnetic starter switches An even more insidious machine-switching danger can bite you after a power outage or when you've tripped an electrical breaker. It's a common mistake to forget to flip off a machine's mechanical on/off switch after the power goes off and then have the machine roar to life unexpectedly when the power comes back on, sometimes with tragic consequences.

Wise machine makers thwart such potential accidents by installing magnetic starter switches on woodworking machines, although such starters are typically fitted only to premium-quality tools.

Most electric-motor-powered machines can be retrofitted with a magnetic starter switch, although they're expensive enough that you probably can afford to fit them only to your most frequently used machines. In addition to shutting off automatically during a power outage, magnetic starters also have internal fuses matched to the machine motor's amperage to provide thermal protection against burnout.

Post Important Information

To make things easier in the event of an emergency, post a list of important phone numbers by the telephone, including ones for your personal physician, your local hospital's emergency room, a poison-control center, and a local hand surgeon in case you need to call one after severing digits. Also, informational charts, such as a poison/antidote chart and a chart that provides instructions on what to do in various kinds of emergencies, can be lifesavers.

GFCI outlets and breakers

About a decade or so ago, the power outlets installed above bathroom sinks started looking strange and different, with funny little buttons. These early ground-fault circuit interrupter (GFCI) outlets were to protect against the all-too-common calamity of electrocution when a hapless person dropped a hair dryer or electric razor into the tub during a bath. When power returns to ground any other way than through the electrical circuit itself (such as through the body of an unwary victim), a GFCI outlet "senses" the current loss and cuts off power in an instant before it can cause bodily harm.

Nowadays, GFCI outlets are common inside homes and shops and around patios. If you work outdoors with power tools, install a GFCI outlet in the box that feeds your extension cords.

Alternatively, you can now buy power strips and plug accessories with built-in GFCI protection. If your shop has a concrete floor or is in a damp area, it wouldn't be a bad idea to protect the entire shop against shocking problems by fitting GFCI circuit breakers.

By cutting off power to the outlet in the event that electricity is traveling to the ground by another path, such as your body, a GFCI outlet mounted in the shop protects against electrocution.

Kid-Proof Your Shop

REMEMBER THAT CHILDREN LOVE TO IMITATE what adults do, and the impulse to play with your tools may be overwhelming. Protect children from getting into trouble by disabling unattended power tools, either by removing their switch keys or padlocking them. Remove the batteries from cordless tools. A lock on the shop door that prevents children from entering is also a wise idea.

You can childproof most modern benchtop machines by simply removing their plastic switch keys. You can prevent unauthorized use of other stationary machines by fitting a small padlock through the hole in the machine's electrical plug prong.

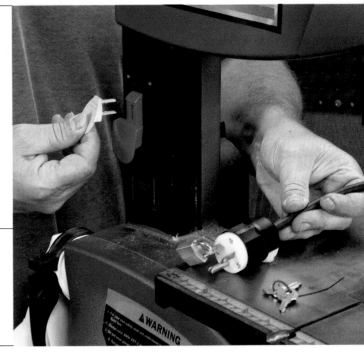